EXODUS
and
LEVITICUS
for
EVERYONE

Also Available in the Old Testament
for Everyone series by John Goldingay

EXODUS
and
LEVITICUS
for
EVERYONE

JOHN
GOLDINGAY

WESTMINSTER
JOHN KNOX PRESS
LOUISVILLE • KENTUCKY

First edition
Published by Westminster John Knox Press
Louisville, Kentucky

10 11 12 13 14 15 16 17 18 19—10 9 8 7 6 5 4 3 2 1

Unless otherwise indicated, Scripture quotations are the author's own translation.

Maps are © Karla Bohmbach and are used by permission.

Cover design by Eric Walljasper, Minneapolis, MN

Library of Congress Cataloging-in-Publication Data

Goldingay, John.
  Exodus and Leviticus for everyone / John Goldingay.
      p. cm. — (The Old Testament for everyone)
  ISBN 978-0-664-23376-1 (alk. paper)
  1. Bible. O.T. Exodus—Commentaries.   2. Bible. O.T. Leviticus—
Commentaries.   I. Title.
BS1245.53.G65   2010
222'.1207—dc22

                                                        2010003678

CONTENTS

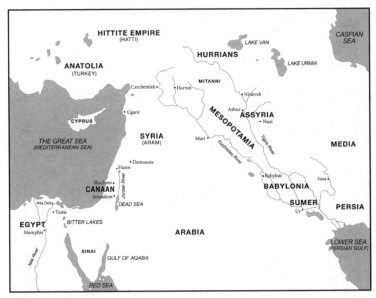

© Karla Bohmbach

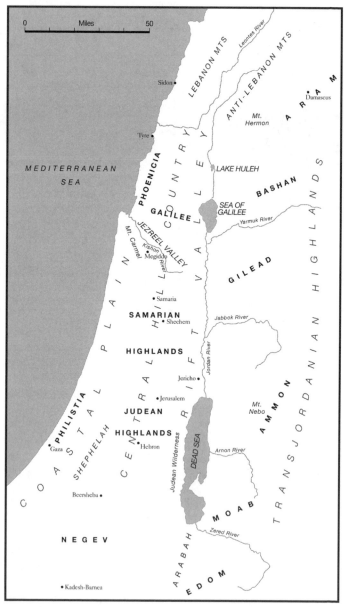

© *Karla Bohmbach*

ACKNOWLEDGMENTS

The translation at the beginning of each chapter (and in other biblical quotations) is my own. I have stuck closer to the Hebrew than modern translations often do when they are designed for reading in church so that you can see more precisely what the text says. Thus, although I prefer to use gender-inclusive language, I have let the translation stay gendered if inclusivizing it would make it unclear whether the text was talking in the singular or plural—in other words, the translation often uses "he" where in my own writing I would say "they" or "he or she." Space confines do not allow for including the whole of the biblical text in this volume; where there is insufficient room for the entire text, I make some general comments on the material I have had to omit. At the end of the book is a glossary of some terms that recur in the text (mostly geographical, historical, and theological expressions). In each chapter (though not in the introduction) these terms are highlighted in **bold** the first time they occur.

The stories that follow the translation often concern my friends as well as my family. None are made up, but to be fair to people, they are sometimes heavily disguised. Sometimes I have disguised them so well that when I came to read them again, it took me time to remember who it was they were describing. In the stories, my wife, Ann, frequently appears. While I was writing this book, she died after negotiating with multiple sclerosis for forty-three years. Our shared dealings with her illness and disability over these years contribute to everything I write, in ways you will be able to see but also in ways that are less obvious. I thank God for her, and I am glad for her sake, though not for mine, that she can now sleep till resurrection day.

I am grateful to Matt Sousa for reading through the manuscript and pointing out things I needed to correct or clarify and to Tom Bennett for checking the proofs.

INTRODUCTION

As far as Jesus and the New Testament writers were concerned, the Jewish Scriptures that Christians call the "Old Testament" *were* the Scriptures. In saying that, I cut corners a bit, as the New Testament never gives us a list of these Scriptures, but the body of writings that the Jewish people accept is as near as we can get to identifying the collection that Jesus and the New Testament writers would have worked with. The church also came to accept some extra books, the "Apocrypha" or "deuterocanonical writings," but for the purposes of this series, which seeks to expound the "Old Testament for Everyone," by the Old Testament we mean the Scriptures accepted by the Jewish community.

They were not "old" in the sense of antiquated or out-of-date; I sometimes like to refer to them as the "First Testament" rather than the Old Testament, to make that point. For Jesus and the New Testament writers, they were a living resource for understanding God, God's ways in the world, and God's ways with us. They were "useful for teaching, for reproof, for correction, and for training in righteousness, so that the person who belongs to God can be proficient, equipped for every good work" (2 Timothy 3:16–17). They were for everyone, in fact. So it's strange that Christians don't read them very much. My aim in these volumes is to help you do that.

My hesitation is that you may read me instead of the Scriptures. Don't do that. I like the fact that this series includes much of the biblical text. Don't skip over it. In the end, that's the bit that matters.

An Outline of the Old Testament

The Jewish community often refers to these Scriptures as the Torah, the Prophets, and the Writings. While the Christian

Old Testament comprises the same books, it has them in a different order:

> Genesis to Kings: A story that runs from the creation of the world to the exile of Judeans to Babylon
> Chronicles to Esther: A second version of this story, continuing it into the years after the exile
> Job, Psalms, Proverbs, Ecclesiastes, Song of Songs: Some poetic books
> Isaiah to Malachi: The teaching of some prophets

Here is an outline of the history that lies at the background of the books (I give no dates for events in Genesis, which involves too much guesswork):

1200s	Moses, the exodus, Joshua
1100s	The "judges"
1000s	Saul, David
900s	Solomon; the nation splits into two, Ephraim and Judah
800s	Elijah, Elisha
700s	Amos, Hosea, Isaiah, Micah; Assyria the superpower; the fall of Ephraim
600s	Jeremiah, King Josiah; Babylon the superpower
500s	Ezekiel; the fall of Judah; Persia the superpower; Judeans free to return home
400s	Ezra, Nehemiah
300s	Greece the superpower
200s	Syria and Egypt, the regional powers pulling Judah one way or the other
100s	Judah rebels against Syrian power and gains independence
000s	Rome the superpower

Exodus and Leviticus

Humanly speaking, the dominant figure in Exodus and Leviticus is Moses, and the King James Bible calls these books the

Second and Third Books "of Moses," but the books do not refer to Moses' writing them, and the way they speak about Moses in the third person rather gives the impression that someone else is writing them. Like most of the Bible, the books are anonymous; they don't tell us who wrote them. One of the features we will notice is that they sometimes have more than one run at the same topic. For instance, they give us two different sets of instructions about the treatment of servants and three sets of instructions about celebrating the pilgrimage festivals in spring, summer, and fall, before the people are settled in the country and are thus in a position where they have much need to use even one set of these instructions. It looks as if what happened is that over the centuries, beginning with Moses, God was continually guiding the community in how to live their lives in connection with matters of worship and everyday life, and was doing so differently as different social contexts required it. Exodus and Leviticus brought together the fruit of this guidance so that it became part of the great work of teaching that constitutes the Pentateuch, the five books of the Torah. The book of Ezra speaks of Ezra's bringing the Torah to Jerusalem from Babylon in 458 BC, some time after the exile, and maybe this indicates that the process of bringing the Torah (and thus Exodus and Leviticus) had now reached its completion. So the books will incorporate material that accumulated over the best part of a millennium, at least from Moses to Ezra.

The King James Bible did not invent the idea of linking the first five books in the Bible with Moses; the idea was around by Jesus' time, and the New Testament presupposes this link. But it is doubtful whether people simply meant to imply that Moses actually wrote the books. There were other books and traditions from their own day that people associated with Moses, even though they will have known that these came from their own day. Calling something "Mosaic" is a way of saying, "This is the kind of thing Moses would approve."

None of these opening five books is really a work on its own, complete in itself. Exodus and Leviticus do not have a real beginning of their own; they presuppose the story in Genesis. There, the promises God made to Abraham found partial fulfillment within Genesis itself, but the book ends with the family of Jacob in the wrong country because of a famine, and Exodus 1–18 takes up this story by getting Jacob's descendants out of Egypt and on their way to their own country. Then for a long time the story stands still. They spend the whole of Exodus 19–40 and Leviticus at Mount Sinai. The time involved is only two years, but the amount of space given to this time shows how important was the stay there and how important was the way Israel worked out the implications of this stay over subsequent centuries. So at the end of Leviticus the people are still on the way; Numbers and Deuteronomy then take them from Sinai to the edge of the promised land.

The five books of the Torah are a bit like the five seasons of a TV series, each ending with a cliffhanger, or at least with questions unresolved, to make sure you come back for the next season. Indeed, the series goes on for another six seasons (making it some sort of record) as the story continues through Joshua, Judges, 1 and 2 Samuel, and 1 and 2 Kings. Exodus and Leviticus are thus actually part of a gargantuan story that runs right through to the books of Samuel and Kings. We know it comes to an end then because turning over the page takes us to a kind of spin-off, a new version of the entire story, in 1 and 2 Chronicles. So Genesis to Kings tells a story taking us from creation via the promise to Israel's ancestors; the exodus; the meeting with God at Sinai; the people's arrival in Canaan; the dramas of the book of Judges; the achievements of Saul, David, and Solomon; and then the division and decline that ends up with many of the people of Judah transported to Babylon. As we have it, this huge story belongs in the period after the last events it records, the exile of Judean people to Babylon in 587 BC. These events form the end of the story that Genesis begins. Realizing that it was completed then sometimes helps us see things in its story.

I say "completed" because I don't assume it was written from scratch then; but strenuous effort to work out the stages whereby it reached the form in which we have it has not produced any consensus on the process whereby this happened. So it's best not to fret about the question. The way the story extends from the beginning of the world to the end of the Judean state does invite us to read the beginning in light of the

4

end, as is the case with any story, and this sometimes helps us to notice points about the story that we might otherwise miss and to avoid misunderstanding points that would otherwise be puzzling. In addition, it is often helpful to imagine the story being told or read to people in the intervening centuries.

Looking at Exodus and Leviticus in one volume of The Old Testament for Everyone series has the advantage that we can consider the whole of the account of Israel at Sinai, which occupies the second half of Exodus and the whole of Leviticus. It is Exodus 1–18 that focuses on the exodus itself. The title "Leviticus" suggests a focus on matters that especially concern the clan of Levi, who were responsible for key aspects of ministry in Israel. We might distinguish two aspects to that ministry. One is looking after the sanctuary, offering sacrifices, and so on. The other is teaching the people what God expected of their lives. Exodus 19–40 and Leviticus cover both of these.

EXODUS 1:1–14

Picking Up the Story

¹So these are the names of the sons of Israel who came to Egypt with Jacob; they came each with his household: ²Reuben, Simeon, Levi, and Judah; ³Issachar, Zebulun, and Benjamin; ⁴Dan and Napthali; Gad and Asher. ⁵Counting every person of those who came forth from Jacob's body, they were seventy, Joseph being in Egypt. ⁶Joseph died, as did all his brothers, and all that generation, ⁷but the Israelites—they were fruitful and they teemed; they grew numerous and very, very strong. The country was full of them.

⁸A new king arose over Egypt who did not recognize Joseph. ⁹He said to his people, "Now. The Israelite people are more numerous and stronger than us. ¹⁰Come on, let's act sensibly with them so they do not become numerous, and when war comes even join together with our enemies and fight against us or go up from the country." ¹¹So they set work supervisors over them to keep them down with their labors, and they built store cities for Pharaoh, Pithom, and Rameses. ¹²But as they kept them down, so they became numerous and were fruitful. And they came to be in dread of the Israelites. ¹³So the Egyptians made the Israelites serve with harshness. ¹⁴They made their lives hard with tough serfdom, with mortar, bricks, and every form of serfdom in the open country. Every form of the serfdom they had them undertake was with harshness.

As I write in the month of May, the TV series are running down or working their way to the kind of cliffhanger I referred to in the introduction, hoping to keep us in suspense for the fall: "Get out of *that* problem/threat"! One or two long-running series are rumored to be nearing their end, and there is some speculation about how the next year will be able to tie up the loose ends. "Does anyone believe that the scriptwriters have any clue how to bring it to an end?" one reviewer asked about a particularly involved series. You can often guess the kind of thing that needs to happen; the question is how the story will get there. When the president got shot at the end of the first season of *West Wing*, did we think he might die? At the end of the season, did we not assume that Josh and Donna would end up together? In the meantime, however, the next season will need to answer questions raised by the previous one, and will begin by giving new, inattentive, or forgetful viewers flashbacks to what has previously happened.

Like those flashbacks, the first paragraph in Exodus summarizes the end of Genesis, mostly in Genesis's own words. The continuity is indicated by the "so" with which the book begins. Jacob's sons are divided into groups according to their mothers.

In describing the Israelites as fruitful, teeming, and numerous, Exodus also reminds the audience of the beginning of the entire series, Genesis 1. There, God commissioned the creation to do that. Israel has done it; it has experienced the creation blessing on a stupendous scale. Describing the people as filling the country further underlines the point, because God's creation commission included filling the earth; in **Hebrew** "earth" and "country" are the same word. Exodus adds a verb that did not come in Genesis. The Israelites became very, very strong. That worries the **Egyptians**, but the Israelites have become an important part of their work force and economy; they want to hold onto them. Their relationship with them is now a little like that of Britain's with India. Britain would have liked to hold onto India, but the tail got too big for the dog. You can try suppression, but in the long run it doesn't work.

Like the arrival of a new presidential administration, a change in the Egyptian dynasty means members of the old staff or government or court lose their positions. Joseph perhaps came to Egypt during the eighteenth dynasty, whose kings included Akhenaten and the childless Tutankhamen. After a coup or two a new dynasty started in the 1290s with Rameses I and his son Seti I, one of whom might have been the Pharaoh who didn't recognize Joseph. The disordered conditions of the transition from one dynasty to another would provide a plausible background for the Egyptian government doing some tightening up. Seti's successor Rameses II (Rameses the Great) is famous for his building projects, and one can imagine these being undertaken by conscript labor with foreign groups such as the Israelites constituting more than their fair share of the labor force. We don't know where Pithom was, but Pi-Rameses was one of the most impressive of Rameses's building projects.

Fixing the story's historical background involves using circumstantial evidence. No sources outside the Old Testament mention Joseph, the Israelites, or Moses. If you are inclined to think the Old Testament is unlikely to have invented the story from scratch (as I am), then you will set the story in this context. If you are not so inclined, you may see it as "just a story" and think it misguided to try to set it in a context at all.

EXODUS 1:15–2:10

How to Resist the Authorities

[15]The king of Egypt said to the Hebrew midwives (one of whom was named Shiphrah, the second Puah), [16]"When you are delivering the Hebrew women, look at the stones. If it is a son, kill him, but if it is a daughter, she may live." [17]But the midwives revered God and did not do as the king of Egypt told them; they let the boys live. [18]The king of Egypt summoned the midwives and said to them, "Why have you done this thing and let the boys live?" [19]The midwives said to Pharaoh, "Because the Hebrew women are not like the Egyptian women, because they are lively. Before the midwife comes to them, they give birth." [20]God dealt well with the midwives, and the people grew numerous and strong. [21]Because the midwives revered God, he made households for them. [22]Then Pharaoh ordered all his people, "Every son who is born you shall throw into the Nile, but every daughter you shall let live."

[2:1]A man from the household of Levi went and took to wife a Levite woman. [2]The woman became pregnant and bore a son, and she saw he was lovely. She hid him for three months [3]but could not hide him any longer. So she got a papyrus container for him, tarred it with tar and bitumen, put the boy in it, and put it in the reeds by the bank of the Nile. [4]His sister stood at a distance so she would know what would happen to him. [5]Pharaoh's daughter came down to bathe in the Nile, while her girls were walking on the bank of the Nile. She saw the container in the midst of the reeds and sent her maidservant, and she got it. [6]She opened it and saw the child. There, the boy was crying, and she felt sorry for him, and said, "This is one of the Hebrews' children." [7]His sister said to Pharaoh's daughter, "Shall I go and summon you someone from the Hebrew women who is nursing, so she can nurse the child for you?" [8]Pharaoh's daughter said to her, "Go!" So the girl went and called the child's mother. [9]Pharaoh's daughter said to her, "Take this child and nurse him for me. I will give you your wages." So the woman took the child and nursed him. [10]When the child had grown, she brought him to Pharaoh's daughter and he became her son. She called him Moses, and said, "Because I 'pulled him out' from the water."

Booker T. Washington was born in slavery but was later the first principal of a Negro college in Tuskegee, Alabama, and was sometimes called the president of Black America. There is a story about a black lawyer fleeing from a lynch mob and coming to Washington's door. Washington gave him protection and helped him escape, but then denied helping the man. His lie may have saved the college campus from destruction and saved other people from being lynched.

The Old Testament's attitude to telling the truth is similar to the one implied by this story. Your mother used to tell you that the Ten Commandments require you to tell the truth, but they don't. They do require you to give true witness in court, but that is a more vital matter. Perjury can cost someone his or her life; stealing a cookie probably won't. Demanding the truth is a way we parents try to control our children, and we use the Ten Commandments to that end. The Old Testament sees truth telling as part of a broader truthful relationship. Where there is a truthful relationship between people, telling the truth is part of that relationship. Where there is no truthful relationship, it does not isolate truth telling as an obligation. Where powerful people are oppressing powerless people, the powerless are not obliged to tell the truth to their oppressors. (So I tell my students, only semi-jokingly, that I am under greater obligation to tell them the truth than they are to tell me the truth.) Revering authorities should be a way of revering God, but when the authorities are requiring murder, all bets are off. You give God what belongs to God as well as giving Caesar what belongs to Caesar. People can pay with their lives for revering God rather than the authorities, but on this occasion God honors that stance, an encouragement to other people faced with their choice.

Specifically, women who are expected to kill their own babies or someone else's babies are not expected to cooperate. In the movie *I've Loved You So Long*, Juliette Scott-Thomas plays a woman who killed her child because she could no longer live with the suffering that its illness was causing it. While she serves time for her crime, she subsequently declares, "The worst prison is the death of a child. You never get out of it." Pharaoh wants to put the **Hebrew** midwives and the Hebrew mothers into that prison. Like Genesis, the women in the exodus story show that they are not people you can assert too much headship over.

Telling us the midwives' names makes them real people; they are not just anonymous functionaries. They are people who revere God. Exodus knows them by name; we know them by name; God knows them by name. We will later discover the names of Moses' parents and his sister; they too are real people (see Exodus 6:20; 15:20). It is less important for the representatives of the **Egyptian** court to be so. Not naming them suggests that they are subordinate to the story. They will have plenty of prominence in Egyptian records, which make no mention of the Israelites. The Old Testament has a different scale of values; it is not Pharaoh and his daughter who count. Pharaoh is someone the newspapers think is important and powerful, yet he can be defeated by three or four women.

Letting the baby girls live also hints at his incompetence (the "stones" may be the birth stool on which a woman knelt when giving birth). Killing the baby boys reduces the size of any potential Israelite fighting force but also reduces the size of the potential Israelite work force; letting the girls live means they can bear many more offspring. Further, his own daughter turns out to be the means of frustrating his strategy. The womanly instincts that prompt the midwives, the mother, and the sister also prompt the princess's actions. If being brought up in the palace equipped Moses for his later role, the Bible never makes that point. If anything, being brought up in the palace is a temptation, not an asset (cf. Hebrews 11).

Pharaoh recognizes that wisdom is important in managing his empire and anticipating its problems, but he does not manifest such wisdom. Egypt had a reputation for its system of higher education and the resources it had gathered for training people in administration, yet the system totally fails it. At the moment of crisis, the people with insight are the women who have no trouble pulling the wool over Pharaoh's eyes and the women who devise a simple plan for pulling the wool over his daughter's eyes (though maybe she is a willing accomplice). The midwives revere God; implicitly, the mother and the sister trust God. Revering and trust are part of wisdom.

In Egyptian, Moses' name means "son" (it is an element in names such as Tutmoses, "Son of [the god] Tut"), but it is nicely similar to a rare Hebrew verb meaning "pull out."

EXODUS 2:11–25

From Guerrilla to Fugitive

[11]During that period, when Moses had grown, he went out to his kinsfolk. He saw them at their labors and saw an Egyptian striking down a Hebrew man, one of his kinsfolk. [12]He turned this way and that, saw that there was no one, and struck down the Egyptian and hid him in the sand. [13]He went out the next day and there—two Hebrew men were fighting. He said to the one in the wrong, "Why do you strike down your fellow?" [14][The Hebrew man] said, "Who made you the man who is an official and an authority over us? Are you thinking of slaying me as you slew the Egyptian?" Moses was afraid. He said, "Then the matter has become known!" [15]Pharaoh heard about this matter and sought to slay Moses, but Moses fled from Pharaoh and lived in Midian. He lived by a well.

[16]Now a priest of Midian had seven daughters. They came and drew water and filled the troughs to water their father's flock, [17]but shepherds came and drove them away. Moses got up and rescued them, and watered their flock. [18]They came to their father Reuel, and he said, "How have you been so quick to come back today?" [19]They said, "An Egyptian man saved us from the shepherds. He actually drew water for us as well and watered the flock." [20]He said to his daughters, "So where is he? Why did you leave the man? Call him so he can have something to eat." [21]Moses agreed to live with the man, and he gave Moses his daughter Zipporah as wife. [22]She bore a son and he called him Gershom, because (he said) "I have become an 'alien' in a foreign country."

[23]During that long period the king of Egypt died, and the Israelites groaned because of their serfdom. They cried out, and their cry for help because of their serfdom went up to their God. [24]God listened to their lament, and God was mindful of his covenant with Abraham, with Isaac, and with Jacob. [25]God saw the Israelites. God acknowledged it.

There is a special kind of irregular verb (popularized by the British TV series *Yes Minister*) that describes the same action differently according to who speaks and who is being referred to. A well-known example is "I am firm; you are obstinate; he is pig-headed." Another might be "I am decisive; you are hasty; he is impetuous." Personally, I am decisive, but I have friends who would call me impetuous. Some are people who avoid being in the car when I am driving. I make decisions and act quickly. The publishers raised an eyebrow or two when I said I would write a thousand words a day for The Old Testament for Everyone series. Decisiveness is not necessarily a strength; you may just make bad speedy decisions.

These first stories about Moses make clear that he was decisive, hasty, and impetuous. His heart was in the right place, but that can be a mixed blessing. Clearly his adoption did not mean he was unaware of his ethnic identity, nor did he come to share the official **Egyptian** attitude to **Hebrew** or Israelite serfs. He takes decisive action, which he intended to be circumspect action, but in that respect he failed, as he discovers when acting the same way the next day.

It does not make him abandon his decisiveness; it is part of his personality. You cannot simply give up aspects of your personality. Subsequently he does not sit by when shepherds appropriate the water some girls have drawn for their flock. Exodus does not comment on the wrongness or futility of the act whereby he delivers someone from being beaten to death or on his intervention in a fight the next day. Nor does it comment on the propriety of the way he rescues the shepherd girls and on the blessing it brings, though it does use the verb "rescue," which the Old Testament often uses to describe God's rescuing the Israelites from their serfdom in Egypt.

Moses has ended up as an alien in a foreign country. With a little license, "Ger-shom" could be understood to mean "Alien there." Was he not an alien in Egypt? He was in a better position than other Israelites to feel at home there. Reuel's daughters describe him as an Egyptian, presumably reflecting the way he dresses and/or speaks. Actually, Moses was never at home anywhere: with his family and his own people, at the Egyptian court, with his Midianite family, or in the promised land (because he will die just before Israel gets there). He lives his whole life as an alien. Maybe that helps him fulfill the calling God gave him.

If you didn't know the story, you would wonder about the connection between these vignettes from Moses' life and the chapter's closing paragraph. Exodus isn't referring to another change of ruler but summarizing the story thus far as background for telling us about the way this caused the Israelites to be groaning, crying out, crying for help, and lamenting. It is not explicit that they are "crying out" to God. They are just crying out in pain. But God has a hard time resisting a cry of protest, whether or not it's explicitly addressed to God. Abel's blood and the victims of Sodom's violence cried out, and these cries reached God. Now Israel's cry does so.

Exodus uses three other words to describe their cry. "Groan" and "lament" underline the pain. The other is "cry for help," a Hebrew word similar to the word for "help" or "deliver." The word points to the thing it asks for. It would surely be so easy to answer. God only has to reverse two letters to transform the situation.

Alongside the four words for pain, Exodus uses four important verbs about God's response. They come in pairs. First, God listened. It is great to have someone listen when you are in pain, but most people who listen to us can do nothing about it. In this case the listener could. Thus, second, God "was mindful of his **covenant**." Translations often have God "remembering," which is fair enough, though the idea is not so much that the covenant has escaped God's memory as that God has not been acting in light of that covenant to give **Canaan** to Abraham's people. Now God decides it's time to do so. God thinks about what needs doing.

13

In the second pair, *seeing* matches *listening*. God had looked at the situation in Sodom and confirmed that the situation was as the cry claimed, and God does the same for Israel. The cry came up to God; God looked down to see. God's acknowledging or recognizing what is going on matches God's being mindful. Translations often have God merely "knowing," but the Hebrew verb for "know" commonly implies acknowledging something, recognizing it, and doing something about it; this fits here.

The vignettes about Moses and this statement about God put us into suspense about what will happen next.

EXODUS 3:1–10

It Was an Ordinary Working Day

[1]Moses was shepherding the flock of his father-in-law Jethro, the priest of Midian, and he had driven the flock to the far side of the wilderness and come to God's mountain, to Horeb. [2]Yahweh's aide appeared to him in a fiery flame out of the midst of a bush. He looked, and there, the bush was burning with fire but the bush was not consumed. [3]Moses said, "I must turn aside and see this great sight. Why does the bush not burn up?" [4]and Yahweh saw that he turned aside to see. God called to him out of the midst of the bush and said, "Moses, Moses!" [Moses] said, "I'm here." [5][Yahweh] said, "Don't come near here. Take your sandals off your feet, because the place you are standing on is holy ground." [6]And he said, "I am the God of your father, the God of Abraham, the God of Isaac, and the God of Jacob." Moses hid his face, because he was afraid to look at God. [7]Yahweh said, "I really have seen the ill-treatment of my people in Egypt, and I have listened to their outcry on account of their bosses, because I have acknowledged their sufferings [8]and I have come down to rescue them from the hand of the Egyptians and take them up from that country to a good, spacious country, a country flowing with milk and sweetness, to the place of the Canaanites, the Hittites, the Amorites, the Perizzites, the Hivvites, and the Jebusites. [9]So now, yes, the outcry of the Israelites has come to me, and I have also seen the oppression that the Egyptians are imposing on them. [10]So now, go, and I will send you to Pharaoh to bring out my people, the Israelites, from Egypt."

14

It was an ordinary working day. My wife, Ann (but she wasn't my wife then—in fact, we hadn't even met), left her university residence in London and took the subway to her medical school. She was just a week or two into her preclinical course and was meeting up with the student with whom she shared a dead body, which they had to dissect before they were let loose on live ones. The student happens also to be called John. Over the corpse, John asked her whether she went to church, and she told him she sometimes did and that she had been confirmed in the Church of England. "Do you know God?" John asked her. The question flummoxed her. She did not know how to think about it. John invited her to go with him to the Anglican mecca near the BBC where another John was the preacher, and the rest is history. On this ordinary working day, Ann suddenly found herself on the threshold of meeting with God.

It was an ordinary working day. Moses was engaged in the family business. His father-in-law is now called Jethro, not Reuel; in Exodus 4:18 he will also be called Jether, though that is not so different. Exodus combines different versions of stories without being troubled by their rough edges; this difference might simply indicate that Moses' father-in-law had more than one name, like Esau-Edom and Jacob-Israel.

As a shepherd, Moses was on the move with the flock. Sinai is not desert like the Sahara, but neither does it resemble a California wilderness where there are grasslands, woodlands, and wetlands. It is arid wilderness; a shepherd has to know where a little winter rain may have made some grass grow. Moses has traveled some way into the wilderness to find it. He is on his own and won't get home for dinner, or even bedtime. There he sees a strange sight. The bush will be something like the spiky acacia.

One can hypothesize natural ways a bush might catch fire, but that would miss the point. Whatever happened to the bush, it attracted Moses' attention. I like to imagine Moses reflecting over coming years that he would have saved himself much trouble if he had simply thought, "That bush is weird. Must get on to find some grass, though." Instead he turned aside and found himself meeting God. God had turned this place into a portal where movement between earth and heaven could take place. Calling it "God's mountain" probably does not indicate a status it already has; otherwise it is not likely that Moses would need warning about its being a holy place. It is this meeting and Israel's later meeting with God here that makes it God's mountain.

Like other Old Testament stories, Exodus is ambiguous about the identity of the figure appearing to Moses. It is initially called a divine **aide**, a heavenly being acting as God's representative, but then the figure speaks as if it actually is God. Suggesting it is a divine aide makes the experience less scary for Moses; the aide represents God and brings God's word but is one stage removed from God. Suggesting that God in person speaks underlines the event's significance; this is not merely a message from heaven delivered by a third party. It is indeed a scary experience, not just subjectively but objectively. Moses needs to keep some distance lest the place's power electrocute him, and not to look at God, lest the light blind him. God's words necessarily convey a mixed message: Come near, but be careful about coming near.

What does Moses know of God? We have been told nothing. God first speaks as "the God of your father"; so God has been involved with Moses' family. The description of this relationship between God and Moses' father becomes more impressive when God goes straight on to add "the God of Abraham, Isaac, and Jacob." There is a straight line from God's involvement with the ancestors to God's involvement with Moses' family. Being involved with Israel's ancestors means God has taken note of their descendants' suffering. Their cry has reached God. God has come down to them. Being their God means God could hardly do anything else. How could God simply sit stony-hearted, as if deaf?

Actually, God often sits as if stonyhearted or deaf. The Israelites were not the only people suffering at the hands of an imperial power in Moses' day, but God did not rescue most of them, and that pattern has continued over the centuries. There is another consideration that makes a difference in Israel's case. In being God to those ancestors, God had been unwise enough to make promises to them, and being God means you cannot get out of keeping your promises. That would make you implode. God promised them that **Canaan** would be theirs, a country with lots of good pasturage for sheep and goats (so it flows with milk), unlike the Sinai wilderness, and a land with lots of date palms (so it flows with "honey"—not bee honey but date honey, a key source of sweetness in the Middle East).

Behind the promise to Abraham, Isaac, and Jacob was God's concern for the whole world; this people is to be a means of bringing blessing to it. That involves getting them out of **Egypt**. So sooner or later, God has to fulfill that promise. All the ducks are getting into a row; all the planets are getting into alignment. The Egyptians need to be put in their place. The Israelites need to be relieved. The Israelites need to have their promise fulfilled. The peoples in Canaan have grown wayward enough to be put in their place. Genesis 15:16 refers to these people in general as **Amorites**; Exodus here gives a more detailed list. The Hittites are the people around Hebron whom Abraham knew there; in this context the Amorites are people east of the Jordan; the Jebusites are the people in Jerusalem; the Hivvites are people north of there; and the **Perizzites** are perhaps village dwellers.

As Moses listened to God, I like to imagine him asking himself, "This is great, but why is God telling me all this? Where is it leading?" I wonder whether he guessed the answer before God got to the outrageous point.

EXODUS 3:11–4:17

Vocation

[11]Moses said to God, "Who am I that I should go to Pharaoh and bring the Israelites out of Egypt?" [12]He said, "I will be with you. This will be the sign for you that I have sent you. When you bring the people out of Egypt, you will serve God on this mountain."

[13]Moses said to God, "Now. If I come to the Israelites and say to them, 'The God of your ancestors has sent me to you,' and they say to me, 'What is his name?' what shall I say to them?" [14]God said to Moses, "I will be what I will be." He said, "Say this to the Israelites, '"I will be" sent me to you.'" [15]God said further to Moses, "Say this to the Israelites, 'Yahweh, the God of your ancestors, the God of Abraham, the God of Isaac, the God of

17

Jacob sent me to you.' This is my name forever, this is my designation to all generations. ¹⁶Go, assemble the elders of Israel, and say to them, 'Yahweh, the God of your ancestors, the God of Abraham, the God of Isaac, the God of Jacob has appeared to me, saying, "I have definitely attended to you and to what is being done to you in Egypt. ¹⁷I have said, I will take you up out of the ill-treatment of the Egyptians to the country of the Canaanites, the Hittites, the Amorites, the Perizzites, the Hivites, and the Jebusites, a country flowing with milk and honey."' ¹⁸They will listen to you and you will go, you and the elders of Israel, to the king of Egypt and say to him, 'Yahweh, the God of the Hebrews—he has met with us. So now, may we go three days' journey into the wilderness to sacrifice to Yahweh our God?' ¹⁹But I myself know that the king of Egypt will not allow you to go, not even by a strong hand. ²⁰I will put out my hand and strike the Egyptians with all the wonders that I will perform in their midst. After this he will let you go, ²¹and I will give this people favor in the eyes of the Egyptians. When you go, you will not go empty-handed. ²²A woman will ask from her neighbor and from the woman staying in her house objects of silver and gold and clothes. You will put them on your sons and your daughters. You will strip the Egyptians."

[Exodus 4:1–17 tells of Moses' further objections and of God's responses.]

In my seminary in England, most students had already been accepted as candidates for ordination, but in my seminary in California many more people come not sure what ministry they may seek or even what denomination they belong to. So we have an Office of Vocational Discernment and Career Services. I find myself in conversation with students wondering whether pastoral ministry will suit them and whether it will be a context where they can exercise their God-given gifts and find fulfillment (or even just find a job). There is nothing wrong with that question, though I feel uneasy about attaching the word "vocation" to it, if we think it has much to do with the way vocation comes to Moses, Jonah, Jeremiah, or Paul. In origin, vocation meant calling, and calling meant summoning. It presupposes the relationship of master and servant. When a master summons a servant to go and do something, it is not designed to be a way for the servant to find fulfillment, nor something the servant has an option about.

When God calls or summons Moses, Jonah, Jeremiah, or Paul, it is not designed to enable them to find fulfillment. Nor is it an invitation they can refuse. At least Moses, Jonah, and Jeremiah find they can't refuse it, and when you have an experience like Paul's on the Damascus road, it doesn't occur to you to try (though we don't know how many people escaped before God summoned these four). God doesn't mind overriding people's wishes and inclinations when a bigger picture requires it. Not that God does this often—maybe once a century—but that shows we are not told Moses' story because it models the way God may relate to us. There was something extraordinary about the way God related to Moses. That is what makes his story important. (But God's capacity for making surreally outlandish demands that run counter to our inclinations and abilities is worth keeping in the back of our minds.)

Fortuitously, Moses' not responding to God by saying, "Okay, I'll be off, then" means he and we learn something from the exchange that follows. "What, me?" Moses first asks. We might have thought that Moses had some useful qualifications. Instead, God grants his premise but denies his conclusion. Moses is not being commissioned on the basis of his experience in the palace, his initiative, or his leadership potential. He will not need any of these to fulfill the strictly subordinate role God has in mind. All he will have to do is relay messages to Pharaoh and perform tricks. What counts is God's "I will be with you." This is not merely a promise that he will feel God is with him but a promise that God will be with him actively whether he feels it or not. If he does not feel it, he will have a sign that God really is with him, though it is a sign that presupposes God's wicked sense of humor. He will see the sign that God is with him only when the exodus is all over. He will have to go through the crisis and the challenge on the basis of trust in God's promise to him, but when he gets back to Mount Horeb, along with the people, he will be able to look back and reflect, "God said 'I am going to do this,' and it happened; this shows God did it."

Second question: Who is this God? Once again Exodus seems to combine several complementary accounts. If the people ask about God's name, the simple answer is "**Yahweh**," but further and significantly that God is the God of Abraham, Isaac, and Jacob. The one intending to act is not only one with that name but one who has been long involved with this people and who made those promises to them. In asking about God's name, they may themselves mean more than "What is the label this God wears?" Names often say something about the person. The people may also be saying, "Tell us something about this God; help us believe what you say." The name "Yahweh" could remind one of the verb "to be"; specifically it is similar to the part of that verb that means "he will be." So Exodus precedes the declaring of the name with the declaration "I will be," and it precedes that with the enigmatic "I will be what I will be." Excuse me? But God has already used that expression in promising Moses, "I will be with you." What kind of God is promising to get them out of **Egypt**? Yahweh is a God who will be there, who will be with them, who will be whatever it is necessary to be in different contexts to achieve that purpose announced to the ancestors.

Moses has more questions or objections (Exodus 4:1–17): "What if they won't believe me?" Moses is given another kind of sign. He can turn a cane into a snake and back again. He can make his hand go all scaly with skin disease, then make it heal. He can turn water from the Nile into blood. That should make them believe there is something special about Moses.

"What about the fact that I am no speaker?" Moses asks. God points out that this is as irrelevant as Moses' earlier "Who am I?" God's being with him also applies to him in this connection. He is just God's servant, like a king's aide. The aide does not have to generate the message, only to repeat the king's message.

"Oh, couldn't you send someone else?" he asks. God is long-tempered, but not infinitely tempered. God does run out of patience, as the Egyptians and the **Canaanites** are about to discover. This doesn't mean God has a change of mind about using Moses. Sometimes God's mind is made up, and you can't change it. God is not prepared to continue the discussion but tells Moses he can have his brother as his spokesman and for goodness' sake to get on with the job.

Why does Exodus give so much space to an account of Moses' commission? God's leaders often need to be drafted. In politics, you have to run for election by the people. Moses runs *from* election by God. Being governed by people who want to exercise power is worrying. The person who leads had to be dragged into a position of leadership: it is a suggestive idea. There are few volunteers among the leaders of Israel or the leaders of the early church.

EXODUS 4:18–23

On Rendering to Caesar

[18]Moses went back to his father-in-law Jether and said to him, "May I go back to my kin in Egypt and see whether they are still alive?" Jethro said to Moses, "Go, in peace." [19]Yahweh said to Moses in Midian, "Go back to Egypt, because all the people who were seeking your life are dead." [20]So Moses took his wife and sons, mounted them on a donkey, and went back to Egypt. Moses took God's staff in his hand. [21]Yahweh said to Moses, "When you go back to Egypt, consider all the wonders that I put in your power and do them in front of Pharaoh. But I myself will strengthen his resolve so he does not let the people go. [22]You are to say to Pharaoh, 'Yahweh has said this: "Israel is my firstborn son. [23]I have said to you, 'Let my son go so that he can serve me,' but you have refused to let him go. Right. I am going to slay your firstborn son."'"

I have just been talking to a student who is a missionary in Indonesia, and we were discussing the dilemma of the church there. He described the church as postcolonial, but I suggested it is still colonial. The gospel came to Indonesia through its being part of the Dutch empire. As East African churches look like British churches, and their forms of worship adapt British forms of worship, Indonesian churches look like Dutch churches, and their theology reflects Dutch theology. It is hard for them to distinguish Dutch culture from Christian faith. It seemed harder for this student to see that the same was true about the U.S. church. The church has always become identified with the empire—British, Dutch, Russian, American. It is in the interests of the empire to appropriate religion as a support. The empire sees itself as god. It can benefit from the support of whatever people call god.

God can return the compliment. God will harness **Assyria**, **Babylon**, **Persia**, and **Greece** to the divine purpose. God does this with **Egypt** in a more paradoxical way. Egypt does its best to hold onto the Israelites rather than letting them go, but as a result ends up giving unwilling testimony to the power of God and plays an unwitting and accidental part in the process whereby God's purpose to bless the nations is achieved. Much later, Rome will likewise crucify the Son of God and thereby also end up giving accidental testimony to the power of the God who raises Jesus from the dead, and play an unwitting and accidental part in the process whereby God's purpose to bless the nations is achieved. Egypt experiences a great defeat in the process. Rome will eventually surrender to the God and Father of our Lord Jesus Christ (though it then cleverly reincarnates itself as Christendom and as the not-very-holy Roman Empire).

The exodus story is the first great conflict in Scripture between God and an imperial power, a superpower. You could say that within the Old Testament it is the only such conflict; God never has much trouble with those subsequent (more impressive) superpowers (when God takes on Rome, it is more of a battle). Pharaoh thinks he is king, thinks he is top dog, virtually thinks he is god. Superpowers regularly do that, and God lets them get away with their delusion for a while as long as it suits God's purpose, but for one reason or another there comes a moment when God deems it necessary to take on the superpower and show who is really King. Such is Pharaoh's moment.

It is the moment when the real King wants to act and do something the human king will be inclined to oppose. God wants to push forward to the next stage of fulfilling the purpose to bless the world through Israel by taking Israel into the country promised to it. Israel has a position in relation to God a little like that of a firstborn son. It is due to receive the firstborn's inheritance or blessing, the gift of a country that belongs to its Father. We know already that Pharaoh doesn't like the idea of the Israelites' deciding to pull up stakes and leave. Like other imperial or developed countries, it looks down on the immigrants in its midst but relies on them to do the jobs that natives don't want to do, and it will be in a mess if they leave.

So this is a moment of conflict between a King and a king or a Father and a serf master. As Father, God has no need to make a point to the serf master; the Father's objective would be fulfilled simply by getting the Israelites out of Egypt. As King, God wants to make a point to the pretend king, his subjects, and the world as a whole that hears about this event.

A prominent theme in the working out of this conflict will be the stiffening or strengthening of Pharaoh's resolve. Traditionally translations speak of the "hardening of Pharaoh's heart"; more literally the words denote making Pharaoh's heart heavy or strong. In English, the heart suggests feelings, but in Scripture, feelings are associated more with the stomach; the heart suggests thinking, taking up attitudes, and making decisions. It is closer to what English refers to as the mind. Strengthening or stiffening the heart suggests making up the mind with some firmness. God is commissioning Moses to put pressure on Pharaoh to let the Israelites go, but God is also going to put pressure on Pharaoh not to do so. Paradoxically, that will help establish who the real king is. A quick and easy victory would do that; prolonging the conflict does it another way. It will suit God if Pharaoh resists the idea of letting God's son go. It will give God more chance to show who is king around here.

How will God go about stiffening or strengthening Pharaoh's resolve? I imagine it is not by manipulating the electrical circuits in Pharaoh's brain or by something analogous to hypnosis so as to make Pharaoh do something he is not inclined to do ("My instinct is to let the Israelites go, but something is stopping me"). Resolve gets strengthened or weakened by argument. I might say to a friend, "If I want have a second helping of fruit pie and cream, will you remind me that I said I want to lose a few pounds and that losing weight will make me feel healthier?" The trouble is that when I am subject to this temptation as I face the fridge late in the evening, there is no one there to argue with me. I have to do my own stiffening of resolve. The preacher seeks to stiffen our resolve by reminding us of what Christ has done for us. Moses seeks to stiffen Israel's resolve by reminding Israel of what God has done for it. Israel, the congregation, or I have to do the resolving; but Moses, the preacher, or my friend does some of the strengthening.

So **Yahweh** declares the intention to strengthen or stiffen Pharaoh's resolve. I imagine Pharaoh hearing this voice saying, "No, don't be soft; it would be stupid to let them go"; but it is Pharaoh who decides whether to listen to this voice. Thus, when Moses and Aaron perform their signs, Exodus more often speaks of Pharaoh's resolve being strong or firm and of Pharaoh's strengthening or stiffening his own resolve than of God's strengthening or stiffening it. The three ways of speaking are all significant. Saying, "Pharaoh's resolve was strong or firm" simply reports the phenomenon. Saying, "Pharaoh strengthened or stiffened his resolve" makes clear that Pharaoh's will is involved; this is not a decision imposed on him from outside. Saying, "God strengthened or stiffened Pharaoh's resolve" makes clear that God is also at work. Referring to God's intention first affirms that God's sovereignty is involved, but in describing how things actually work out, Exodus refers first to Pharaoh's resolve being strong or firm (Exodus 7:13, 14, 22) and to Pharaoh's stiffening his own resolve (Exodus 8:15, 32) before speaking of God's strengthening Pharaoh's resolve (Exodus 9:12). That order again makes clear how significant is Pharaoh's human involvement. He is not just a puppet in God's hands.

EXODUS 4:24–31

The Migrant Returns

[24]On the way, at a lodging place, Yahweh met up with [Moses] and sought to kill him. [25]Zipporah got a flint and cut off her son's foreskin, touched his feet, and said, "Because you are a bridegroom of shed blood to me!" [26]And he drew back from him. (At that time she said, "a bridegroom of shed blood," with reference to the circumcision.)

[27]Yahweh said to Aaron, "Go and meet Moses in the wilderness." He went and met up with him at God's mountain and kissed him. [28]Moses told Aaron all the words God had sent him with and all the signs he had commanded him with, [29]and Moses and Aaron went and assembled all the elders of the Israelites.

[30]Aaron spoke all the words Yahweh had spoken to Moses and did the signs before the people's eyes, [31]and the people believed. When they heard that Yahweh had attended to the Israelites and had seen their ill-treatment, they bowed low in prostration.

The last two people I had helping me care for my disabled wife were from the Philippines. Although both were the wives of students at our seminary, it is no coincidence that both were Filipinas. There are many Filipina caregivers in the United States and Britain; indeed, I have seen advertisements for caregivers in the Middle East and elsewhere that said, "Filipina preferred." Many such will hope to go "home" one day (our last caregiver found it too cold in Southern California!), and a Filipina student of mine has noted how Moses' story illumines the stories of Philippine migrants in the West. For them as for Moses, migration means dislocation, invisibility, marginality, and alienation. Although I am also a foreigner, as a Caucasian tenured professor I don't suffer from those experiences, but I do experience some uncertainty of identity. I am not a U.S. citizen, but I am out of touch with Britain, and if I went back, I would not go back to the same place but to a culture that has changed. I don't speak like someone from the United States, but back in Britain people would laugh at the way my accent and idioms have been affected by living in the United States. The position of Filipino/a migrants is much trickier. Part of them longs to go home; but there were reasons why they left "home," and going home means returning to the situation that made them leave—particularly their family's economic needs.

For Moses, returning means facing other questions about family; he has a family in Midian and a family in **Egypt**. It also means facing questions about his own identity. Returning involves him in a near-death experience. God knows that the old Moses has to die if he is to fulfill his vocation. Inevitably this affects his family, though it need not have affected them the way it does. It pulls Moses' wife and son into a new relationship with him and his vocation.

Many aspects of the story of Moses' son's circumcision are unclear. Whose feet did Zipporah touch, and why, and is "feet" a euphemism for genitals (as it sometimes is)? Why had Moses failed to circumcise his son? It is the sign of the covenant, of sharing in **Yahweh**'s promise to give Abraham's descendants the country where Moses is to lead them. What was he thinking? Is it a sign of unfaith? You could not blame him for losing faith. God had made a **covenant** with the ancestors, a covenant all about the future. They would find a settled, secure position in **Canaan** instead of being like undocumented aliens. But for generations they have not been in the country at all. What has happened to God's covenant commitment? Has God forgotten it? Certainly God has not been mindful of it.

The covenant concerned the future and did not make much demand of the ancestors in the present. They simply had to accept the covenant sign. It is that single, simple sign that Moses has neglected. God has not been mindful of the covenant promise. Moses has not been mindful of the covenant sign.

He needn't worry about the threats to his life that he knew about and was scared about, but there is another threat he has not thought about. Mysterious in yet another sense is God's trying to kill Moses and failing. I guess God wasn't trying too hard. The point was presumably to pull Moses to his senses. Fortunately, even a Midianite woman knows a man needs to be circumcised (it was a common practice in Middle Eastern culture, though God had given it a new significance in making it the sign of a covenant with Abraham and his people). How fine that it is Zipporah who has to take the decisive action to save Moses. Once again he owes his life to a woman's initiative. Once again the exodus story would have derailed had it not been for a woman's action.

We do not know how long Moses has been in Midian (Jewish tradition says it was forty years, and Acts 7:30 presupposes that). Who knows what Moses' family would make of his return with his Midianite family after all this time? It is good that God appears to Aaron as well as Moses. It is easy to imagine that the return of this migrant claiming that God has commissioned him to lead the Israelites out of **Egypt** would provoke a skeptical reaction among the Israelites. It is as well that God has also anticipated this, both in appearing to Aaron and in giving Moses (and now Aaron) the signs to perform.

So the people believed. It is the sixth time the verb has come up in Exodus 4. The other five times suggest that Exodus is talking about people believing Moses, as they related Moses' doubt about whether people would believe him and God's promise that one way or another they will. God's promise finds fulfillment. Exodus is not talking about their believing in God, though it implies they do, because when they have listened to the message about God's having seen their affliction and having determined to take action on their behalf, they bow low in prostration.

EXODUS 5:1–6:1

Whose Service Is Perfect Freedom

[1]Afterward, Moses and Aaron went and said to Pharaoh, "Yahweh has said this: 'Send my people Israel off so they may hold a festival for me in the wilderness.'" [2]But Pharaoh said, "Who is Yahweh that I should listen to his voice about releasing Israel? I do not acknowledge Yahweh, nor will I send Israel off." [3]They said, "In that the God of the Hebrews has met with us, may we go a three days' journey into the wilderness and sacrifice to Yahweh our God? Otherwise he may strike us with epidemic or sword." [4]But the king of Egypt said to them, "Moses and Aaron, why should you take the people away from their work? Get to your labors."

[5]So Pharaoh said, "Right. The people of the country are now numerous, and you will make them cease from their labors?" [6]That day Pharaoh commanded the bosses over the people and their own overseers: [7]"You shall not continue to give the people straw for the bricks, as yesterday and the day before. They themselves can go and collect straw for themselves. [8]But the quantity of bricks they were making yesterday and the day before, you are to impose on them. You shall not reduce it, because they are slacking—hence they are crying out, 'Let's go and offer sacrifice to our God.' [9]Service is to weigh heavy on the men so that they may work at it and not listen to deceptive words."

[10]So the people's bosses and their own overseers went out and said to the people, "Pharaoh has said this: 'I am not giving you straw. [11]You go and get straw for yourselves from wherever you may find it, because there is no reduction in your service, at

27

all.'" [12]The people scattered through all Egypt to gather stubble for straw, [13]while the bosses hurried them up: "Get your work finished, each day's assignment, just like when you had the straw." [14]The Israelites' overseers, whom Pharaoh's bosses had put over them, were beaten, saying, "Why have you not finished your prescription of bricks, as yesterday and the day before, either yesterday or today?" [15]So the Israelites' overseers came and cried out to Pharaoh, "Why do you act like this with your servants? [16]No straw is given to your servants but they are saying to us, 'Bricks! Make bricks.' Now. Your servants are being beaten, but the offense is your people's." [17]But he said, "You are slacking, slacking. That's why you are saying, 'May we go to sacrifice to Yahweh?'"

[Exodus 5:18–6:1 relates how the Israelites' overseers protest to Moses and Aaron for making their situation worse, and Moses protests about this to Yahweh.]

Tomorrow I shall preside at a "service" in church. In what sense do we "serve" God by singing hymns and so on? Indeed, is it God that we are serving? Yesterday, one of my colleagues on the seminary's chapel committee asked me what was my evaluation of the chapel worship over the past year. Maybe I should have replied, "Well, you had better ask God for an evaluation, not me!" It is easy to assume that the criterion for evaluating worship is whether we feel good afterward. But "service" is one of the Old Testament's most common words for "worship." Servants do not serve their master for their own sake. (Well, actually, they do, but they have to forget this while they are involved in their service. Only if they focus on serving their masters will they benefit from it themselves.)

Service is a major theme in the exodus story, though English translations use words such as *worship*, *bondage*, and *slavery* as well as *service* to translate **Hebrew** words that are related. Pharaoh makes them *serve* (that is, work for the **Egyptians**) with harsh *service* (Exodus 1:13–14). Later, their service gets tougher (5:9, 11; 6:9). When they want to leave, he bids them get back to their service (5:18). They cry out because of their service (2:23) and speak of themselves as Pharaoh's *servants*

(5:15, 16), but their cry by reason of their service reaches God (2:23). God hears their cry when the Egyptians make them serve, and God intends to bring them out from their service (6:5, 6). Their escape means being brought out of a country of servants (13:3, 14), and Pharaoh suddenly realizes it was stupid to let them go from serving the Egyptians (14:5).

Facing the waters of the Reed Sea, the Israelites agree they would have been better off staying to serve the Egyptians; "Leave us alone so we can serve them," they claim they said in Egypt, though Exodus has not told us that (14:12). The sign God promised Moses when first appearing to him was that when he has brought the people out of Egypt, they will serve God on this mountain (3:12), and God's challenge to Pharaoh is thus, "Let my son go so that he can serve me" (4:23) or "Let my people go so that they can serve me" (7:16; 8:1, 20; 9:1, 13; 10:3). No doubt there is a sense in which they can serve God in Egypt, but they are also under Pharaoh's authority, and he decides what happens to them. After the epidemic of locusts, Pharaoh's officials urge him to let the Israelites go to serve their God, and he says the men can indeed go to serve God; after the terrible darkness falls on the country he says the men, women and children can go to serve God (10:7, 8, 11, 24). Moses points out that they will need animals with which to serve God (10:26). After the death of the firstborn Pharaoh does let the people go with the animals to serve God (12:31). Passover and the flat bread festival will be a service with which they will serve (12:25–16; 13:5).

So here in Exodus 5, God does not just say, "Let my people go" but "Let my people go so that they may serve me." God also declares that they are to "hold a festival for me." It would be quite appropriate to refer to this as "making a pilgrimage." Muslims are expected to make a pilgrimage to Mecca some time in their life, and the word for this pilgrimage, *hajj*, is related to the word Moses uses here. Pilgrimage recognizes that there are places that are special to a faith. Christians may make pilgrimage to Jerusalem and Galilee because of the importance of what happened there; later in the Old Testament, Israelites will make pilgrimage to Jerusalem as the place

29

where God especially deigned to be present among them. Here, their God has already appeared at a mountain in the wilderness and declared the intention to deliver them from Egypt, so they must go and meet with God there. This does not mean God is not present with them in Egypt; the idea that there are special places that have been shown to be portals between earth and heaven can coexist with the knowledge that God is everywhere. This requirement does, however, raise the question of whether Moses is being completely honest about the purpose of their leaving. If Pharaoh lets them go for three days, will they really come back? Is this really a pilgrimage or an exodus? Perhaps if Pharaoh were willing to let them go for a three-day pilgrimage, they would not need to be so keen to leave Egypt altogether.

Moses' third description of their service is that they will offer "sacrifice." This involves killing an animal and burning some or all of it so it goes up in smoke to God. Servants serve their masters by providing them with food. There were religions in Israel's world that took that rather literally. Their gods could be born, marry, die—and eat and drink. Israelites knew their God was not humanlike in that way; at least, in theory they knew that, though no doubt many of them fell into that way of thinking. The Old Testament still risks referring to worship as a way of "serving" God. The Israelites knew worship was done for God's sake. Only if they worshiped on that basis would they find that they had benefited from it. Further, the prominence of sacrifice in Old Testament worship means worship is costly to worshipers. You do not just come to worship with loving feelings in your heart. You come with expensive offerings.

Christians can seem to give too much attention to worshiping God and neglect serving God in the world, for instance by caring for the poor. The Old Testament critiques that. There is an opposite possibility, of focusing on serving God out in the world and not being involved in worship. Exodus reminds us of the importance of worship by the way it uses this word for "service" to mean "worship," and in effect it defines worship as making sacrifices to God and making pilgrimage. That kind of thing is no use at all to the world, but it constitutes action that recognizes that God is God and honors God as God.

EXODUS 6:2–7:13

My People—Your God

²God spoke to Moses and said to him, "I am Yahweh. ³I appeared to Abraham, Isaac, and Jacob as El Shadday, but my name Yahweh I did not make known to them. ⁴I also established my covenant with them to give them the country of Canaan, the country in which they resided simply as aliens. ⁵I have also now personally listened to the lament of the Israelites whom the Egyptians are treating as serfs, and I have been mindful of my covenant. ⁶Therefore, say to the Israelites, 'I am Yahweh. I will bring you out from under the labors of the Egyptians and rescue you from their serfdom. I will restore you by an outstretched arm and by great acts of authority. ⁷I will take you for myself as a people and I will be God for you, and you will acknowledge that I am Yahweh your God, the one who brings you out from under the labors of the Egyptians. ⁸I will bring you to the country I swore to give Abraham, Isaac, and Jacob. I will give it to you as a possession. I am Yahweh.'" ⁹Moses spoke thus to the Israelites, but they did not listen to Moses because their spirit was worn out and their serfdom harsh.

[Exodus 6:10–7:13 summarizes God's instructions to Moses about going to see Pharaoh, Moses' hesitation, and God's commission to both Moses and Aaron. It also includes a list of the heads of the Israelite households and of the members of Moses' family.]

I am discussing their wedding with a young couple in my student Bible-study group. The wedding is a lovely thing to be involved in, and not only because it will happen within sight of the beach but because it brings home to me as a Brit one of those quaint features of U.S. culture: people devise their own marriage service as if they were the first people who ever got married. When they are reinventing the wheel, however, a couple will always include a mutual commitment: "Will you take this man as your husband? Will you take this woman as your wife?" There is an analogy between the marriage relationship and the relationship between us and God. There are limits to the analogy, in that there is a hierarchical aspect to our relationship with God that is not present in the marriage relationship as God designed it, but both are characterized by mutuality. That mutuality is seen, for example , in God's self-giving to us and ours to God, God's self-surrender to us and ours to God, God's commitment to us and ours to God.

That is the form of relationship described in this second account of God's commissioning Moses, which forms a reprise of the first account in Exodus 3:1–4:17. Having access to two versions of a story, the compilers of the **Torah** often include both because the event is important and/or because the second account has distinctive things to say. Here, God first recalls making a **covenant** commitment to Israel's ancestors, the commitment God has been thinking about. The time has come to do something about the promise this covenant involved. But there was nothing very mutual about that covenant. All God was doing was making a promise for the future. All the ancestors had to do was implement the sign of circumcision.

Covenants do not have to be mutual, but now God is going to introduce mutuality into the covenant, making it more like a marriage. This is now possible because God is making the covenant not merely promise but actuality. It could seem that God had forgotten the covenant commitment, as Moses perhaps had in failing to circumcise his son, but God is now mindful of it. God is going to bring the people out of **Egypt** and take them into the country God had promised, and therefore God can look for a more solid response than merely a sign like circumcision.

"I am Yahweh," God says. In Genesis, God made that declaration to Abraham and Jacob, but Genesis did not quite mean this literally. God here notes that the actual name **Yahweh** was not revealed to them. There was not untruth involved in portraying them as in relationship with Yahweh, because Yahweh really was relating to them, but Yahweh did not literally use that name. As Exodus 3 described more fully, there is now a new name to go with a new stage in God's relationship with them and a new stage in God's activity among them. Henceforth in Exodus and elsewhere, God often begins speaking with this self-introduction, "I am Yahweh." The implication then will be not that they do not know who God is. It is more like the president saying, "I am John F. Kennedy" or "I am Ronald

Reagan" or "I am Barack Obama." It means "I am the one who has the power to do what I am about to announce. You can believe what I say."

In speaking of covenant action (as opposed to covenant promise), God introduces another key word, **restore**. Leviticus 25 and 27 will talk about the way restoration works in the human family, but Exodus 6 and 15 first talk about God's acting as restorer. While the human reality provides the image for understanding God's position and activity, God's reality and instincts underlie the Torah's expectations about the human family. Israel is part of God's family to whom God accepts family obligations. Israel has been pushed into the position of a debt servant who has lost possession of his land, but it will get free from its servitude and get back to "its" land.

That will be the way Yahweh becomes God for Israel and Israel becomes a people for Yahweh. Exodus has made quite clear that this is already the relationship, but God's action in restoring Israel will carry with it Israel's having a new form of commitment to Yahweh. The relationship involves not merely a promise that Israel accepts but an act that Israel responds to.

To put it another way, Israel will "acknowledge" Yahweh. That verb complements the earlier talk of serving, celebrating, and sacrificing. A Christian understanding of God often sees it as involving a relationship that feels intimate, warm, and inward, a sense of being near to God and cherished by God. The Old Testament believes in a relationship like that, but it doesn't call it "knowing God." When it talks about people not knowing God (or not knowing the Torah), what it has in mind is that they don't acknowledge God (or the Torah) in their thinking and in their lives. It is the other side of the fact that God doesn't merely know about us and have a warm relationship with us. God acknowledges us and makes a commitment to us. God does more than merely know about the people's oppression in Egypt (and more than merely be present with the people in their suffering). God acknowledges it, recognizes it, and does something about it (Exodus 2:25). God affirmed this in the first account of Moses' commission (Exodus 3:7). In this account God flips the coin. God acknowledges us; we are expected to acknowledge God.

33

EXODUS 7:14–8:7

The Nine Natural Disasters

[14]Yahweh said to Moses, "Pharaoh's resolve is firm. He refuses to send the people off. [15]Go to Pharaoh in the morning. There he will be, going out to the water. Station yourself to meet him at the edge of the Nile. The staff that turned into a snake—take it in your hand. [16]You are to say to him, 'Yahweh, the God of the Hebrews, sent me to you to say, "Send my people off so they may serve me in the wilderness." Now. You have not listened so far. [17]Yahweh has said this: "Because of this you will acknowledge that I am Yahweh." Now. I am going to strike the water in the Nile with the staff in my hand, and it will turn into blood. [18]The fish in the Nile—they will die. The Nile will stink. The Egyptians will be loath to drink the water from the Nile."'[19] And Yahweh said to Moses, "Say to Aaron, 'Take your staff and stretch out your hand over the waters of Egypt, over its rivers, its canals, its ponds, over every body of water, so that they become blood. There will be blood in all Egypt, even in wood and stone [vessels].'" [20]Moses and Aaron did so, as Yahweh commanded. [Aaron] lifted the staff and struck the water in the Nile before the eyes of Pharaoh and his servants, and all the water in the Nile turned into blood. [21]The fish in the Nile—they died. The Nile stank. The Egyptians could not drink the water from the Nile. There was blood in all Egypt. [22]But Egyptian experts did this with their spells, and Pharaoh's resolve stayed strong and he did not listen to them, as Yahweh had spoken. [23]Pharaoh turned and went to his house. He did not give his mind even to this. [24]All the Egyptians dug around the Nile for water to drink, because they could not drink the water in the Nile.

[25]Seven days passed after Yahweh had struck the Nile. [8:1]Yahweh said to Moses, "Go to Pharaoh and say to him, 'Yahweh has said this: "Send my people off so they may serve me. [2]If you refuse to release them: right, I am going to smite all your territory with frogs. [3]The Nile will teem with frogs. They will climb up and come into your house, into your bedroom, and onto your bed, and into the house of your servants and among your people and in your ovens and your mixing bowls. [4]Yes, among you and your people and all your servants the frogs will climb up."'" [5]And Yahweh said to Moses, "Say to Aaron, 'Stretch out your hand with your staff over the rivers, the canals, and the

> ponds, and make the frogs come up on Egypt.'" ⁶Aaron
> stretched out his hand over the waters in Egypt, and the frogs
> came up and covered Egypt. ⁷But the experts did this with their
> spells and made the frogs come up on Egypt.

As I came out of my office the other day, a little group of students were strolling past and greeted me with the comment,
"Oh, it's the one and only Dr. Goldingay!" I was able to respond,
"Actually I'm not the 'one and only.'" My daughter-in-law is just
finishing a PhD, and I had been wondering whether there are
any other Dr. Goldingays apart from my wife and me, so I did
a search and discovered a Dr. Goldingay in Australia, who is
an expert in frogs. It would be nice to consult him about this
bit of Exodus. The movie *Magnolia* came to a climax with a
scene in which thousands of frogs fall from the heavens. A sign
on the side of the road says, "Exodus 8:2." The significance of
the frogs is not obvious, but apparently part of the background
to the movie scene is that there are reports from time to time
of the sky raining frogs or other small creatures (but not cats
and dogs) during a storm, because somehow the wind sucked
up the frogs from a stretch of water and dropped them some
distance away.

What is the relationship between the "natural" epidemics
and disasters in Exodus and other "natural" events? Exodus
relates nine such events before the death of **Egypt's** children:
water turning into blood, frogs, gnats, flies, cattle disease, boils,
thunder and hail, locusts, and darkness. To some degree all can
be paralleled in events in one human community or another. Or
they can be understood a little less than literally: for instance,
the bloodlike appearance of the Nile might not suggest actual
blood but the presence of some organism that turned the water
red. If you are inclined to "natural" explanations of things, you
can see these stories as magnified accounts of "natural" events.
It would be important, however, not to stop there, because Exodus has a series of bigger things to say.

Exodus is about the God of the **Hebrews** intervening in the
political, military, and social affairs of Egypt. God is interfering in
its political policies in the way it handles an immigrant community such as the Israelites. God is interfering in its social policies

by not countenancing the way it treats its serfs. While God is going to be active as a warrior, taking on the military might of the Egyptian war machine at the Reed Sea, God is also lord of nature. That is how not only Genesis but also Exodus began, with the flourishing growth of Israelite families, and it is where both Genesis and Exodus continue, with a further, more-negative demonstration of God's lordship over nature in these "natural" calamities. Israel's God is not one who rules only in politics and history or only in nature. Yahweh is lord in all these realms.

Exodus asserts that Israel's God is lord in relation to all the resources Egypt thought it could rely on. The natural disasters begin with the water of the Nile. Egypt was quite properly proud of its Nile, and it looked down on countries like **Canaan** that had to rely on rain to make its crops grow and had to wonder each year whether there would be enough rain. The Egyptians pictured rain as a kind of second-rate substitute for the Nile, which they knew they could rely on. Its water supply was always there. Except that suddenly it was not. God could deprive Egypt of its water supply as easily as God could shut up the heavens so that there was no rain in Canaan. Let the Egyptians not think they were invulnerable to the intervention of the God of Israel!

Exodus also asserts that nature, like humanity, is subordinate to God's purpose and that God is prepared to be as ruthless in relating to the natural world as in relating to the human world. When Jesus shows himself prepared to curse a fig tree as a kind of prophetic sign, he shows he has the same attitude to nature as his Father had in sending disease on all the livestock in Egypt to try to get a point home to the Egyptians. When leaders do the right thing, their people and their country profit. When leaders fail, both suffer.

The Egyptian "experts" are involved in all this. They are not mere magicians but the scientists of the day, the people who know how to manipulate the environment, an important resource to Pharaoh in managing the country. They are like White House staff or people in government research agencies. They can make things happen the way Moses and Aaron can. But the story makes fun of them. They, too, could turn a staff into a snake (but Aaron's staff swallows theirs!) and turn water into blood or multiply frogs (wouldn't it be more useful if they could do the opposite?). They can't multiply gnats, however, and they acknowledge that this must reflect "the finger of God." They won't be able to protect themselves from the blisters that affect everyone in Egypt (Exodus 9). Exposing their feebleness and inability to compete with Moses is another way the story shows that the God of Israel who works through Moses and Aaron is the real God.

EXODUS 8:8–32

Praying for the Enemy

[8]Pharaoh summoned Moses and Aaron and said, "Plead with Yahweh to remove the frogs from me and my people, and I will send the people off so they may sacrifice to Yahweh." [9]Moses said to Pharaoh, "You may have the honor over me in connection with when I plead for you, your servants, and your people for the cutting off of the frogs from you and your houses. Only in the Nile will they be left." [10]He said, "Tomorrow." [Moses] said, "According to your word, so that you may acknowledge that there is no one like Yahweh our God. [11]The frogs will move away from you, your houses, your servants, and your people. Only in the Nile will they be left." [12]Moses and Aaron went out from Pharaoh, and Moses cried out to Yahweh about the frogs he had brought on Pharaoh, [13]and Yahweh acted in accordance with Moses' word. The frogs died in the houses, the courtyards, and the open country. [14]They piled them up, heap after heap. The country stank. [15]Then when Pharaoh saw there was relief, he stiffened his resolve and did not listen to them, as Yahweh had spoken.

[16]Yahweh said to Moses, "Say to Aaron, 'Hold out your staff and strike the country's dirt so it becomes gnats in all Egypt.'" [17]They did so. Aaron stretched out his hand with his staff and struck the country's dirt, and gnats came on human beings and cattle. All the country's dirt became gnats in all Egypt. [18]The experts did this with their spells to produce gnats, but they could not do it, so when the gnats came on human beings and cattle, [19]the experts said to Pharaoh, "This is the finger of God." But Pharaoh's resolve stayed strong, and he did not listen to them, as Yahweh had spoken.

²⁰Yahweh said to Moses, "Early in the morning, take your stand before Pharaoh. There he will be, going out to the water. You are to say to him, 'Yahweh has said this: "Send my people off so they may serve me. ²¹Because if you do not send my people off: well, I am going to send swarms of flies on you, your servants, your people, and your houses. The houses of the Egyptians will be full of swarms of flies, and also the ground that they walk on, ²²but on that day I will distinguish the region of Goshen on which my people stand so that there is no swarm of flies there, in order that you may acknowledge that I Yahweh am in the midst of the country. ²³I will establish a redemption between my people and your people. Tomorrow this sign will come about.'" ²⁴Yahweh did this. Heavy swarms of flies came into Pharaoh's house and into the house of his servants. In all Egypt the country was devastated because of the swarms of flies. ²⁵Pharaoh summoned Moses and Aaron and said, "Go, sacrifice to Yahweh your God within the country." ²⁶Moses said, "It would not be right to do so, because what we sacrifice to Yahweh our God is offensive to Egyptians. If we sacrifice what is offensive to Egyptians before your eyes, will they not stone us? ²⁷We will go three days' journey into the wilderness to sacrifice to Yahweh our God, as he says to us." ²⁸So Pharaoh said, "I myself will release you so you may sacrifice to Yahweh your God in the wilderness. Only do not go any great distance. Plead for me." ²⁹Moses said, "I am going out from your presence and I will plead with Yahweh so that the swarms of flies move away from Pharaoh and his servants and his people tomorrow. Only, Pharaoh must not again act deceitfully by not releasing the people to sacrifice to Yahweh." ³⁰So Moses went out from Pharaoh's presence and pleaded with Yahweh. ³¹Yahweh acted in accordance with Moses' word and removed the swarms of flies from Pharaoh, his servants, and his people, and not one was left, ³²but Pharaoh stiffened his resolve this time, too, and did not send the people off.

I think it's easier for my church to pray for the present U.S. president than it was to pray for his predecessor. They like the present president; they find it easy to identify with him (he is African American and so are most of them); and they like his attitudes and his commitments. Other churches will have the opposite feelings. But how easy it is doesn't make any difference to whether you pray for the president. There are people who become the confidantes, counselors, confessors, and prayer partners of presidents, and they have to perform an analogous but much more complex balancing act. It is no use just being the president's yes-man, always reassuring him he is doing his best. Sometimes you have to confront him, precisely because you are his friend. You have to be something like an Israelite prophet, who at different times confronts the king, brings him God's word, encourages him, and prays for him

Moses' relationship to Pharaoh is actually that of a prophet. A king runs an earthly court where issues get discussed, decisions are made, and modes of implementation are decided. A prophet may have no right of access to this court. But there is another court to which he does have access and to which the king does not, the meeting of the court in the heavens where even more far-reaching issues get discussed, decisions are made, and modes of implementation get decided. A prophet gets to know what this court is planning and has the right to take part in its deliberations. When prophets come to someone and declare, "God has said this," they are acting like an envoy sent from the king's court who says, "The king has said this."

One might expect Pharaoh to pray on his own behalf, and perhaps he does that, but by asking Moses to pray for him, he indicates recognition of who Moses is, as well as who Moses' God is, and recognition of the special position of a prophet in God's court. He therefore twice bids Moses to "plead" for him with God when this heavenly court meets. One might have thought that Moses would refuse and/or that God would decline to listen to the plea, at least after the first time Pharaoh reneged on his word: "Next time, Pharaoh, let's have the action first, then we'll have the prayer and the relief." Praying for your oppressors isn't like that. You carry on praying for them even when they carry on deceiving you. Moses pleads like someone speaking in court on behalf of a friend. He cries out to God on Pharaoh's behalf; Exodus uses the verb that elsewhere describes Israel's own crying out to God. He cries out on behalf of the people's oppressor in the way Israel itself cries out about this oppressor.

One reason is that praying for them works in favor of God's purpose as well as in favor of Pharaoh. It is a way of turning the other cheek. It declines to acknowledge the power differential between the superior person and the subordinate person; indeed, it reverses it. Pharaoh is asking Moses for something! Pharaoh acknowledges that in this connection he is not the person with power and authority; Moses is. Praying for our oppressors exercises an authority God has given us, takes up a position that reframes the way we look at the authority differential between us and the people who have power over us. When we are the people in power, knowing that people over whom we have power are praying for us makes us reframe our own position. There is thus a nonchalance and irony in Moses' words: "You may have the honor over me in connection with when I plead for you." It's like a father saying to a child, "You decide for us." Pharaoh can have the "power" to specify when the prayer is answered, and Moses will see it is answered and thereby show where the power actually lies. Pharaoh's exercise of power with regard to the prayer will magnify Moses' exercise of power with regard to it.

In chapters 9–10 Moses will pray for Pharaoh again after saying he is well aware that Pharaoh's profession of repentance is false. The prayers and their answers demonstrate Moses' power, and they function as part of what leaves Pharaoh without excuse. His troubles sometimes start reframing his thinking, but this reframing doesn't last long. How strange not to be permanently changed by having one's prayer answered! For Pharaoh, the result of praying, receiving an answer, and then ignoring its implications is to deepen his culpability. Every time God sends some calamity on the country, it gives him an opportunity to come to his senses. Every time he fails to do so, he sinks deeper into guilt.

EXODUS 9:1–21

Knowledge and Acknowledgment

[Verses 1–12 relate further afflictions, an epidemic among Egypt's animals and a devastating rash on human beings and animals.]

[13]Yahweh said to Moses, "Early in the morning, take your stand before Pharaoh and say to him, 'Yahweh, the God of the

40

Hebrews, has said this: "Send my people off so they may serve me. [14]Because this time I am going to send all my blows on your spirit and on your servants and your people, in order that you may acknowledge that there is no one like me in all the earth. [15]Because by now, had I sent my hand and hit you and your people with an epidemic, you would have disappeared from the earth. [16]Yet for this purpose I have let you stand, for the purpose of getting you to see my power and for the sake of proclaiming my name in all the earth. [17]You are still exalting yourself against my people so as not to send them off. [18]Now. This time tomorrow I am going to make it rain very heavy hail, such as has not happened in Egypt from the day of its founding until now. [19]So now, send to bring into safety your livestock and everything that you have in the open country. Any human beings or cattle that find themselves in the open country and do not gather in the house, the hail will fall on them and they will die.""" [20]Any of Pharaoh's servants who revered Yahweh's word hurried his servants and livestock to their homes, [21]but whoever did not apply his mind to Yahweh's word left his servants and livestock in the open country.

Over recent years the world has watched with dismay the ruin of Zimbabwe. There are ways in which the sins of the fathers are being visited on the children; Britain and other colonial powers have to accept some responsibility for the postcolonial experience of such countries. Yet some of these countries do worse than others in a way that does not relate to that history. Zimbabwe or Rhodesia (as it was) is rich in minerals and agricultural potential but saw nothing but decline beginning in the 1990s. The willfully unwise policies of its government seem to have been a big factor in this decline and an even bigger factor in the catastrophic hastening of this decline over the subsequent decade. As one watched reports on TV, one asked, "How can leaders be so foolish? Why can't they see?"

One of God's aims in bringing this series of disasters on Pharaoh is so that he "may acknowledge that there is no one like [God] in all the earth." The theme runs through the story. "I do not acknowledge Yahweh," Pharaoh said when Moses first asked him to release the Israelites (5:2). When these epidemics start arriving, Pharaoh was told, "You will acknowledge that I am Yahweh, . . . and so will your people" (7:5, 14). It is a strange expression; it means more than it sounds. It implies that **Yahweh** is the only God who counts; to acknowledge that this is Yahweh is to acknowledge that this is the one God who counts and to bow down to that God. In fact, it is to "acknowledge that there is no one like Yahweh our God" (8:10). Further, Pharaoh will be driven to "acknowledge that I Yahweh am in the midst of the country" (8:22). That's rather sassy on Yahweh's part. Surely this country belongs to the gods of **Egypt**? Oh, I don't acknowledge the gods of Egypt, says Yahweh. I can be present and active where I like. The God of the **Hebrews** will act so that Pharaoh will be forced to acknowledge that the earth belongs to Yahweh and that Yahweh makes a distinction between Egypt and Israel (9:4; 11:7).

Eventually Pharaoh's ministers of state see the point and surely risk their lives with the boldness of their confrontation of Pharaoh: "Do you not yet acknowledge that Egypt is lost?" (10:7). Can he not see they are like animals caught in a trap? Yet they keep returning to the trap to let it spring shut on them again. "Egypt is lost" is a strong expression: Egypt is dead, destroyed, finished. It's an exaggeration, but anyone can see that the country is going through a series of calamities that have brought it to its knees. But Pharaoh can't see it. There are none so blind as those who won't see.

In Exodus 9, the particular means designed to pull Pharaoh toward acknowledging God is the way God protects the Israelites from the disasters that come on Egypt. In connection with the first three disasters (the blood, the frogs, and the gnats), there was no mention of how they affected the Israelites, though the story stresses their effect on the Egyptians in particular. Only in Exodus 8 in connection with the flies does the question surface. There God "set apart" the Goshen region where Israel lived, so that there would be no flies there. In Exodus 9, first God exempts the Israelites from the catastrophe to the livestock. God "sets apart" the Israelite livestock and the Egyptian livestock. Likewise the terrible darkness that afflicts the country in chapter 10 exempts the region where the Israelites live, in the way one area of a city can retain lighting when another area experiences a power outage. God will do the same with the last and most terrible disaster (11:7).

42

There is a neat link between the word for "setting apart" (*palah*) and the word for "redeeming" (*padah*). There is only one letter's difference between them. In Exodus 8:22–23 God declared the intention to set apart the region of Goshen and thereby establish a redemption between Israel and Egypt. There are two connections in which Exodus talks about redemption that might help us understand the idea.

Suppose someone has to become an indentured servant, working as a servant to someone else; perhaps the family farm has failed and the family cannot support itself and has got into debt. If someone in your extended family has resources, he can "redeem" you—pay what you borrowed and thereby make it unnecessary for you to be someone's servant. He thus gives you back your freedom. In effect, that is what God is doing for the Israelites. Because of a famine they had to go to Egypt and eventually became servants or serfs to the Egyptians. Now they are being treated like members of God's family to whom God is accepting an obligation to procure their freedom. There isn't exactly a price God pays in this connection; the stress in the idea of redemption lies on the procuring of their release. So talk of "redemption" is similar to talk of "**restoration**" (6:6).

The other context is the obligation to give the firstborn to God, as an aspect of the awareness that all life comes from God, belongs to God, and is owed to God. One recognizes this fact symbolically by giving God the firstborn, the one who opens the womb. With animals that can be sacrificed you may directly do that, but with animals such as donkeys and with human beings you "redeem" the firstborn by making a donation to the work of the sanctuary that is equivalent to the firstborn's notional value. You thereby free this firstborn to live an ordinary life. Metaphorically speaking, Israel is God's firstborn son; Israel has a position of privilege and responsibility in relation to God and in relation to the rest of the human "family." At the moment, Egypt is preventing Israel from fulfilling that role, but God wants this firstborn son back (4:22). So it is as if God is prepared to redeem him. The language is paradoxical. Instead of Israel's paying the price to God to redeem its own firstborn, God pays the price to redeem Israel. Indeed, there is again not exactly a price God will pay in this connection, and it is not clear to whom God would pay it—not Pharaoh! (When this image came to be used to describe Christ's achievement on the cross, the early church theologian Origen asked whom Christ paid our ransom price to, and said it was Satan; which similarly involves pushing the idea of "redemption" too literally.)

In doing this God sets the Israelites and the Egyptians apart. In the end, God is interested in "redeeming" and blessing Egypt as much as Israel, but to achieve this, in the short term God treats them in very different ways.

EXODUS 9:22–35

Pharaoh Flip-Flop

[22]Yahweh said to Moses, "Stretch out your hand toward the heavens so that hail may come on all Egypt, on human beings and cattle and all the herbage in the open country in Egypt." [23]So Moses stretched out his staff toward the heavens. As Yahweh sent thunder and hail, lightning fell on the ground, and Yahweh rained hail on Egypt. [24]Hail came with lightning flashing about in the midst of the hail, very heavy, such as had not come in all Egypt since it became a nation. [25]In all Egypt, the hail hit everything in the open country, both human beings and cattle; all the herbage in the open country it hit, and every tree in the open country it shattered. [26]Only in the region of Goshen, where the Israelites were, was there no hail. [27]Pharaoh sent and summoned Moses and Aaron and said to them, "This time [I acknowledge] I have sinned. Yahweh is in the right and I and my people are in the wrong. [28]Plead with Yahweh so that this may be quite enough supernatural thunder and hail, and I will send you off. You will stay no longer." [29]Moses said to him, "As I go out of the city, I will spread my hands to Yahweh. The thunder—it will stop, the hail—it will fall no longer, so that you may acknowledge that the earth belongs to Yahweh. [30]But you and your servants: I know that you do not yet revere Yahweh." [31](The flax and barley were ruined, because the barley was ripening and the flax was budding, [32]but the regular wheat and hulled wheat were not hit, because they ripen late.) [33]From Pharaoh's presence Moses went out from the city and spread his hands to Yahweh, and the thunder and hail stopped and the rain did not pour on the earth, [34]but when Pharaoh saw

that the rain, hail, and thunder had stopped, he did wrong again; he stiffened his resolve, he and his servants. [35]So Pharaoh's resolve remained strong and he did not send the Israelites off, as Yahweh had spoken by means of Moses.

In the rough and tumble of U.S. politics, you have to be very careful about changing your mind, or you may be accused of flip-flopping. It's appropriate that there should be a term for an unprincipled change of mind or change of policy, one that may be designed merely to try to win votes from people who opposed the policy you previously espoused, or one that indicates you are not very good at thinking things through. Yet there are occasions when presidents or governments need to change their minds and their policies in light of developments in events or in thinking. John Maynard Keynes is credited with the comment "When the facts change, I change my mind. What do you do, sir?" In this connection it's a shame when accusing someone of flip-flopping becomes itself a way of getting votes, a cheap way to discredit an opponent. The assumption is that people like to think of their leaders as clear thinking and decisive; deriding them as flip-floppers marks them as lacking in judgment and indecisive.

Pharaoh is the Bible's great flip-flopper, the man who is always changing his mind, and neither because he needs to get elected nor because the facts have changed. His initial reaction to the request from a crowd of foreign serfs to be allowed to go and hold a religious festival in the wilderness (Exodus 5–6) was quite reasonable and logical. Maybe his declining to be too impressed by Aaron's tricks that could be at least partly emulated by his own experts (Exodus 7) was an indication that he was not going to flip-flop too readily. Subsequently he starts doing so. He asks Moses to pray for the frogs to be removed and promises to send Israel off, but reneges on the promise. Then during the epidemic of flies he tries to get a compromise from Moses by suggesting that the people offer sacrifice within the country rather than leaving it, or that they go into the wilderness but not too far (in case they never come back to work as serfs!); he again asks Moses to pray for the flies to go away but subsequently reneges on his suggestion (Exodus 8).

Now in light of the hail Pharaoh makes what looks like a confession that takes him forward and takes the situation forward. "This time," he says, speaking as if he has indeed come to a new position, "I have sinned. Yahweh is in the right and I and my people are in the wrong." It is an astonishing confession. It precisely matches the way Israelites are expected to make confession. Confession doesn't involve going into great emotional outpourings about how sorry we are. It involves acknowledging facts, owning what we have done. So Pharaoh's confession matches the one David makes when Nathan gets him to face up to the wrongdoing he has been hiding from (2 Samuel 12) and the confession Psalm 51 makes, after which it goes on to grant (like Pharaoh), "You are in the right in your speaking; you are in the clear in your decision" (the decision to send trouble as a consequence of the wrongdoing). It also matches confessions Jeremiah reports Judah making, or imagines Judah making (Jeremiah 14–15), but there Jeremiah goes on to report or imagine God's skeptical response; God suspects a mismatch between words and heart, and Moses wisely suspects the same mismatch in Pharaoh. He does not yet "revere" God. The previous time Exodus used this verb it described the midwives who on this basis took no notice of a previous Pharaoh's instructions. Moses knows that Pharaoh has not yet caught up with the midwives.

With hindsight, we know where this flop-flop will end, but when you are in the midst of the story in real life, you do not. Every time God acts in mercy on Pharaoh it gives him a real chance to change. Moses knows that Pharaoh does not yet revere God. Not yet. It could still happen.

EXODUS 10:1–29

More Prayer, More Flip-Flop

[1]Yahweh said to Moses, "Go to Pharaoh, because I have stiffened his resolve and his servants' resolve so as to set these signs of mine in his midst [2]and so that you may recount in the ears of your son and your grandson how I dealt ruthlessly with the Egyptians, and [recount] my signs that I set among them, so

that you may acknowledge that I am Yahweh." ³So Moses and Aaron went to Pharaoh and said to him, "Yahweh the God of the Hebrews has said this: 'How long do you refuse to humble yourself before me? Send my people off so that they may serve me. ⁴Because if you refuse to send my people off: well, I am going to bring a locust swarm on your territory tomorrow. ⁵It will cover the surface of the country; people will not be able to see the country. It will eat the remains of what survived, left over for you from the hail. It will eat every tree that grows for you, from the open country. ⁶They will fill your houses and the houses of your servants and the houses of all the Egyptians, which your fathers and grandfathers have not seen, from the day they came on the land until this day.'" And he turned and went out from Pharaoh's presence.

⁷Pharaoh's servants said to him, "How long will this be a trap for us? Send the people off so they may serve Yahweh their God. Do you not yet acknowledge that Egypt is lost?" ⁸So Moses and Aaron were brought back to Pharaoh, and he said to them, "Go, serve Yahweh your God. Who are the ones who are going?" ⁹Moses said, "With our young and old we will go, with our sons and daughters, with our flocks and herds we will go, because we will have a festival for Yahweh." ¹⁰He said to them, "May Yahweh be with you as I send you and your little ones off! See, you have wrongdoing in mind. ¹¹Definitely not. You men, do go and serve Yahweh, as this is what you are seeking." And they were thrown out from Pharaoh's presence.

¹²So Yahweh said to Moses, "Stretch out your hand over Egypt with the locust swarm, so it may come over Egypt and eat all the herbage in the country, anything the hail left." ¹³So Moses stretched out his staff over Egypt and Yahweh drove an east wind through the country all that day and all night, and when morning came, the east wind had carried the locust swarm. ¹⁴The locust swarm came over all Egypt and settled in the entire territory of Egypt, very heavy. There had not been a locust swarm like it before it, and after it there would not be. ¹⁵It covered the surface of the entire country, and the country was dark. It ate all the herbage in the country and all the fruit on the trees that the hail had left. Nothing green was left of the trees or the herbage of the open country in all Egypt. ¹⁶Pharaoh quickly summoned Moses and Aaron and said, "I have sinned against Yahweh your God and against you. ¹⁷But now, will you carry my

wrongdoing only this time. Plead with Yahweh your God that he just remove this death from me." [18]He went out from Pharaoh's presence and pleaded with Yahweh, [19]and Yahweh diverted a very strong west wind, carried the locust swarm, and threw it into the Red Sea. Not one of the swarm remained in all the territory of Egypt. [20]But Yahweh stiffened Pharaoh's resolve and he did not send the Israelites off.

[Verses 21–29 report another calamity, the descent of a preternatural darkness, but once again Pharaoh is not prepared to let the Israelites go without any conditions, and the chapter ends up with an angry standoff between Pharaoh and Moses.]

I've just been reading a paper by one of my students titled "Prayer in the Scriptures." The student astonished me first by reporting a poll indicating that 72 percent of people in the United States pray at least several times a week. Then he surprised me by reporting another study indicating that people in the church who pray are apparently more likely to pray for other people than for themselves. At least, of the prayers left in a prayer box, only 5 percent were for the author alone; 81 percent were for family and friends, and 11 percent for global issues. When the student came to prayer in the Bible, his first reference was to Pharaoh's requests to Moses for prayer, and Moses' prayers in response.

As Moses puts it here, Pharaoh has not yet humbled himself before **Yahweh**. It is a telling verb. The king of **Egypt** has been set on keeping the Israelites down, keeping them in their place (1:11–12). Moses turns the tables on Pharaoh by using the same word to refer to his obligation to submit himself to God. Another verb that recurs here is "refuse": Pharaoh keeps refusing to do what Yahweh says (4:23; 7:14; 8:2; 9:2; 10:3–4). The question is, When is Pharaoh going to acknowledge that he is not God and Yahweh is?

Actually Pharaoh continues flip-flopping. When he says, "May Yahweh be with you as I send you and your little ones off!" perhaps he means this positively, but I think more likely he implies (as my mother would have put it), "If you think I am going to let go of you all like that, you've got another 'thing' coming." Pharaoh knows that if he lets the Israelites take their families as well as their animals, there is no reason for them ever to come back to resume their position as his serfs. So let the men go on their own. The massive locust storm soon has him confessing his sin and asking Moses to plead with Yahweh again. Once again with a straight face he says, "Just this one time." Then, he adds the plea to Moses to "carry" his wrongdoing. There are two noteworthy features about the way Pharaoh speaks. God made a wind "carry" the locusts in, and God will in due course "carry" them away, and in between Pharaoh pleads with Moses to "carry" his wrongdoing. But then "carry" is the regular Old Testament word for "forgive." What you do when you forgive someone's wrongdoing is carry it. You accept its burden and accept responsibility for its consequences, rather than making the other person suffer for it. Once again, Exodus pictures Pharaoh using just the words a king ought to use in these circumstances. One effect will be to remind Israelites who listen to the story, and especially their kings, about something. Pharaoh models the right way for a king to speak with a prophet when he knows he has done wrong, and it reminds the Israelites and their king not to flip-flop in these circumstances (as Zedekiah once did: see Jeremiah 34).

Pharaoh has at last and at least come to see what his ministers have already seen. They talked about Egypt being lost. He wants Moses to plead with God to "remove this death from me," this epidemic that is bringing death to him and his people because the locusts have eaten everything that grows. But when God does that, he again changes his stance. The preternatural darkness that follows makes him try again at compromise: the families may go with the men, but the flocks and herds must stay (10:24). Moses cleverly but truly points out that it is no use going out for a festival without some animals to sacrifice; but they hardly need to take all of them, and Moses' insistence that "not a hoof is to remain" may hint that he knows that Pharaoh knows that he knows that Pharaoh is right about the Israelites' not coming back once they leave. Its more direct point is that whereas Pharaoh keeps seeking a compromise, both Moses and Yahweh are less and less inclined to make one. This is a contest for the highest stakes, a contest to the death. The standoff at the end of chapter 10 expresses the point clearly. An irresistible force is meeting an immoveable object.

But the object will have to move in the end. Moses will express his anger, and so will God. And Pharaoh will not only bid the Israelites go to serve God as Moses said, with their flocks and herds, but will add "and bless me also."

EXODUS 11:1–10

Knowing and Acknowledging Again

[1]Yahweh said to Moses, "There is yet one more blow I shall bring on Pharaoh and on Egypt. After that, he will send you off from here. When he sends you off, it will be complete. He will finally throw you out from here. [2]You may speak in the ears of the people so that they ask for objects of silver and gold, each man from his neighbor and each woman from hers." [3]Yahweh gave the people favor in the eyes of the Egyptians. Moses himself was also very great in Egypt in the eyes of Pharaoh's servants and of all the people.

[4]Moses said, "Yahweh has said this: 'At midnight I intend to go out in the midst of the Egyptians [5]and every firstborn in Egypt will die, from the firstborn of Pharaoh who sits on the throne to the firstborn of the servant who is behind the millstones, and all the firstborn of the cattle.' [6]There will be a loud cry in all Egypt such as has not been and will not be again. [7]But at any of the Israelites a dog will not growl, at a person or an animal, so that you may acknowledge that Yahweh distinguishes between Egypt and Israel. [8]All these servants of yours will come down to me and bow down to me saying, 'Go out, you and all your people who follow you.' After that I will go out." He went out from Pharaoh's presence in angry fury.

[9]So Yahweh had said to Moses, "Pharaoh will not listen to you, in order that my wonders may multiply in Egypt," [10]and Moses and Aaron had performed all these wonders before Pharaoh, but Yahweh had strengthened Pharaoh's resolve and he did not send the Israelites off from his country.

The other day I was stopped for speeding, and the highway patrolman asked me the same question that a British policeman once asked me in these circumstances: "Sir, do you know the speed limit on this road?" Yes, I said, and I was able to give the right answer; it was 65 mph, and I was doing rather more than that. If I had been in Israel and had been asked the question, it would have seemed more complicated, at least in Old Testament times, because the verb for "know" also means "acknowledge" or "recognize" and thus obey (I don't think the verb works that way in modern **Hebrew**, so if I am ever stopped for speeding in Israel, that is one thing I needn't worry too much about). Like some other Hebrew words, it presupposes a link between the way we think and the way we act. When I was stopped by the police, I knew the speed limit in my head, but I was not acknowledging it with my right foot. That is often the prophets' complaint about people. They *know* the **Torah**, but they do not *acknowledge* it.

It is not only Pharaoh that **Yahweh** wants to draw into acknowledging Yahweh. These signs are designed also to draw Israel into that acknowledgment. The logic is one Paul will pick up in Romans 1–3. The people of God can be good at recognizing other people's falling short of God's standards and be inclined to exempt themselves. Paul's argument shows how "all have sinned and come short of God's glory." It's true of Jew but also of Gentile, of agnostic but also of believer, of Muslim but also of Christian. Exodus knows that Israel has as much need to acknowledge Yahweh as **Egyptians** have. God's commission of Moses in Exodus 6 included reference to how the exodus will bring about that acknowledgment. If Yahweh's being that kind of God really gets under their skin, it will revolutionize their lives.

Moses is to tell his son (the one he had failed to circumcise?!) and his grandson about the tough way Yahweh treated Pharaoh so that they may make that acknowledgment (10:2). Moses stands for all Israelites in relation to their children and grandchildren. The king of Egypt (or **Assyria** or **Babylon** or **Persia**) will often be controlling their destiny, and they will be tempted to stop trusting in Yahweh. They need their trust in Yahweh sustained. One way to sustain it is to keep retelling the story of God's ruthless treatment of the imperial power that dominated them at the beginning of their story. Yes, Israel needs to keep acknowledging that Yahweh is God. Yahweh's encouraging Pharaoh to keep resisting pressure to release the Israelites means more and more signs of Yahweh's power, and these will encourage that acknowledgment.

God makes the point again in connection with the deaths of the firstborn, which will affect the Egyptians but not the Israelites, "so that you may acknowledge that Yahweh makes a distinction between Egypt and Israel." Little people like Israel can assume they count for nothing over against the superpowers of the day. This story makes it possible for them to look at things differently. God is not on the side of the superpowers.

Throughout, the exodus story alternates two ways of understanding events. There are two wills being worked out in the story, God's and Pharaoh's. Pharaoh is stiffening his resolve not to let go of his Israelite labor force. At the same time, God is stiffening Pharaoh's resolve, encouraging him not to let the Israelites go (all the while bidding him to let them go!). The final catastrophe will bring about a total capitulation.

There are several linked aspects to God's will. God is intent on ending the Israelites' suffering and also on enabling them to focus on serving God rather than having to give their energy to serving Pharaoh in building projects that just serve his interests. God is intent on showing Pharaoh who is God and who is in control of the world, and on Israel itself recognizing this. Further, God is intent on this being a story that will bring that truth home to the world—to people like us who still read the story. In order to achieve the first two of these ends, it would be fine to get the Israelites out of Egypt as easily and as quickly as possible, but in order to achieve the other three ends, it is useful if it takes longer. So God is quite happy to encourage Pharaoh not to give in too easily. His ever-increasing stupidity and its coming to a climax in the terrible catastrophe that is imminent would have frightening implications for the leader of any great power. Such a leader cannot afford to fall into the trap of thinking he or she is God, which may bring down terrible calamity on the people. It also contains great encouragement for later Israel and for other powerless nations and people. Great leaders and great powers fall, and great is the fall thereof.

Exodus announced one way of putting this when Moses was first sent to bid Pharaoh to let the Israelites leave. Israel is God's firstborn: that is, Israel is the one whom God intends to privilege in connection with its having a special responsibility and role to fulfill for its Father in relation to the rest of the human family. Pharaoh is trying to hold onto this firstborn and use it to fulfill his own ends. Like a mafia boss sending a message to a foolish small fry who thinks he can defy the big guy, God offered friendly advice to Pharaoh. It would be wise to let go of my firstborn; otherwise I will take yours. Yet for all the impressiveness of Egyptian wisdom, wisdom is not Pharaoh's strong suit. He has come to make too much of himself, and this is the moment when the chickens come home to roost. Jesus will warn that when people fail to give food and drink, hospitality and clothing (which would be quite a good way to describe how the Egyptians had treated the Israelites) to members of his family, they depart into eternal fire (Matthew 25). Exodus is less frightening; only the firstborn of the nation pay the price, and it is only a this-worldly price.

The note about the generosity of ordinary Egyptians makes a similar point in a very different way. They are quite happy to make gifts to the Israelites that will be used to build a sanctuary for God. In this sense they join in serving God.

There is some jerkiness about this section of Exodus, presumably issuing from the way it combines different versions of the story. At the end of chapter 10 we would have assumed Moses had left Pharaoh, but in 11:4 he still seems to be in Pharaoh's presence. So this means the hot anger with which Moses leaves Pharaoh links with the standoff at the end of chapter 10. It is the first time Moses has become angry (maybe we should infer some anger when he killed the Egyptian in his youth). We have had one or two references to God's being angry, and maybe Moses is now learning to be more like God. Anger is an important energy-producing emotion for people who are called to do the right thing when it involves firm and aggressive action, or even simply to react in the right way to wrongdoing like Pharaoh's.

EXODUS 12:1–27

Anticipatory Celebration

[1]Yahweh said to Moses and Aaron in Egypt: [2]"This month is to be the beginning of the months for you. It is to be the first of the months in the year for you. [3]Speak to the whole Israelite

community as follows. On the tenth of this month they are to get for themselves, each man, a lamb for the family, a lamb for the household. ⁴If the household is too small for a lamb, he and his neighbor near his house are to get one, according to a count of the people. They are to account for the lamb, each person, according to what it [the household] will eat. ⁵Your lamb is to be whole, male, a year old. You may get it from the sheep or the goats. ⁶It is to be in your care until the fourteenth day of this month, then all the congregation of the Israelite community is to slaughter it at twilight. ⁷They are to take some of the blood and put it on the two doorposts and the lintel of the houses where they will eat it. ⁸They are to eat the meat that night. They are to eat it roasted over a fire, with flat bread and bitter herbs. ⁹Don't eat any of it raw or boiled (boiled in water) but roasted over a fire, including its head, with its legs and entrails. ¹⁰You are not to leave any of it until morning. What is left of it until morning, you are to burn in the fire. ¹¹This is how you are to eat it: your robes hitched up, your shoes on your feet, your cane in your hand. You are to eat it hurriedly. It will be Yahweh's Passover. ¹²I shall go through Egypt that night and strike down every firstborn in Egypt, human beings and animals. On all the Egyptian gods I will execute acts of authority. I am Yahweh. ¹³But for you the blood will be a sign on the houses where you are. I will see the blood and pass over you. No blow to bring destruction will come on you when I strike Egypt down. ¹⁴And this day is to be for you a memorial. You are to celebrate it as a festival for Yahweh. Through your generations you are to celebrate it."

[Verses 15–27 give further detail on the observance, with particular reference to eating flat bread for a week.]

I am sometimes asked, "What do you miss about England?" One of my joke replies is that I miss a magnificent chocolate-and-cream pastry called an "elephant's foot" that they sell at a bakery where we often had Saturday lunch. Another reply is "proximity to Israel." The last time we went there, two years before our move to the United States, the trip came immediately after Easter, which that year came at the same time as Passover. We were driving through the Galilee mountains and stopped at a fast-food stand at lunchtime, where I tried to buy a sandwich. The man looked at me in disbelief. Of course there were no sandwiches. It's Passover week, for goodness' sake. There is no bread from which you can make sandwiches this week. I felt really stupid. I almost got the impression that the man thought I might be from the rabbinic police, trying to catch Jews who were not observing Passover properly. It was one of those moments when you realize that the observances and other realities of which Scripture speaks are not just things from the past or stories in a book but contemporary realities. Passover is not just an event from a nation's past in the way that King Arthur or William the Conqueror might be for me. It is *the* event from the past that shapes the present for Jewish people.

One symbol of this fact is that the month of Passover, which corresponds to the latter part of March and the beginning of April, is now to mark the beginning of the year. Israel did not take that literally, and neither do modern Jews (the year begins in September), but in terms of faith, theology, and self-understanding the year begins in spring, because Passover marks the beginning of Israel's move as a nation from the service of Pharaoh to the service of God. Good Friday thus also falls in March or April, because Jesus was crucified at Passover time, and the Last Supper was a Passover meal. Holy Communion thus links with Passover, though Passover more vividly reenacts the event it commemorates and brings home its significance to people.

Like Thanksgiving in the United States or Christmas in Britain, Passover is a family occasion, though it is more than that. It is not individual nuclear families that celebrate it (then spend a week experimenting with recipes for leftover turkey). A household would be closer to what Western thinking would call an extended family, and its head (the "person" in verse 3) would negotiate sharing a lamb with the household next door if the family wasn't big enough to eat the whole. We think in terms of a Passover lamb, but the word could as easily refer to a kid goat. It will be a male, because females are more valuable as producers of milk and potential mothers of the next generation, whereas males are mainly good for eating.

The lamb will make for the kind of festive meal an Israelite family might have on other occasions, with some herbs to make it spicy and some pita. The rules about a week eating flat bread may also reflect an observance relating to the beginning of the grain harvest, but these "ordinary" observances are given new meaning. The whole event comes to remind people of the exodus. So you eat it all that night because you are leaving tomorrow, and you even dress in light of that fact. You eat flat bread because you haven't got time to make proper bread with leaven to make it rise. You don't take all the time in the world over it. You must be ready to go.

The strange aspect of the event is the daubing of blood on the door. God is about to bring about that last terrible catastrophe, killing the firstborn throughout **Egypt**. The blood on the door will mark this as a home God can "pass over"; it is marked as an Israelite home. Excuse me, does God not know which are Israelite homes (and anyway, are the Israelites not all together in that ghetto in Goshen)? Well, maybe, but it often seems God prefers to look and see rather than rely on omniscience, as at the Babel Tower and at Sodom. In calling this a sign "for you," however, Exodus also hints at the significance of daubing the blood for the people. It is their proclamation of who they are; they mark themselves as Israelites and not Egyptians. Further, it reassures them they will be safe when the ax falls and **Yahweh** lets the Destroyer do his work (verse 23; he is apparently an **aide** who does the actual killing).

It will be an exercise of authority and power against the Egyptian gods. It's the only time Exodus mentions the Egyptian gods. Otherwise the narrative is all about a conflict between Yahweh the God of Israel and the human king of Egypt. The king of Egypt certainly believed in some gods, but it is a rule about politics that the gods are ancillary to you rather than your being the servant of God, and the bigger your empire, the more that will be true. So the conflict between Yahweh and Pharaoh is one designed to put in his place the person who for practical purposes behaves like God (indeed, Egyptian kings were thought to be in some sense incarnations of a god). This comment by Yahweh also suggests a different point. It is the responsibility of gods to look after their people, right? So Yahweh's ability to breeze in and kill all the firstborn in Egypt shows that there is not much to be said for the gods of Egypt. Yahweh has the power to act decisively in Egypt. It doesn't matter what the Egyptian gods think.

The Old Testament does not have an idea of a final judgment and of people being under God's wrath and going to hell. That is something you find only in the New Testament, where the objects of God's wrath are not only one nation but the whole world. But Christ's death then functions like the Passover lamb's death. Passover is not a sacrifice, and the Passover lamb is not a sacrificial lamb; what happens to its blood is different from what happens to the blood at a sacrifice. The New Testament came to understand the Passover lamb as a sacrifice and to apply the image to Jesus, but this involved seeing new meaning in the Passover. If you are "marked" by Christ's blood, as the door of an Israelite's house was marked by the lamb's blood, then that protects you from the Destroyer when God implements his sovereignty over the world that resists his authority. It marks you as someone who through what Christ has done belongs to the people whom God had already claimed as his own and who have recognized that claim.

EXODUS 12:28–13:16

The 3 a.m. Scream

[28]The Israelites went and acted; as Yahweh commanded Moses and Aaron, so they did. [29]And in the middle of the night Yahweh struck all the firstborn in Egypt, from the firstborn of Pharaoh who sits on the throne to the firstborn of the captive who was in the dungeon, and all the firstborn of the cattle. [30]Pharaoh got up in the night, he and all his servants and all the Egyptians, and there was a loud crying out in Egypt, because there was no household where there was not someone dead. [31]He summoned Moses and Aaron in the night and said, "Up, get out from the midst of my people, both you and the Israelites. Go and serve Yahweh as you said. [32]Both your flocks and your herds—take them as you said. Go. And bless me also." [33]The Egyptians were firm with the people, quick to send them off from the country, because (they said), "We are all going to be dead." [34]So the people took their dough before it was leavened, their mixing bowls wrapped in their clothes, on their shoulder. [35]The Israelites had acted in accordance with Moses' word and asked the Egyptians for objects of silver and gold, and

clothes, [36]and Yahweh had given the people favor in the eyes of the Egyptians so they granted their request, and they stripped the Egyptians.

[37]The Israelites traveled from Rameses to Sukkot, 600,000 men on foot apart from little ones. [38]A mixed crowd also went up with them, and flocks and herds, very extensive livestock. [39]They baked the dough they brought out from Egypt into flat bread loaves because it was not leavened, because they were thrown out of Egypt and were not able to delay, and also they had not made provisions for themselves. [40]The period the Israelites lived in Egypt was 430 years. [41]At the end of 430 years, that very day all Yahweh's armies came out of Egypt. [42]It was a night of keeping watch for Yahweh in bringing them out of Egypt. For the Israelites through their generations this night is one for keeping watch for Yahweh.

[43]Yahweh said to Moses and Aaron, "This is the Passover ordinance. While no one born of a foreigner may eat of it, [44]any person who is a servant, acquired for money, but you have circumcised him—then he may eat of it. [45]A resident or employee may not eat of it. [46]It will be eaten in one house. You may not take any of the meat outside the house. You may not break any bone of it. [47]The whole Israelite community is to do this. [48]If a person lives with you as an immigrant and observes Passover for Yahweh, every male belonging to him is to be circumcised, then he may take part to observe it; he will be like a native of the country. But anyone who is uncircumcised may not eat of it. [49]There will be one instruction for the native and for the immigrant who lives among you.

[Exodus 12:50–13:16 gives more instructions on consecrating the firstborn to Yahweh on the celebration of Passover and the flat bread festival and on the marking of that with a sign on people's hands and foreheads.]

It was midnight, not 3 a.m., but in the Western world where we organize our own time rather than following nature's time, midnight is not the middle of the night; it is about the time I put out the light. So think of yourself as having been asleep for several hours when suddenly you are woken by a terrible scream. Or imagine you live at a time of genocide in Poland or Armenia or Rwanda, and you belong to the wrong ethnic group, and you hear a crowd approaching and there are shots. . . .

Oddly, in the order of events in Exodus the rules about how to observe Passover are detailed before the Passover event actually happens. That section of Exodus makes for a dramatic pause before we read about the actual Passover event, but it also adds a suggestive note to the regulations for celebrating Passover. God gave Moses and Aaron the instructions for celebrating the Passover while they were still in **Egypt**. Before the event has even happened (and when as an Israelite you might be entitled to a little skepticism about whether it ever will happen), God told Israel how to celebrate it, generation in, generation out, and Israel held the first celebration. Christians will devise ways of celebrating Christ's birth, death, and resurrection, and the outpouring of the Spirit, but (apart from the resurrection) it will be long after these events that they start having those celebrations. Israel starts celebrating God's great act of deliverance before it happens.

Now the Passover event does happen. As often happens to nations, the **Egyptians** are the victims of their leadership's stupidity. They have benefited from the wisdom and shrewdness of their leaders and have avoided being drafted for building work because immigrants such as the Israelites have been doing it. Now they pay the price for the nation's resistance to **Yahweh**, even attending showers for Israelites who are about to leave!

Six hundred thousand men implies a company of two or three million with the women and children, which would mean the Israelites were as numerous as the Egyptians and far more numerous than the population of **Canaan**, or than the Israelites themselves ever were when they lived in Canaan through Old Testament times, or than the peoples in Palestine in the first half of the twentieth century. But the word for a thousand can also mean a family, and something like six hundred families fits the scale of things. The reworking of the numbers so that "family" becomes "thousand" then underlines how wondrous was God's act of deliverance, and/or it symbolizes the sense in which the whole of later Israel was involved in the exodus.

Likewise the 430 years need not indicate literal chronology. First Kings 6 dates the building of the temple 480 years after the exodus, and that is not a literal chronological note; the actual period was much shorter. A similar period elapsed from the building of Solomon's temple to the rebuilding of the temple after the **exile**. Figures such as these are part of a chronological scheme for picturing the shape of Israel's story, like Matthew's schematizing of the story in terms of sequences of fourteen generations (Matthew 1:1–17). Ascribing a neat pattern to it is a way of indicating that the whole story is under God's control and reflects the working out of God's orderly plan.

The 600,000 plus their families were not the whole company. There was also a mixed crowd of non-Israelites—Egyptians who had become convinced that Yahweh was God and was Israel's God, and/or who saw no future for themselves in Egypt for one reason or another, and/or who had fallen in love with Israelite girls; and/or members of other ethnic groups (other **Hebrews**). That links with notes that appear in the ordinance for Passover. Like modern countries, Israel will have many foreigners in its midst, there for the same reasons as that mixed crowd that joined the exodus, but also (for instance) because they are involved in trade. How is Israel to relate to them?

We might ask, What sort of visa do they have? Israel asks, Can they take part in Passover? Are they more like foreigners or Israelites, more like members of the Israelite congregation, members of the people of God, or more like the adherents of another religion? How does God relate to them? The answer is that they have to choose. If they are the kind of immigrants or traders who are just staying in the village or the town but will eventually go back home and continue worshiping their old gods, then they are welcome to earn their living here, but it would be inappropriate to have them join in the festival when Israel celebrates God's great act of redemption. If they want to become part of this **covenant** people, they can be circumcised and then take part. They and other people will always be aware that they belong to another ethnic group, but Israel is totally open to people from other ethnic groups joining the covenant community. You do not have to be born an Israelite in order to be part of God's people.

EXODUS 13:17–14:31

One Kind of Fear Turns to Another

[17]When Pharaoh had sent the people off, God did not guide them by the road to the Philistines' country because it was near, because [God said], "In case the people have a change of heart when they see battle, and turn back to Egypt." [18]God made the people go around by the wilderness road, by the Reed Sea. The Israelites went up from Egypt organized into companies. [19]Moses took Joseph's bones with him, because he had made the Israelites solemnly swear, "God will definitely attend to you, and you are to take up my bones from here with you." [20]They traveled from Sukkot and camped at Etham at the edge of the wilderness, [21]with Yahweh going before them by day in a cloud column to guide them on the way and by night in a fire column to give them light, so that they could go day or night. [22]The cloud column by day and the fire column by night would not depart from before the people.

[14:1]Yahweh spoke to Moses: [2]"Tell the Israelites they are to turn back and camp near Pi-hahirot, between Migdal and the sea. You are to camp near Baal-zaphon, opposite it, by the sea. [3]Pharaoh will say of the Israelites, 'They are lost in the country. The wilderness has closed in on them.' [4]I will strengthen Pharaoh's resolve and he will pursue them, so that I may gain honor through Pharaoh and all his army, and the Egyptians may acknowledge that I am Yahweh." They did so. [5]When the king of Egypt was told that the people had fled, the resolve of Pharaoh and his servants toward the people changed. They said, "What is this that we have done, that we have sent Israel off from our service?" [6]He harnessed his chariot and took his people with him; [7]he took six hundred picked chariots and all the other Egyptian chariotry, with officers over all of them.

[8]So Yahweh strengthened the resolve of Pharaoh king of Egypt and he pursued the Israelites. As the Israelites were leaving with hands high, [9]the Egyptians pursued them. They overtook them camping by the sea, all Pharaoh's chariot horses, his riders, and his army, near Pi-hahirot, opposite Baal-zaphon. [10]As Pharaoh got near, the Israelites looked up. There: the Egyptians were marching after them. They were very fearful. The Israelites cried out to Yahweh,[11]and said to Moses, "Was it for lack of graves in Egypt that you took us to die in the wilderness? What

61

is this you have done to us in getting us to come out of Egypt? [12]Is this not the thing we told you in Egypt, 'Leave us alone and we will serve the Egyptians, because serving the Egyptians is better for us than dying in the wilderness'?" [13]Moses said to the people, "Do not be fearful. Take your stand and look at Yahweh's deliverance, which he will effect for you today. Because the Egyptians you have seen today you will not see any more, ever again, forever. [14]Yahweh—he will fight for you. You—you can stay quiet."

[In verses 15–31 Yahweh then bids Moses tell the Israelites to advance towards the sea and lift his staff over the sea and split it. Yahweh splits the sea by sending a strong wind and the Israelites begin to cross, with a wall of water on either side. When the Egyptians follow, Yahweh sends them into a panic and causes their chariots to get stuck. The sea returns, and they drown. The Israelites see what happens, revere Yahweh, and come to trust in Yahweh and in Moses.]

This weekend our rector is on a discernment retreat, and next weekend he is away preaching at a church in another city. I was a bit slow on the uptake, and someone else had to whisper to me that this is code for his wondering whether he should leave if that church asks him to move there. Having your pastor leave is a bit scary. He has been with us for eight years and has been a great gift for us. (He has given me lots of scope to be involved in the ministry, too.) Losing your pastor isn't like facing the Egyptian army, but it raises some similar issues. Can you face the future? Whom do you trust? Change can be hard: we prefer the situation we know.

In the streets of Tel Aviv you used to come across bits of old railway track (they have probably been cleaned up now), the remains of the railway line from Damascus to Cairo on which trains have not run for some time. South of Tel Aviv, they take the obvious, flat route along the coast all the way to **Egypt**. That might have seemed the obvious route for the Israelites from Egypt to **Canaan**, but Canaan was part of the Egyptian empire (the Philistines were not actually there yet—Exodus describes the geography in terms that make sense to people reading the story later). There was much traffic along this route precisely because it was the obvious one. The Egyptians would guard it, and going that way would mean hitting trouble. So God took them by an inland route, but that involved crossing the Reed Sea, the "sea of rushes" (the word is the one that came in Exodus 2 where Miriam left Moses in the reeds by the Nile).

Frustratingly, the story gives us lots of concrete detail about the way the Israelites went, but we cannot actually locate any of the places it mentions. The Reed Sea might be one of the northern arms of what we call the Red Sea, either side of Sinai, or it might be an area of marshy lakes within Sinai. Things that we know about Egyptian geography and history also don't help us establish how the exodus happened. The only hard detail that we can link with Egyptian records is the reference to Rameses in Exodus 1. Maybe this helps us focus on the way the story put the stress on how God guided the Israelites. When God guides you and you end up trapped in a cul-de-sac, it's reasonable to react the way the Israelites did. They still get in trouble, but it does not mean God abandons them.

As usual, God has a bigger picture in mind. We would have thought that the Israelites' escape from Egypt meant the exodus story was over. All they need do now is to march to the promised land. Taking Joseph's bones fulfills the wishes of the whole ancestral family: that is, to know that one day they will have their rest in the promised land as a place that belongs to the family and not merely one where they live as aliens. But it transpires that neither God nor Pharaoh is finished. God encourages Pharaoh not to give in quite yet.

Maybe we are not surprised that Pharaoh flip-flops once again and asks whether the disadvantages of letting the Israelites leave outweigh the advantages. Each time there is a disaster, things look different once the disaster is over. From God's angle, it is obvious that Pharaoh has admitted defeat, but it's not clear whether he has really acknowledged who is God. So God is happy to have one final confrontation whereby to get honor through him and his army. Once again it is emphasized how events demonstrate that **Yahweh** is God. The great power's leader thinks his will decides what happens in the world, and his people and other peoples are inclined to believe him. Yahweh's victory at the Reed Sea will give a final proof that this is not so.

The Israelites go from having their hands held high in praise and/or confidence and/or triumph to abject fear. They cry out to God, which is the right thing to do, but their words to Moses indicate how terrified they are. Like the disasters in Egypt, the parting of the sea has been explained as a natural event; a strong wind blew at just the right moment to let the Israelites through and then abated and caught the Egyptians as they followed. Such explanations undermine the story's concern to relate how the event proved that Yahweh is God and that the great power's leader is much less powerful than he thinks. Its point comes at the chapter's close: "When Israel saw the great power Yahweh exercised on the Egyptians, the people feared Yahweh and trusted in Yahweh and in his servant Moses." Hebrew uses the same word for being afraid and for revering, for a negative fear and a positive submission. At the beginning of the story the midwives feared God in a good sense rather than fearing Pharaoh and doing what he said. At the end of the story Israel gives up fearing the future and fearing Pharaoh in a bad sense because it has seen the reason for fearing God in a good sense. That it is a good fear is indicated by the fact that it goes along with trusting in Yahweh. The Israelites have caught up with the midwives.

EXODUS 15:1–21

Moses and Miriam Sing and Dance

¹Then Moses and the Israelites sang this song for Yahweh. They said:

> "I will sing for Yahweh because he is so exalted:
>> horse and its rider he threw into the sea.
> ² Yah is my strength and my song:
>> he became my deliverance.
> This is my God—I will glorify him:
>> my father's god—I will exalt him.
> ³ Yahweh is a warrior;
>> Yahweh is his name.
> ⁴ Pharaoh's chariotry and his army he threw into the sea;
>> the pick of his officers were drowned in the Reed Sea.

⁵ The deeps covered them;
    they went down into the depths like a stone.
⁶ Your right hand, Yahweh, was majestic in power;
    your right hand, Yahweh, shattered the enemy.
⁷ In the greatness of your majesty you tore down your
       opponents;
    you sent off your fury, it consumed them like straw.
⁸ At the blast of your nostrils waters piled up;
    floods stood up like a wall;
    deeps solidified in the heart of the sea.
⁹ The enemy said, 'I will pursue, overtake;
    I will divide plunder, my appetite will have its fill.
    I will bare my sword, my hand will subdue them.'
¹⁰ You blew with your blast, the sea covered them;
    they sank like lead in the mighty waters.
¹¹ Who is like you among the gods, Yahweh;
    who is like you, majestic in holiness,
    awesome in glory, doing wonders?
¹² You stretched out your hand;
    earth swallowed them.
¹³ In your commitment you have guided the people you restored;
    in your strength you have led them to your holy abode.
¹⁴ Peoples have heard and trembled;
    anguish has gripped the inhabitants of Philistia.
¹⁵ Then the chiefs of Edom have been terrified;
    the leaders of Moab—trembling has seized them;
    all the inhabitants of Canaan have melted.
¹⁶ Terror and dread have fallen upon them;
    through the power of your arm they have become as still
      as a stone,
Until your people have passed, Yahweh,
    until the people you acquired have passed.
¹⁷ You have brought them and planted them on your own
      mountain,
    the place for you to dwell that you have made, Yahweh,
    the sanctuary, Lord, that your hands have established.
¹⁸ Yahweh will reign
    for ever and ever!"

¹⁹Because Pharaoh's horses, his chariotry, and his riders went into the sea, and Yahweh let the water of the sea come back on

them, whereas the Israelites went on dry ground in the midst of the sea.

²⁰Miriam the prophetess, Aaron's sister, took a tambourine in her hand, and all the women went out after her with tambourines and dancing. Miriam chanted for them, "Sing for Yahweh, because he is so exalted: horse and its rider he threw into the sea."

A few weeks before my disabled wife died, we were in a restaurant where they have a live band, one of my absolute favorites, playing swing, blues, and rockabilly. My feet and hands were tapping, or perhaps thumping and stomping (I can't understand how anyone can sit still when listening to music). The lead guitarist's girlfriend could see that Ann couldn't dance with me and came across to ask if I would like to dance. I first made the excuse that I was no good at dancing, but then confessed that Ann's not being able to dance with me meant it would churn me up too much to dance at all (but I much appreciated the thoughtful invite). Music arouses complicated mixed feelings. For me, dancing suggests both joy and grief.

A Jewish midrash about the Reed Sea story brings this out (a midrash is an edifying story linked with Scripture; many such stories seek to explain something puzzling about Scripture). It starts from the way the Israelites are not told to rejoice at Passover, as you might expect, and explains that the angels wanted to rejoice at the Reed Sea, but God told them not to do so: "My handiwork [the **Egyptians**] is drowning in the sea; would you recite song before me?" "Do not gloat at the fall of your enemy" (Proverbs 24:17), one version of the story adds.

Yet it was evidently fine for Moses and the Israelites to sing, and for Miriam and the other women to dance. As the women started off the exodus story, they round it off. When God acts to bring judgment, to show who is really God, or to put down oppressors, there is reason for grief and sadness and for joy and praise. You could call this the first psalm in the Bible. Many psalms praise God for rescuing the people from distress and oppression, and one can imagine their being sung in the temple. Miriam and Moses don't wait until they can get to church before declaring God's praise. Praise begins out in the world. Their song emphasizes a note running through the exodus story. The great power's leader thought he was the preeminent power in his world, and that made him think he was god, but God has shown who is God. Pharaoh would have said his gods were very powerful; now God has shown that they are nothing.

Miriam's being a prophet may explain the last part of the song. When God breaks into the structures of a patriarchal world, this can involve making women into prophets or "judges" (like Deborah), as happens at the beginning of the story in both Testaments. Their prophecy can take the form of an act of praise that sees the far-reaching significance of what God has done. This song does so. Philistia, Edom, Moab, and company have not yet reacted as it describes, but it speaks of how they will react if they are wise. Israel has not yet arrived in **Yahweh**'s land and started worshiping in Yahweh's sanctuary there, but the Reed Sea event establishes that Israel will do so, because it provides a basis for declaring that "Yahweh will reign for ever and ever."

As with the rest of the exodus story, Egyptian records make no reference to a catastrophe like this one. In a news report relating to some archaeological discoveries, the *New York Times* quoted an Egyptian archaeologist: "There is no evidence of the exodus. It's a myth." It then quoted another: "A pharaoh drowned and a whole army was killed. . . . Egyptians do not document their crises." They did document a claim to have defeated Israel, on the "Merneptah stele," a thirteenth-century stone inscription relating to the Pharaoh who succeeded Rameses the Great. It is the most solid evidence from outside the Old Testament that Israel was around at the most likely time when the exodus would have happened. But the emphasis on the exodus running right through the Old Testament also makes it hard to believe that the story was simply made up.

EXODUS 15:22–17:7

Surviving in the Wilderness

²²Moses got Israel to move on from the Reed Sea and they went out into the Shur Wilderness and walked for three days in the wilderness, and found no water. ²³They came to Bitter and

could not drink the water from Bitter because it was bitter; hence it was called "Bitter." [24]The people complained at Moses: "What shall we drink?" [25]He cried out to Yahweh, and Yahweh pointed to some wood. [Moses] threw it into the water and the water became sweet. [Yahweh] made an authoritative rule for them there; he tested them there. [26]He said, "If you listen attentively to the voice of Yahweh your God, do what is upright in his sight, give ear to his commands, and keep all his rules, I will not bring on you any of the diseases I brought on the Egyptians, because I am Yahweh your healer." [27]Then they came to Elim. There were twelve springs of water there and seventy palm trees. They camped there by the water.

[16:1]The whole community of the Israelites traveled from Elim and came to the Sin Wilderness, between Elim and Sinai, on the fifteenth day of the second month after their leaving Egypt. [2]The whole community of the Israelites complained against Moses and Aaron in the wilderness. [3]The Israelites said to them, "If only we had died by Yahweh's hand in Egypt when we sat by pots of meat and ate our fill of bread! Because you have brought us out into this wilderness to kill this whole congregation with hunger!" [4]Yahweh said to Moses, "Right. I am going to rain bread for you from the heavens so that the people may go out and gather the day's allocation each day, so that I may test them, whether they will live by my instruction or not."

[Exodus 16:5–36 tells how Yahweh made vast numbers of quail fall on the camp in the evening, and in the morning a breadlike substance appeared. Henceforth a day's supply appeared each day, and two days' supply on Friday. Yahweh bade Israel keep some in a container in the sanctuary to remind them of how they were looked after in the wilderness. Exodus 17:1–7 tells of another occasion when they ran out of water and complained against Moses, and God then provided.]

A former colleague of mine used sometimes to say of a seminary student, "He [I don't remember it ever being a she] needs to learn to love the church." The comment would be aroused by the student's reaction to some piece of apparent inefficiency or arbitrariness or shortness of vision on the part of the church. I would nod sagely at this comment. Then the other week someone rebuked me for the way I had been going on (so he implied) about the church's failures, and he reminded me of the New Testament's high opinion of the church and the optimism it holds about it. I felt suitably chastised while also confused; I thought I was right in what I had said (!), though I also knew he was right about the high view the Scriptures have of the importance of the church.

The Scriptures manifest a similar ambivalence about Israel. It is God's people, God's chosen, God's means of reaching the world, a body God definitely intends to take to its destiny. As Romans 11 puts it, eventually Israel as a whole is going to be saved. On the other hand, in 1 Corinthians 10 Paul also takes up the dynamics of passages such as these stories in Exodus of what happened when the Israelites ran out of water or food, and he notes what they tell us about Israel's failures and their consequences. Any given generation of Israel or the church can forfeit its place within God's purpose.

The Israelites had their hands high when they marched out of **Egypt**. After their deliverance at the Reed Sea I imagine their hands were high when they marched into the wilderness, but they soon discover that God's defeat of Pharaoh by no means solves all their problems. It only introduces them to the next challenge. When God does something new and creative, it is tempting to think that everything now is going to be wonderful, but the early church soon found it was having to deal with people being put in jail and people falsifying their pledges and with one group complaining about another group being neglected when food was distributed (Acts 4–6). It was repeating Israel's experience, even in the sense that it involved down-to-earth questions like whether you have enough to eat and that it issued in division in the community. Israel complained to Moses and Aaron; one Christian group complained against another.

The Psalms make clear that it is fine to complain against God about things that happen to us and about the way people are treating us (though admittedly they don't include God's replies to the prayers that appear there, and it wouldn't be surprising if God sometimes responded as straight as Israel spoke). The Israelites don't complain against God but against Moses and Aaron; it requires less courage to criticize your human leaders than to criticize God. Fortunately Moses knows what to do when people complain against you. He cries out to God, the way the Israelites themselves had cried out to God when Pharaoh's army was advancing on them (the problem is they are not doing this now). Perhaps he is crying out about the way the people are complaining against him, as leaders need to do if they are to handle that pressure rather than giving as good as they get and turning the relationship into one of mutual recrimination. Perhaps he is crying out to God on their behalf, the way he had once cried out to God on Pharaoh's behalf (!), which is certainly a key aspect of a leader's job. God's response is to tell him to throw a tree branch into the pool of bitter water they had found. This will have seemed a silly suggestion, but maybe Moses could imagine it was not. After all, he had considerable experience of God's doing exotic tricks.

Exodus adds that the story establishes a principle of God's dealings with the people. An experience like the one they have just gone through is a kind of testing. Their failure doesn't actually matter. They need to learn from what happened. The rule is, live your life in accordance with God's bidding, and God will make things work out. They then come to a place with abundant water, which encourages their faith.

The way they then complain about their food supply suggests they have learned nothing ("Sin" is just the Hebrew name of the wilderness—it's not the Hebrew word for "sin"). Indeed, things have gotten worse, and time has given a rosy glow to their life in Egypt compared with the reality Exodus has described: "You brought us out of Egypt to starve us to death." "It's God you're complaining about, not us. God will act so spectacularly, it will show it was God who brought you out, not me," Moses and Aaron reply.

The concrete way the provision of food will test them is that it will come daily except at the weekend; they will get two days' supply on Friday so they don't have to do anything to make sure they have enough to eat on the Sabbath. This puts them into daily reliance on God. Whether they collect a lot or a little, they have enough. When they try to collect extra to make sure they have some for the next day (who could blame them?), it goes rotten. But it doesn't do that on Saturday. Further, if they fail to prepare for the Sabbath, they find nothing arrives that day. This is the first reference to an obligation to observe the Sabbath (at creation God kept the Sabbath, but there was no mention of this as a human obligation). It is another crazy divine expectation. How could you risk not having enough to live on by doing nothing one day in seven? It makes no economic sense. That is part of the story's point. Sense lies in trusting that things will work out if we do what God says.

Our ancestors all followed the guidance of the cloud column, and they all went through the Reed Sea as a kind of baptism, Paul says in 1 Corinthians 10. They all drank the water, and they all ate the food. But most of them fell in the wilderness. Remember that their stories were written for us to learn from. Don't think you couldn't go the same way, he urges.

EXODUS 17:8–18:27

The First Enemy and the First Convert

[8]Amalek came and fought with Israel at Rephidim. [9]Moses said to Joshua, "Choose some men for us and go out and fight with Amalek. Tomorrow I am going to take my stand on top of the hill with God's staff in my hand." [10]Joshua did as Moses told him by fighting with Amalek, while Moses, Aaron, and Hur went up to the top of the hill. [11]As Moses would raise his hand, Israel would prevail, but as he would rest his hand, Amalek would prevail. [12]So when Moses' hands were heavy, they took a stone and put it under him. He sat on it, while Aaron and Hur supported his hands, one on this side and one on that. So his hands were steadfast until sundown [13]and Joshua overwhelmed Amalek and its people with the sword. [14]Yahweh said to Moses, "Write this in a document as a memorial and set it in Joshua's ears, how I shall totally blot out Amalek's memory from under the heavens." [15]Moses built an altar and called it "Yahweh My Banner," [16]and said, "A hand [raised itself] against Yah's throne! Yahweh will have war against Amalek from generation to generation."

[18:1]Jethro the priest of Midian, Moses' father-in-law, heard all God had done for Moses and his people Israel, how Yahweh had brought Israel out of Egypt. [2]Now Jethro, Moses' father-in-law, had taken Zipporah, Moses' wife, after she had been sent away, [3]and her two sons (of whom one was called Gershom, because—he said—"I have been an alien in a foreign country" [4]and the other was called Eliezer, because "the God of my father has been my help and rescued me from Pharaoh's sword"). [5]Jethro, Moses' father-in-law, brought both his sons and his wife to Moses in the wilderness where he was camped at God's mountain. [6]He had said to Moses, "I, Jethro, your father-in-law, am coming to you with your wife and her two sons with her." [7]Moses went out to meet his father-in-law. He bowed low and kissed him. Each of them asked the other how he was, and they went into the tent. [8]Moses recounted to his father-in-law all that Yahweh had done to Pharaoh and the Egyptians for Israel's sake, all the hardship that had met them on the way and how Yahweh had rescued them. [9]Jethro rejoiced over all the good that Yahweh had done for Israel when he rescued them from the power of the Egyptians. [10]Jethro said, "Yahweh be praised, who rescued you from the power of the Egyptians and from Pharaoh, when he rescued the people from the power of the Egyptians. [11]Now I acknowledge that Yahweh is greater than all gods, because in this thing they asserted themselves against them." [12]So Jethro, Moses' father-in-law, got a burnt offering and sacrifices for God, and Aaron and all the elders of Israel came to eat bread before God with Moses' father-in-law.

[Verses 13–27 go on to tell of Jethro's advising Moses on how to cope with the pressure of making decisions and offering guidance to people, suggesting that Moses appoint some other people to fulfill those tasks while he focuses on approaching God on the people's behalf and mediating God's teaching to them.]

We just watched a movie called *The Reader*. One of its central characters is a German girl who in about 1940 worked as an S.S. guard in Auschwitz, had been living ever since with the guilt of that, and to the very end never escapes that guilt. Another is a man who was too young to have been directly involved in the war but who therefore belongs to a generation of Germans that is needing to come to terms with what the war meant. In Jewish thinking, Hitler was the twentieth-century Amalekite. The president of Israel referred to Amalek in his letter declining to show mercy to the Nazi war criminal Adolf Eichmann. In the Second World War, however, alongside people who got sucked into collaborating with the Nazis were people who resisted and who as Gentiles took risks and sometimes sacrificed their own lives to protect Jews. Some did so because they recognized the Jewish people as God's people; some did so out of simple human instincts. The movie *Schindler's List* tells of one such Gentile. The Jerusalem Holocaust Memorial, Yad VaShem, commemorates them as well as commemorating the Jews who died.

The Amalekites and Jethro represent these two attitudes to Israel and to the Jewish people over the millennia. Ironically and in some way significantly, both Amalek and Jethro were descendants of Abraham. The relationship between Israel and the two peoples of Amalek and Midian (to which Jethro belonged) is not like its relationship with **Egypt**. It is a relationship within the family. The same was true of the relationship between the Nazis and the Jews; most of the Nazis were Christians, as were most of the people who sought to protect the Jews. (It hurts Christians to describe the Nazis as Christians because we see their behavior and attitude as incompatible with Christian faith; but they were professing Christians.)

So the Amalekites attack the Israelites as they make their journey through the wilderness. Exodus gives no reason for the attack. Perhaps they thought they could appropriate the Israelites' flocks and herds. Living in the wilderness south of **Canaan**, perhaps they felt threatened by the Israelites' advancing their way. Greed, resentment, and fear have often fueled anti-Semitism. But Exodus gives no reason, and this underlines the link between the mystery of hostility to Israel and the Jewish people that has been a recurrent aspect of Israelite and Jewish experience.

What do you do when Amalek attacks you? Jews today sometimes critique their grandparents' generation for the submission with which they walked to the death camps and determine that Amalek or Hitler will never have that experience again (we have to keep this in mind when seeking to understand the Middle Eastern situation; some Jews see the Palestinians or Iranians as another version of the Amalekites). Moses and Joshua provide them with a contrary model. Moses again assumes control of the power God had given to him at the Reed Sea and directs the forces of heaven in the battle that follows, with the amusing need for him to be given physical

73

support as he does so. The way the battle works shows it is not merely a this-worldly one but one where God's forces are active in ensuring that Israel is not defeated. It resembles the conflict with Pharaoh, except that here for the first time the Israelites are involved in fighting; they do not just watch while God acts. Joshua wins a vital victory, though it does not involve annihilating Amalek; indeed, it is not explicit that the Israelites killed anyone (maybe the Amalekites fled from the Israelites when they saw they were prepared to fight rather than lie down and be killed!). Thus the promises with which the story closes are important for the future, and they remain important for the Jewish people.

The story of the Midianite Jethro offers a contrast. Moses has the chance to tell his father-in-law what God had done for Israel in rescuing them from Pharaoh and then from the troubles they have had on their journey through Sinai (like the problems about food and water and the attack of Amalek). Jethro bursts out in praise and brings his offerings to show he means it. It is quite a reaction from a Midianite priest. One should perhaps not call him the first convert; maybe that was Hagar in Genesis, and then there are all those other people who accompanied the Israelites when they left Egypt. But he is the first person whose detailed conversion story we are told. He also stands as a reminder of a better promise than the one concerning the destruction of Amalek, a promise that God will bring about that drawing of the world to acknowledge Israel's God.

After seeing Jesus, the "wise men" do not become disciples; they go back home to resume their lives. Yet they can never be the same. After offering Moses some fatherly advice, Jethro does not stay with Israel; he goes back home to resume his life. Yet he can never be the same.

EXODUS 19:1–25

Two Kinds of Preparation for Meeting God

¹At the beginning of the third month after the Israelites came out of Egypt, that day they came to the Sinai Wilderness. ²They moved on from Rephidim and came to the Sinai Wilderness,

and camped in the wilderness. Israel camped there in front of the mountain [3]and Moses went up to God. Yahweh called to him from the mountain: "You are to say this to the household of Jacob and tell the Israelites, [4]'You yourselves saw what I did to the Egyptians. I lifted you on eagles' wings and brought you to me. [5]So now, if you really listen to my voice and keep my covenant, you will be for me a treasured possession among all the peoples. Because all the earth is mine, [6]but you in particular will be a priestly kingdom, a holy nation.' These are the words you are to speak to the Israelites." [7]Moses came and summoned the elders of the people and set before them all these words that Yahweh instructed him. [8]All the people answered as one, "All that Yahweh spoke we will do." So Moses took the people's words back to Yahweh, [9]and Yahweh said to Moses, "Now, I am coming to you in a thick cloud so that the people may hear when I speak with you and also may trust in you forever."

So Moses reported the people's words to Yahweh [10]and Yahweh said to Moses, "Go to the people and make them holy today and tomorrow, and get them to wash their clothes. [11]They are to be ready for the third day, because on the third day Yahweh will come down before the eyes of all the people on Mount Sinai. [12]You are to set bounds for the people round about, saying, 'Be careful not to go up the mountain or touch its border. Anyone who touches the mountain is definitely to be put to death. [13]No hand is to touch him because he is to be simply stoned or shot with arrows. Whether it is an animal or a person, he is not to live.' When the horn sounds out, they may go up the mountain."

[In verses 14–25 Moses passes on Yahweh's instructions and God comes down onto the mountain to the accompaniment of smoke, earth tremor, and thunder. God again warns people about not breaking through to look at God.]

When Israel was occupying Sinai in the early 1970s, you could catch a plane from Tel Aviv to an airstrip near the Monastery of Saint Katharine and then catch an Israeli bus to the foot of the mountain itself. I have a photo of the incongruous bus stop sitting in the middle of the desert with the unforgettable shape of Mount Sinai rising behind it out of the plain. Climbing the mountain was an extraordinary experience. All the way up I was saying to myself the words from Psalm 24, "Who may climb the mountain of the Lord?" (Never mind that the psalm is referring to Mount Zion.) The psalm answers with a variety of challenges about your behavior and your lifestyle. At the same time I was overcome by the wonder of this being the very mountain where God appeared to Moses and to Israel. (Never mind that no one knows for sure whether it is the actual Mount Sinai, though it is the only one with a long tradition of identification as such; and if it is not, then the actual mountain is another one like it.) It was both an emotional and spiritual experience, and a morally challenging one. (Of course for many people on the weekend, organized by the Israeli Nature Society, it was simply an adventure or a vacation.)

When the Israelites arrived at Sinai, they first had a morally challenging experience—or perhaps one should call it a relationally challenging one. It marks a new stage in the **covenant** relationship between God and Israel. We often think of Sinai as the occasion when the covenant came into being, but God was already in covenant relationship with Israel; the exodus happened because God was mindful of that covenant (Exodus 2:24). What happens at Sinai is a kind of renegotiation of the terms of this covenant, as will happen again when Christ comes. When God made a covenant with Israel's ancestors, it was 99 percent a commitment purely on God's part, a promise about something God was going to do. There were no specific requirements laid on Abraham except that the males should be circumcised. The situation has now changed. God has initiated the process whereby the covenant promise is being fulfilled. The people are on their way to the country God promised them. God has rescued them from their servitude to **Egypt**. (Admittedly, if you were an Israelite, you might think the language about eagle's wings was a bit rich. "Eagle's wings? Excuse me, we walked. That's why it took us two months to get here.")

So now God can reasonably think that the commitment between God and Israel should become more mutual. If the Israelites also now keep the covenant, as God has, they can have a special position in connection with God's purpose in the world. "Priestly kingdom" (literally, "a kingdom of priests") and "holy nation" is a twofold way of describing the same thing. The stress lies on the first of the two words in each phrase. There is a sense in which they are a nation like any other nation, and in due course they will be ruled by kings and be a kingdom like any other kingdom; but they are a holy nation and a priestly kingdom.

Their being a priesthood stands in some tension with their being a kingdom. Being a kingdom means one person has supreme power. Describing them as a kingdom of priests reminds them (and reminds the monarch) that they all have a close, priestly relationship with God. God's description of them here is the origin of the expression "a priesthood of all believers." It is easy for pastors and people to think that pastors have a special relationship with God, but God implies that this is not so. Pastors may have power, but all the people have the special relationship. (There is no idea here that as a priesthood Israel has a ministry to other peoples. The focus lies on the privilege of their priestly position. The **Torah** does assume that they are to be the means of bringing blessing to the world, but it does not use "priesthood" language in this connection.)

Being holy stands in a different tension with being a nation. Nations have natural ways of functioning; Egypt has illustrated what nations are like. Being a holy nation involves being in the world but not of the world. Can you survive in the world on that basis? Israel's experience in due course seemed to suggest that it could not and that it needed to be like other nations in order to survive (notably, by having a king to lead it in battle— by being a kingdom, in fact). The church has likewise usually found that it cannot function in the world on that basis, so its structures and procedures are the same as those of other organizations. God's words put a demanding but also encouraging vision in front of it.

"All that **Yahweh** spoke, we will do." Ah, if only!

As well as putting a relational and moral challenge before the people, God's appearance at Sinai puts before them a spiritual and emotional one (though that is a relational one, too). For some Christians, God is a rather frightening person, and they are more comfortable with Jesus; the description of God in the latter part of Exodus 19 confirms their worst fears. For others,

God is a loving Father, and they are put off by the description here. Exodus offers both sorts of Christian something to learn.

One way to come at it is to start from the New Testament, from where Hebrews 12 takes up the Sinai story. It notes how terrifying was God's appearance at Sinai, and it draws a contrast with the position of Christians. We might think that it is about to rejoice that Christians do not have to think in terms of fear, but it does not do that. The contrast it notes is that the Israelites were merely listening to God on earth. "How much less will we escape, if we turn away from the one who warns us from heaven?" Hebrews 12:15 asks. If we turn away, God's speaking to us will also be terrifying. The Sinai audiovisual phenomena and the warnings God gives Moses are designed to get Israel to take God's God-ness really seriously, but they and we need not be afraid of God, because they and we have already seen how much God cares for them and us. So (says Hebrews 12:28–29, like Exodus 19), "Let's worship God acceptably, with reverence and awe, because our God is a consuming fire."

EXODUS 20:1–21

A Rule of Life

[1]God spoke all these words: [2]"I am Yahweh your God who brought you out of Egypt, out of a household of serfs. [3]You will not have other gods over against me. [4]You will not make yourselves a sculpture or any likeness of anything in the heavens above, on the earth below, or in the waters under the earth. [5]You will not bow down to them; you will not serve them. Because I, Yahweh your God, am a passionate God, visiting the waywardness of parents on children, on the third and fourth [generation] in respect of people who oppose me, [6]but showing commitment to a thousand [generations] in respect of people who give themselves to me and keep my commands. [7]You will not lift up the name of Yahweh your God in respect of emptiness, because Yahweh will not acquit someone who lifts up his name in respect of emptiness. [8]Be mindful of the Sabbath day to make it holy. [9]Six days you can serve and do all your work, [10]but the seventh day is a Sabbath for Yahweh your God. You will not do any work, you, your son or daughter, your male or

female servant, or the resident alien within your settlement.
[11]Because in six days Yahweh made the heavens, the earth, the
sea, and all that is in them, and rested on the seventh day. That
is why Yahweh praised the seventh day and made it holy.
[12]Honor your father and mother, so that your days may be long
on the ground that Yahweh your God is going to give you. [13]You
will not murder. [14]You will not commit adultery. [15]You will not
steal. [16]You will not give false testimony against your neighbor.
[17]You will not covet your neighbor's household: You will not
covet your neighbor's wife or his male or female servant or his
ox or ass or anything your neighbor has."

[Verses 18–21 take further the people's witnessing of the scary
accompaniments of God's appearing and take further Moses'
reassurance of them.]

As a seminary professor in England, it was my task to ask the
students who were my particular pastoral responsibility about
their rule of life. The idea of a rule of life had become popular, though maybe the idea was more popular than actually
keeping a rule. A rule of life might cover the pattern of your
church worship, your Bible reading and prayer, your fasting
and giving, and your reflection on your relationship with God.
It might also cover how much time you spent shopping or taking exercise, how much you drank and ate, what time you went
to bed, how much hospitality you offer people, whether you go
on retreat and spend time in silence. It might cover how you
handled tricky areas of life such as sex. Many Christians used
to be hesitant about the idea of a rule of life because it seemed
legalistic, but it doesn't have to be. Ask someone a few questions about those areas of life, and you are pretty sure to generate an agenda for a conversation that can last quite a long time.

Churches can have a rule of life, and the Ten Commandments are the beginning of Israel's rule of life. The Old Testament does not refer to them as "ten commandments," only
as "ten words (the word *decalogue* is a Latin-derived word
that originally meant "ten words"). Indeed, in form they look
as much like definitions as commands, though "You will" or
"You will not" is also a strong command. They have some overlaps with the rule of life the church needs. They address the

individual Israelite men who are the heads of families. While many can be extended to people in general, they do hold up to the light the responsibilities and temptations of the heads of families in a patriarchal society.

They begin from the point God made at the beginning of Exodus 19. God brought Israel out of their serfdom in **Egypt**. That gave God the right to lay down expectations of Israel if they want to be in relationship with God. It is to be an exclusive relationship. The first command is not concerned to deny the existence of other gods (the Old Testament is more inclined to demote them to being the real God's underlings) but to deny Israel the right to treat them as gods. There are at least two contexts in which they will be tempted to do that. They will live cheek by jowl with local peoples in **Canaan** who seek the help of other gods to make their crops grow and their animals and families fertile, and to enable them to stay in contact with their family members after they die in order to get their wisdom and help. The heads of Israelite families (and thus the families themselves) are to rely on **Yahweh** for all these needs.

They are not to make statues to help them worship. This is another countercultural requirement; people like something visible to help them worship. The trouble is that a statue can never truly represent the active and talking nature of the real God. In effect, worshiping with the help of a statue means worshiping a different god. It thus makes the real God passionately angry. God rescued them from the service of Pharaoh so they could serve God; they have no business bowing down to other gods as if they were free to serve them. The consequences within the family will be horrific. They will affect not just the parents but the children, grandchildren, and great-grandchildren. Family life is like that. (But if they accept this constraint, God's **commitment** will have much more far-reaching consequences.)

They must not associate Yahweh with things that have nothing to do with Yahweh and actually have no reality. They could do that by waging their own wars and calling them Yahweh's, or building a sanctuary to suit them and saying this is Yahweh's will, or making their decisions and calling them Yahweh's, or appointing the government they want and calling it Yahweh's.

They are to see to the observance of the Sabbath. The house-holders are to do so and to make sure everyone else can do so, even the animals. There is to be no sending the servants out to plow on the Sabbath when you are able to rest. This command has the longest rationale; it will be one of the most difficult to accept when the householder knows there is work on the farm to be done and that failing to do it risks the family's having nothing to eat next year.

The householder is to honor his parents, who will now be old and not as useful to the family economy as they once were, and who may be inclined to interfere with the decisions he knows need to be taken. The family is basic to the way Israel is to work, and failing to honor one's parents imperils the fundamental structure of the society. It thus imperils its very existence.

They are not to murder anyone. The KJV has "You shall not kill," but the command uses not the ordinary word for kill but a word for slaying someone without warrant. It does not preclude execution (though we do not have indications that Israel practiced much capital punishment, even though the **Torah** will allow for it). Nor does it preclude war. It presupposes that relationships can get so fraught in the family and the community that one person might want to kill another, and it looks that reality in the face.

They are not to have affairs. That is another reality of life in Israel as in the church and in society. It again imperils the family and thus the society. For all the excitement, fulfillment, and affirmation that a man can find in an affair, it is off limits.

They are not to steal. Your neighbor's ox and his ass are his livelihood. His sheep and goats, his olives and his grain, are his means of sustaining his family. You imperil his family by taking them.

They are not to testify that their neighbors have done something that they have not. That can be a "legal" way of achieving the same ends as murder or stealing, and it is just as forbidden.

They are to look to the inner attitude that lies behind many of those outward acts. Their neighbor's wife may be better at managing the household (more like the woman in Proverbs 31); his servants may be more hardworking; his animals may be sturdier. You could do your job much better if you had them.

Be content with and do your best with what you have, says the command. Trust that things will be okay.

EXODUS 20:22–22:14

Coping with Crises

[22]Yahweh said to Moses, "You are to say this to the Israelites: 'You yourselves saw how I spoke with you from the heavens. [23]With me you will not make gods of silver and you will not make gods of gold for yourselves. [24]An altar of earth you will make for me, and you will sacrifice on it your burnt offerings and fellowship sacrifices, your sheep and oxen. In every place where I cause my name to be commemorated, I will come to you and bless you. [25]But if you make an altar out of stones for me, you will not build it of cut stone, because when you have wielded your cutter on them, you will have treated them as ordinary. [26]You will not go up on my altar by steps, so your nakedness will not be exposed on it.'

[21:1]"These are the rules you are to set before them. [2]When you acquire a Hebrew servant, he is to serve six years. In the seventh he is to leave free, for nothing. [3]If he comes single, he leaves single. If he has a wife, his wife leaves with him. [4]If his master gives him a wife and she bears him sons or daughters, the wife and her children belong to her master. He leaves alone. [5]If the servant explicitly says, 'I love my master, my wife, and my children. I will not leave free' [6]his master is to take him near God and take him near the door or the doorpost, and the master is to pierce his ear with an awl. He is his servant forever. [7]When someone sells his daughter as a servant, she does not leave as male servants do. [8]If her master is not pleased with her, and he had designated her for himself, he is to let her be redeemed. He does not have the power to sell her to a foreign people, because he broke faith with her. [9]But if he designates her for his son, he is to deal with her in accordance with the rule for daughters. [10]If he gets himself another wife, he will not withhold her food, her clothing, or her conjugal rights. [11]If he does not do these three things for her, she may leave for nothing, without payment."

[Exodus 21:12–22:14 lays down rules for dealing with murder, manslaughter, assault, fighting, and disputes over property, and for when an animal kills a man.]

When I worked as a pastor, the Inland Revenue treated me as self-employed rather than as an employee. I am not sure why this was, and I didn't feel self-employed. I had a boss (my rector) who made it clear that he was my boss, and I had employers (the church) who made it clear that they were my employers. Some time later I was a boss, because I was the principal of a seminary (in U.S. terms, a cross between being president and provost), though of course I was employed by the seminary and was responsible to the board of trustees. I enjoyed being the boss for a while but eventually needed to get out of the responsibilities it brings and get back to being just an ordinary professor; which is what brought me to California. In the novel *East of Eden*, John Steinbeck describes a Chinese man (a university graduate) who tells why he was content to be a servant. He has a master who looks after him, and while he has to work, his master has to work *and* worry.

During the seventeenth, eighteenth, and nineteenth centuries, most people who came to America from Europe came as indentured servants. They were often people without jobs, or convicts, who found a new life in America by working for a period of years to pay for their passage. During the latter part of that period, almost all the people who came from Africa came after being captured into slavery, and they had no prospect of freedom. Translations use the English word "slave" in passages such as Exodus 21, but it is misleading. The Old Testament does not have a word for "slave" because the idea of slavery is a European one, known in **Greece**, Rome, Britain, and America, but not in the Middle East. There, people were more like indentured servants in that the law gave them some protection; their masters could not do what they liked with them, and they served only for a limited period.

Their servitude was thus a way of their getting a new start in life, like that of people who came to America from Europe rather than from Africa. One reason for becoming someone's servant was going into debt. Your farm had failed; you had nothing to eat for the next year; and working for someone opened up the possibility of a new start. You would let your son or daughter become a servant first because that opened up the possibility of your being able to keep going, get back on your feet, and keep the family together. Selling yourself into service would be a last resort. If you could get back on your feet, you could pay your debt to the man who had made a loan to keep you going, for which your son or daughter's work was paying, and thus "redeem" them. Selling your daughter in this way would be a way of arranging her marriage to the master or his son; you would eventually be arranging her marriage anyway.

The rules in Exodus 21 give some protection to servants, with a particular concern for girls in that position. Later in the chapter they prescribe punishment for a master who kills a servant, though not for "merely" injuring him; the master has then punished himself by depriving himself of the servant's work. The rules also meet something of the master's interests; it would be no use making the conditions of service so weighted in favor of the servants that a master would never take on a servant. That would defeat the object of providing needy people with a way of surviving and getting a new start. The possibility that someone might want to sign on as a servant for life (like the Chinese man) shows that this servitude must have been nothing like slavery. These rules have a lot to teach a culture where people who become poor and/or get into debt have little way of getting out of the poverty trap and find their entire life as a family collapsing.

The reference to a **Hebrew** servant may mean the rule also covers non-Israelites; it may even have them especially in mind. In any country, many servants were foreigners. The story of Ruth illustrates the point. It begins with Elimelech and his family having to leave Israel for Moab because of a famine. That would be the kind of circumstance that took a family to a foreign country to find a way of surviving there. Exodus 21 later bans kidnapping people (so that they could become your servants), the way slaves were brought to America.

Exodus 21:12–22:14 covers a random-looking collection of "things that happen." Their randomness indicates that this collection of rules is not a law code, designed to deal systematically with the sorts of thing that typically cause problems in communities, and available to be consulted in a "legal" kind of way. It is more a set of sample cases to give the community and the village elders an idea of how to deal with issues, so they can work out from these examples how to deal with other issues that arise. It includes the basic rule of "an eye for an eye." As far as we know, no one ever treated this as if it were a literal law, any more than Jesus' telling you to pluck out your eye was a literal law. What it does is set limits to the compensation someone has a right to seek when one gets injured. Likewise, as far as we know no one was ever executed for offenses such as belittling one's parents, or most of the many "capital" offenses in Israel's rule of life. Saying "such a person should be put to death" is a way of saying, "This is a really wicked thing to do; terrible consequences may follow."

Israel's rules to regulate servitude and other matters have equivalents in other Middle Eastern peoples' social codes. A distinctive feature of Israel's version is the way it begins with some rules about worship. God comes first in Israel's rule of life. The precise way its rule works then shows a concern to distinguish Israel from other peoples precisely while working out some social procedures that were quite like theirs. Other peoples had images of their gods because people find these helpful, but the way God appears to Israel at Sinai shows that its God is not the kind you can make a statue of. Other peoples had magnificent, elaborate stone altars for sacrifice. Just a simple one made of earth or natural stone will do, God says, and beware of accidentally exposing yourself on it.

EXODUS 22:15–23:19

You Know the Feelings of an Alien

[15]"If a man seduces a girl who is not betrothed and sleeps with her, he is to make the proper marriage payment for her as a wife for himself. [16]If her father absolutely refuses to give her to him, he is to weigh out silver in accordance with the marriage payment for girls. [17]A medium: you will not allow her to live. [18]Anyone who has sex with an animal is definitely to be put to death. [19]Someone who sacrifices to a god other than Yahweh alone is to be 'devoted.' [20]An alien: you will not wrong or ill-treat him, because you were aliens in Egypt. [21]Any widow or orphan: you will not oppress them. [22]If you oppress them at all, when they cry aloud to me, I will listen attentively to their cry. [23]My

anger will blaze and I will slay you with the sword. Your wives will become widows; your children orphans. ²⁴If you lend money to my people, to an oppressed person who is with you, you will not be like a lender to him. You will not make him pay interest. ²⁵If you take your neighbor's coat as a pledge, before sunset you will return it to him, ²⁶because it is his only covering, his protection for his skin. What is he to sleep in? When he cries out to me, I will listen, because I am gracious.

²⁷"You will not belittle God or curse a leader among your people. ²⁸Your fullness [of harvest] and your pressing [of grapes]: you will not delay them. The firstborn of your sons: you will give him to me. ²⁹You will do this with your oxen and your flocks. It will be seven days with its mother; on the eighth day you will give it to me. ³⁰You will be holy people to me. You will not eat meat from an animal savaged in the wild; you will throw it to the dogs.

²³:¹"You will not carry empty reports; do not join hands with the faithless to be a malicious witness. ²You will not follow a majority in doing wrong; you will not testify in a case in bending after a majority, in bending it. ³But you will not honor a poor man in his case. ⁴When you come across your enemy's ox or donkey straying, you will positively take it back to him. ⁵If you see your enemy's donkey lying down under its load and you would refrain from lifting it up, you will definitely lift it up with him. ⁶You will not bend a decision for a poor person in his case. ⁷False statements: stay distant from them. The innocent, the faithful: do not slay them, because I do not treat the faithless as faithful. ⁸Bribes: do not take them, because bribes blind people who can see and overturn the statements of the faithful. ⁹An alien: you will not ill-treat him; you yourselves know the feelings of the alien, because you were aliens in Egypt."

[Verses 10–13 cover letting the land lie fallow one year in seven and letting the needy eat of what grows naturally, keeping the Sabbath, not praying to other gods, and observing the festivals.]

There are aliens who freely choose to live in a foreign country, and there are aliens who felt they were driven to do so (and then there are the aliens who come on spaceships). I am an alien and that occasionally causes me a problem. On our first Independence Day in the United States, I flew a British flag as a joke and discovered that my neighbors took the United States' independence too seriously for this to be funny. I had things to learn about the culture if I was not to get into trouble. After twelve years I can still accidentally offend people by the way I say things. I have taxation without representation, but it is my choice. Most aliens in the United States or in Britain, whether or not they have papers, have a choice only in a formal sense. They are in a foreign country because circumstances drove them there, like Elimelech and his family in the story of Ruth. They probably wish they were home. They do the jobs citizens don't want to do. They are marginalized. When recession comes, they are among its first victims. They are unlikely to have as good health care as the average citizen. It is easy to take advantage of them.

Many of those dynamics will have applied to aliens in Israel, but a traditional culture adds some extra factors. To live, you need food. There are no supermarkets; people grow their own food. To grow food, you need land; but the land belongs to the people to whom the country belongs. It is distributed among its families, so you can find a secure way to live only if in some sense you belong to a family.

In Exodus 20–23 there are rather few explicit references to the way faith in God affects the expectations it expresses, and many of its rules are similar to the expectations expressed in other Middle Eastern documents, such as the "law code" of Hammurabi, who was a great **Babylonian** king a few centuries before Moses. I put "law code" in quotes because it was no more a law code than the ones in the **Torah**. It was not a statute book, a basis for the practice of law in Babylon, but a statement of the way society ought to operate, or of some concrete examples of the principles Hammurabi claimed to be committed to. It might seem surprising that the teaching of the Torah was similar to other people's teaching, but the Old Testament and New Testament assume that God did not leave the world outside Israel with no understanding of God and of how to live. Some such understanding was built into being human. So it is not surprising that other Middle Eastern peoples have insights similar to Israel about how society should run (and about God). You could perhaps forfeit the awareness of the basics about God and about morality; but you were then forfeiting something given to you by creation.

It is also not surprising if God's particular involvement with Israel issued in some special insights (technically, we are talking about special revelation as opposed to general revelation). Thus God comes first in Israel's rule of life. Then there is the recurrent reminder about the Israelites' background in their rescue from **Egypt**: "You were aliens in Egypt. . . . You yourselves know the feelings of an alien." Concern for the immigrant does not appear in Hammurabi's code. God's act of deliverance should shape the Israelites' lives, for it reflects God's nature. The God who heard the Israelites' cry will also hear the cry of people whom Israelites ill-treat. In other words, God's grace applies to other people, not just to me, especially when I am not generous to them. Consistent with that fact is the encouragement to lend to someone in need. In our culture, lending to someone in need is a way to make money, but in the Torah's vision, lending is a way to help people get back on their feet, preferably before things get bad enough for them to have to become servants to pay off their debts. Maybe you even have to be prepared to lend to your enemy. Certainly you have to be prepared to help your enemy; when Jesus tells people to love their enemies, he is making explicit something that the Torah implies.

It is easy for us to feel positive about such concerns, but it is also easy for us to pick and choose which bits of the Torah we like. We like to think we do that on the basis of being Christian, but more likely we do it on the basis of the culture to which we belong. To do justice to the Torah, we need to get inside the way it talks when it seems odd and not just use it to affirm what appeals to us. The comments about the girl who gets seduced illustrate one or two points. The Torah has no regulations for the regular process of marriage; that is an affair between families, and the Torah assumes people know what to do about it. It deals only with marginal situations that cause conflict in the community. It works with the fact of the "double standard," which makes it easier for a man to get away with sex outside marriage than for a girl. One reason is that it is the girl who gets pregnant; who will have responsibility for the baby? The Torah works with the assumption that marriages are arranged through families, a system that does not appeal too much in the West but looks as if it can hardly work worse than our system. (The Torah does not assume that a father would marry his daughter off against her wishes, to judge from a story such as that of Rebekah.)

EXODUS 23:20-33

How to Get into the Promised Land

[20]"Now. I am going to send an aide ahead of you to take care of you on the way and bring you to the place I have prepared. [21]Take care in relation to him. Listen to his voice. Do not defy him, because he will not put up with your rebellions, because my name is in him. [22]But if you really listen to his voice and do everything I say, I will be an enemy to your enemies, a foe to your foes, [23]because my aide will go ahead of you and bring you to the Amorites, the Hittites, the Perizzites, the Canaanites, the Hivites, and the Jebusites, and I will annihilate them. [24]You will not bow down to their gods, you will not serve them, you will not do as they do, but completely demolish them and break up their columns, [25]and serve Yahweh your God. He will bless your bread and water, and I will remove sickness from your midst. [26]There will be no one miscarrying or infertile in your country. The full number of your days I will bring to completion. [27]My terror I will send off ahead of you, and it will throw into panic all the people among whom you come. I will make all your enemies turn their back before you. [28]I will send off hornets ahead of you, and they will drive out the Hivites, the Canaanites, and the Hittites. [29]I will not drive them out ahead of you in one year, in case the country becomes a desolation and the animals of the wild become too many for you. [30]Little by little I will drive them out before you until you are fruitful and possess the country. [31]I will set your border from the Reed Sea to the Philistine Sea and from the wilderness to the Euphrates, because I will give into your hand the inhabitants of the country, and you will drive them out ahead of you. [32]You will not seal a covenant with them or their gods. [33]They will not live in your country in case they cause you to offend me because you serve their gods, because it would be a snare to you."

Modern people get concerned about the Israelites annihilating the **Canaanites**. As far as one can tell, it only became an issue in modern times. Although Christians explain their concern by referring to Jesus' exhortation to love one's enemies, until a couple of centuries ago Christians didn't see the Old Testament story as conflicting with that. The New Testament shows no hesitation about the achievements of Joshua and rather sees him as a great guy, and Augustine commented that loving our enemies didn't mean we had to love God's enemies. While it might be that we see things more clearly than do the New Testament and Augustine, we should at least consider the possibility that there is something odd about us in our modern culture and that it is not that we are more enlightened.

In this first description of the way the Israelites will get into the country, they are not told to kill anyone. It is God who will do the killing. This may seem more or less as bad. Is God not someone who loves all peoples? Again, the New Testament assumes so, but it does not stop Jesus from talking about the way his loving Father will send trillions of people to hell. God juggles a personal commitment to loving all people with a personal commitment to taking action against wrongdoing, lest it spoil the whole universe. For God there is a judgment call involved in deciding whether a particular moment is one for mercy or one when it is necessary to say, "That's it!"

For the peoples of Canaan, God has just made the judgment call against them. The **Torah** has already indicated a recognition that God cannot throw people out of Canaan simply on the basis of eminent domain or compulsory purchase: "I need your country to give to the Israelites, so I am throwing you out." In Genesis 15:13–16 God explained to Abraham that it would be a long time before his descendants could enter into possession of the country where they were living as immigrants because the sinfulness of the people there was not yet bad enough. By implication, God now has a basis for throwing them out.

What was so bad about them? The nearest the Old Testament gets to explaining is to talk about their wicked religious practices, notably the sacrifice of children. That is a well-evidenced-enough practice, though they were not the only people in the ancient world who went in for that practice. So an element in the explanation of their fate is that they were in the wrong place at the wrong time. They did not get away with things that other peoples got away with. That links with another consideration that surfaces here. God is set on establishing Israel in Canaan as a people that lives God's way. Living among the Canaanites, however, might mean that the influence of the Canaanites on the Israelites is as far-reaching as the influence of the Israelites on the Canaanites.

Which is how it turned out. The Israelites ended up sacrificing their children and in other ways living like the Canaanites, and that is how the Israelites ended up being thrown out of the country: **Ephraim** in the eighth century, and **Judah** in the sixth. The principle that applied to the Canaanites also applied to the Israelites. In connection with Exodus 15:22–17:7 we noted Paul's assumption that the principle that applied to Israel applies to the church. We don't have a country to gain or lose in the way the Canaanites and the Israelites did, but we have a destiny or a position to inherit or to imperil. That is one reason that we do well to feel uneasy about the way God deals with the Canaanites. If God could do that to them, God could do it to us. We had better listen to what God's **aide** says to the Israelites.

The exhortation in Exodus is not just intended for Israelites on the way from **Egypt** to Canaan. The link between how the Canaanites lived and how Israel lived reminds us that these stories do more than relate things that were going on between God and Moses and Israel in the thirteenth century BC. As Paul points out, they were written down so that people in subsequent centuries could learn from them. Asking how they made sense to people in Israel listening to the stories helps us perceive aspects of them. Many of the rules in Exodus 20–23 would make little sense to a crowd of Israelites in the wilderness. They have little application to their lives. It is Israelites settled in Canaan that they address. The same applies to this closing section of what God tells Moses to tell the people. It will make most sense to people living in the country over the centuries. That also fits with the way the address says things that stand in tension with one another. God intends to drive the **Canaanites** out of the country. God will send holy terror and unholy hornets ahead of the Israelites to turn the Canaanites into a state of panic. So why are the Canaanites still there in the country? Well (the address goes on to make clear) there are disadvantages to throwing the Canaanites out. The address provides its listeners with a variety of theological insights and resources to help them understand what God is doing with them.

Israel spent nearly all its life pressed by enemies—local powers such as the Philistines or the Edomites, big powers such as the **Egyptians** or **Assyrians**. God promises that Israel will not be overwhelmed by these. In contrast, for many of these centuries Israel can listen to this story and think "**Perizzites**? Hittites? Jebusites? Haven't seen many of them lately. God fulfilled this promise. So maybe I can trust God to deal with Philistines and Assyrians." At the same time, Israel was often involved in the kind of activity this address warns about, such as serving the gods of these peoples and recycling the "columns" (pillars as symbols of the gods). It was tempting to assume that the gods the Canaanites worshiped were the entities that knew how to make crops grow; the Canaanites had been successfully relying on them for years. Israel is told that **Yahweh** is key to having bread to eat and to fertility, good health, and long life.

As it listens to these words, every generation is urged to listen to what God or God's aide is saying to it now, as it continues on the journey towards the fulfillment of its vocation to be a priestly kingdom and a holy nation.

EXODUS 24:1–18

Seeing God

[1]He said to Moses, "Come up to Yahweh, you and Aaron, Nadab and Abihu, and seventy Israelite elders. Bow low from afar. [2]Moses alone is to come near Yahweh; they are not to come near and the people are not to come up with him."

[3]Moses went and told the people all Yahweh's words and all the rules. All the people responded with one voice and said, "All the things Yahweh said, we will do." [4]Moses wrote down all Yahweh's words. Early in the morning he built an altar at the foot of the mountain, and twelve columns for the twelve Israelite clans. [5]He sent some Israelite young men and they offered

up burnt offerings and sacrificed oxen as fellowship sacrifices. [6]Moses took half the blood and put it in basins, and half the blood he cast on the altar. [7]He took the covenant book and read it in the hearing of the people. They said, "All that Yahweh said, we will do, we will obey." [8]Moses took the blood, cast it on the people, and said, "Here is the blood of the covenant that Yahweh has sealed with you on the basis of all these words."

[9]Moses and Aaron, Nadab and Abihu, and seventy Israelite elders went up [10]and saw the God of Israel. Under his feet was something like a sapphire pavement, like the heavens themselves for purity. [11]Against the "pillars" of the Israelites he did not raise his hand. They beheld God, and they ate and drank.

[12]Yahweh said to Moses, "Come up to me on the mountain and be there. I will give you the stone tablets with the teaching and the command that I have written to teach them." [13]So Moses and his assistant Joshua set off, and Moses went up onto God's mountain. [14]To the elders he said, "Stay here for us until we come back to you. Here are Aaron and Hur with you. Anyone who has things to say can approach them."

[15]So Moses went up onto the mountain, and the cloud covered the mountain. [16]Yahweh's splendor dwelt on Mount Sinai; the cloud covered it for six days. On the seventh day he called to Moses from the midst of the cloud. [17]The appearance of Yahweh's splendor was like consuming fire on the top of the mountain before the eyes of the Israelites. [18]Moses went into the midst of the cloud and went up the mountain. Moses was on the mountain forty days and nights.

A Christian song by Michael W. Smith called "Open the Eyes of My Heart, Lord" declares, "I want to see You; to see You high and lifted up, shinin' in the light of Your glory." Another song, "I Want to Know You," by Andy Park, several times repeats the plea, "I want to see your face." When singing these songs, I am always also asking myself what I mean, and what the other people in the congregation mean. I guess I do know what we mean; that opening line "Open the eyes of my heart" tells me. We are asking for an inner sense of being in God's presence. Other songs rejoice in the idea of seeing the Lord "face to face" at the resurrection. There is also a visionary kind of seeing the Lord, a sense of physically seeing. Then there is the more literal physical seeing that the disciples experienced.

I'm not sure what kind of seeing Exodus 24 refers to, and I'm not sure Exodus knows. One indication is the confusing way it tells its story. You keep getting a sense that you know what is going on, but then the logic of the story jumps. Last night we watched a movie called *Home* about a woman coming to terms with having cancer and about the way this affects her relationship with her husband and her daughter, and how it makes her revisit her childhood and her mother's illness. It jumps from portraying her daughter, to portraying her as an adult behaving a bit the way she did as a child, to portraying her as a child. You have to keep adjusting your perspective. It's basically a true-story movie, and the jumpiness helps to convey the historical truth. So in Exodus, who goes up the mountain? Moses? Moses and Aaron with Nadab and Abihu? Hur? Seventy elders? Some people who are "pillars" of the community? Joshua? And who sees what? And how many times does Moses climb the mountain? The frequency here is in addition to the number of times he does so in Exodus 19 (it took me four hours, and Moses is eighty years old).

Part of the genius of this way of telling a story is to make some realities clear yet leave you with an appropriate sense of mystery. If Exodus could give us a straightforward report of Moses and company meeting with God, as if it were like the disciples meeting with Jesus, this would surely be misleading. It would trivialize the event. A meeting with God that actually happened is bound to be indescribable. Paradoxically, by making it impossible to work out exactly what happened, Exodus gives us a true impression of its momentous, unrepeatable nature.

Something else makes a paradoxical contribution to this effect. You could also compare Exodus 24 with a movie whose director didn't appoint a continuity person. It looks as if Israel had a number of versions of their story, as the early Christians had a number of versions of the Jesus story. Having a number of versions of the events at Sinai meant having a number of ways of trying to describe the indescribable. When Israelites composed the book we call Exodus, their instinct was to include several accounts of what happened. There may have been other versions that they omitted, though we have no way of knowing what these were. They preserved the ones in which they perceived the ring of truth, without attempting to turn them into one neat narrative without rough edges.

When people read this story, they know it is making a series of vital affirmations. God really met with Israel at Sinai. The average Israelite was protected from the scary aspect of that meeting; the people's leaders met with God on the people's behalf. Key to God's meeting with them was sealing the new version of the **covenant** relationship, so the people who hear this story can have assurance about God's relationship with them. Key to the covenant sealing being effective is Israel's making its own commitment to God; so the people who hear this story need to affirm that commitment for themselves. God did make sure that Israel knew how it was expected to live in the future; so the people who hear this story can be sure that they know God's expectations.

The actions with the animals' blood are not regular sacrifices but a special ceremony that can be associated with the making of a covenant. A story in Jeremiah 34 illustrates what it means when it speaks of the people having cut a calf in two and walking between the pieces. Outside the Bible, we know of a document that records a treaty between Syria and **Assyria** that involves dismembering a lamb and requires the Syrian king to pray that he may be treated the same way if he breaks the treaty. Thus when Exodus speaks of "sealing" the covenant, it more literally refers to this as "cutting" the covenant. The ceremony involved cutting up the animals and spattering the blood on the people and also on the altar, which stands for God. God and people are thereby saying, "May I be dismembered and my blood be spattered if I break this covenant."

EXODUS 25:1–26:30

How to Build a Church—I

[1]Yahweh spoke to Moses: [2]"Speak to the Israelites so that they take an offering for me. You are to take the offering from every individual whose resolve impels them. [3]This is the offering you are to take from them: gold, silver, copper; [4]blue, purple, and scarlet yarns, fine linen, goats' hair, [5]tanned rams' skins, dolphin

skins, acacia wood; ⁶oil for lighting, spices for the anointing oil and the aromatic incense; ⁷onyx stone and stones for setting in the ephod and the breast piece. ⁸They are to make me a sanctuary, and I will dwell in their midst. ⁹In accordance with everything that I am going to show you, the pattern of the dwelling and the pattern of all its accoutrements, so you are to make it.

¹⁰"They are to make a chest of acacia wood two and a half cubits long, a cubit and a half wide, and a cubit and a half high. ¹¹Overlay it with pure gold, overlay it inside and outside, and make a gold molding on it all around. ¹²Cast four gold rings for it and put them on its four feet, two rings on one side of it and two on the other. ¹³Make poles of acacia wood and overlay them with gold, ¹⁴and insert the poles into the rings on the sides of the chest, so as to carry the chest by them. ¹⁵The poles are to be in the rings of the chest; they are not to be removed from it. ¹⁶Put into the chest the declaration that I will give you.

¹⁷"You are to make an expiation cover of pure gold, two and a half cubits long and a cubit and a half wide, ¹⁸and to make two gold cherubs (of hammered work you are to make them) at the two ends of the cover. ¹⁹Make one cherub at one end and the other cherub at the other end, and make the cherubs one with the cover at its two ends. ²⁰The cherubs are to be spreading out their wings upwards, shielding the cover with their wings, and with their faces towards each other; their faces will be towards the cover. ²¹Put the cover on the chest, on top, and put into the chest the declaration that I will give you. ²²I will meet you there and speak with you from above the cover, from between the cherubs that are above the declaration chest, all that I shall command you for the Israelites."

[Yahweh goes on to give instructions for making a gold table for the "presence bread," a six-branched gold candelabrum for the sanctuary, the curtains that form its walls, the covering of hides that goes over it, and the supports that hold these in place.]

At our church we have just begun inviting ourselves to make offerings for work that needs to be done to the buildings. We have a list of priorities, like the replacement of some wooden beams that have rotted in the rains (it is California) and the building of proper handicap access (that was my personal priority because I had to lift my wife's wheelchair up a step or two in order to get into church each Sunday). The vestry (the church committee) agreed on the list of priorities and then wrote the membership about them. I have no doubt that our little congregation will give generously. At least as important is the way people give of their skills. One person is good at fixing electrical things, and someone else is a skilled woodworker; he carved the cross in the church. One woman is a great cook; I still salivate at the thought of her red velvet cake. On the Feast of St. Barnabas (our patron saint) the other week, someone e-mailed us with a reminder about the day and some comments on what Barnabas has to teach us. Someone else leads the singing when the organist is on vacation, and there are even people who preach sermons. . . .

The sanctuary or dwelling that Exodus describes will need offerings that overlap with both the offering of money and the offering of abilities. Money has not been invented yet; there is no danger of people thinking they have done their duty by writing a check. Most of the gifts will come from the people's own possessions or will require their having things from the local area (yes, there are creatures something like dolphins swimming off Sinai, and local people do catch them and use their hides as leather). From the shopping list God gives Moses, we also see the point about the Israelites' going-away shower before they left **Egypt**. Unwittingly, perhaps, the Egyptians will contribute to the making of **Yahweh**'s sanctuary. In due course, Exodus will talk about the skills that will also be required for the work the people have to undertake.

They will be making a "sanctuary" that is a "dwelling" (the King James Bible called it a "tabernacle"). The idea of having a place where God will "dwell" among them is a new one. In the past God was "the God of Abraham, Isaac, and Jacob," the God associated with people who were always on the move and the God who was with them wherever they were. God was not one who lived in a particular place. In the present, God is one acting in their midst; God has just now brought them out of Egypt and is about to take them into **Canaan**. They will settle, and God will settle there too. The "dwelling" will be located in a particular place in Canaan, and they will always know God is there and can be prayed to there. At the same time, the **Hebrew**

97

word suggests a place where someone "stays" (as we put it); "staying" is less permanent or fixed than "living" there. The structure will be moveable.

As a "sanctuary," a holy or sacred structure, it is a special place, set apart for ordinary usage in a way appropriate for the distinctive holiness of the God who comes to stay there. For Christians, it points to a paradox. The coming of Christ terminated the need for a sacred place; the people of God are the "place" where God dwells. Yet Christians soon found themselves setting apart special places for worship, and in the United States a place of worship is commonly called a sanctuary. That reflects a human need for a place set apart, a need to which God graciously condescends.

The detailed instructions begin with some of the significant elements in the sanctuary. First there is a chest, a bit more than a yard long, a bit more than half a yard wide and high (a cubit is about half a yard or half a meter). The King James Bible refers to it as an "ark," but the word means a box, though it is only occasionally used to refer to chests used for other purposes. In the King James Bible it is "the ark of the **covenant**," but again Exodus does not use the ordinary word for "covenant" but a word that means a solemn declaration. So the "ark of the covenant" is the "declaration chest." The link with covenant is that the "declaration" concerns the kind of expectations God has "declared" to Israel in connection with the covenant, specifically the ten commands. The chest has no great significance in itself; its point is to contain the two tablets expressing the basis for Israel's covenant relationship with God, which God will give Moses at the end of giving him the specifications for the sanctuary.

Likewise the "**expiation** cover" has no significance in itself at this point, though its name suggests it is significant in connection with people's relationship with God (the King James Bible calls it the "mercy seat"). Here the focus lies on the cherubs attached to either end of it. We are not to think of cherubs as baby-angel figures, as they are in modern English. They are impressive enough to stand guard at the gates of Eden to stop people forcing their way in, so perhaps they act here as guardians of the chest. They are imposing creatures with wings, so that in Ezekiel's visions they can fly and transport God's throne around the heavens. They thus represent God. You cannot make an image of God, but the images of the cherubs suggest the presence of God whose invisible throne they support. Indirectly they witness to the real presence of the invisible God. Enthroned above them, God will meet with Moses (the "you" throughout refers to Moses in particular) to reveal the further instructions God wants to give Israel, when the Sinai revelation is over and God still wants to stay in communication with the people.

EXODUS 26:31–27:21

How to Build a Church—II

[31]"You are to make a curtain of blue, purple, and scarlet thread, and woven fine linen. It is to be made as a creative work, with cherubs. [32]Put it on four posts of acacia overlaid with gold, with their hooks of gold, on four silver bases. [33]Put the curtain under the clasps and take the declaration chest there behind the curtain. The curtain will separate the holy place from the holiest place for you. [34]Put the expiation cover on the declaration chest in the holiest place. [35]Place the table outside the curtain and the candelabrum opposite the table to the south side of the dwelling, with the table on the north side. [36]Make a screen for the tent doorway, of blue, purple, and scarlet thread and woven fine linen, the work of an embroiderer, [37]and make for the screen five posts of acacia and overlay them with gold, with their hooks of gold, and cast for them five copper bases.

[27:1]"You are to make the altar of acacia wood, five cubits long and five cubits wide (the altar will be square) and three cubits high, [2]and to make its horns on its four corners (its horns are to be one with it), and overlay it with copper. [3]Make its buckets for removing its ashes, its shovels, basins, forks, and fire pans: make all its utensils of copper. [4]Make a grating for it, a mesh made of copper, and make on the mesh four bronze rings at its four corners. [5]Put it under the altar ledge downwards; the mesh is to be halfway up the altar. [6]Make poles for the altar, poles of acacia wood, and overlay them with copper. [7]The poles are to be inserted into the rings and the poles are to be on the two sides of the altar when it is carried. [8]Make it hollow, of boards. As it was shown you on the mountain, so they are to make it. [9]And make a courtyard for the dwelling."

[In 27:10–21 Yahweh gives specifications for the hangings that delimit the courtyard, one hundred cubits by fifty cubits, with their supports, a screen for the entrance, all made of similar materials to those already specified. These verses then prescribe the bringing of olive oil for the light that is to burn all night outside the curtain in front of the chest.]

When I was a toddler in the latter part of the Second World War, family lore says that I used to watch the "fireworks" and the "bonfires" from my second-floor bedroom. These were actually bombs falling on the RAF airstrip that is now Birmingham International Airport and fires that during the bombing devastated the nearby city of Coventry, including its fourteenth-century cathedral. A decade or so later I visited the ruins of the cathedral at a time when a new cathedral was being built. Does God really want cathedrals? Wouldn't there have been some better way of spending those resources in God's name? The question was being asked again when we moved to Los Angeles and the Roman Catholic archdiocese was building its new cathedral. Wouldn't the money be better spent on the poor? Why would God want a sanctuary like this one Exodus describes? Why would God have wanted to give such detailed instructions for its building? Why would God then have wanted these instructions for its building to be included in his book?

While the instructions concerning the sanctuary would be needed when it was being built, there would be no need to write them down. Putting them into writing made them available to people living long afterward. It is instructive to imagine people reading them as they read about the building of David and Solomon's temple or about the **Second Temple** built after the exile, or as they took part in the building or planning of these. The First Temple was David's idea, not God's, and God had mixed feelings about it (see 2 Samuel 7). That relates to the sense in which sanctuaries exist for our sake, not God's. We have noted that there were no sanctuaries in Genesis and no sanctuaries in the early decades of the church. Yet soon Christian congregations were building sanctuaries. God did not need special places to meet with people, but people did. Here in Exodus, too, God was meeting people where they were in their need (as physical human beings) for a physical place.

There was a specific reason for God's unease with David's desire to build a palace for God, based on the fact that David himself had one. God liked being on the move rather than being stuck in one place. The instructions for building the wilderness sanctuary would remind people of this fact. This sanctuary was a glorified tent, not a glorified palace. The instructions keep incorporating reference to the portable nature of the dwelling's elements. It could stay on the move, as the God who was accessible to people there would stay on the move. The temple was an imposing structure on the top of the hill in Jerusalem, towering above ordinary people. The wilderness sanctuary was a magnificent dwelling in the midst of the people in their encampment, on a level with them. When the temple had been burnt and devastated by the **Babylonians**, these instructions for the wilderness sanctuary would remind people of some truths about God and them that they perhaps needed to take more account of as they contemplated rebuilding it.

Partly for reasons of climate, when Western people think of a sanctuary we think of a large building inside which the whole congregation meets for worship. The Temple Mount in Jerusalem gives you more of an idea of the dynamic of the temple or the wilderness sanctuary. The sanctuary itself is a small sacred structure (five by fifteen yards) that especially belongs to God, surrounded by a yard the size of a small soccer field. People can gather there to be with God, especially for big worship occasions, or just to hang out and actually play soccer as they do on the Temple Mount. It is the part of the structure where God welcomes people, as opposed to God's private rooms; God's dwelling works the same as a family dwelling, and the yard is the scene of family gatherings. The sacrificial altar stood there because of its significance for this meeting. Here families and individual men and women would bring the offerings that expressed their love and commitment to God, their gratitude for what God had done for them, and their desire to make up for wrong they had done. The details of its construction are unclear, as is the significance of the horns, though they perhaps stood for divine strength (like the horns of a bull).

Two thirds of the actual sanctuary comprises the "holy place," where stands the table with the presence bread and the candelabrum. Exodus does not explain the significance of these and other features of the sanctuary, but one can imagine that they would remind people of the way God provided their "daily bread" and the light they needed on their way. (If anybody wondered whether the bread was food for God, their faith would soon point out that this did not fit what they knew of God.)

The other third of the sanctuary is the "holiest place" that most powerfully symbolizes the presence of God. The chest with the declaration given by God was there. On one hand, the existence of the courtyard expresses the reality of being in the actual presence of the God who wants to be in fellowship with the people. On the other, the separateness of the holiest place reminds them of the real distinction between the heavenly God and created humanity, and it safeguards against their confidence becoming a wrong kind of familiarity. Between the two "rooms" of the sanctuary is the curtain with its embroidered cherubs, corresponding to the cherub statues over the chest. They constituted another reminder of the presence of God there.

EXODUS 28:1–29:37

How to Ordain a Priest

[1]"You yourself are to have your brother Aaron brought forward to you, and his sons with him, from among the Israelites, to act as priests for me: Aaron, Nadab and Abihu, Eliezer and Ithamar, Aaron's sons. [2]Make sacred garments for your brother Aaron, for splendor and beauty. [3]You yourself are to speak to all the people who are skilled in heart, the people I have filled with a skillful spirit, so that they make Aaron's garments for his consecration to act as priest for me. [4]These are the garments they are to make: a breastplate, an ephod, a robe, a woven tunic, a headdress, and a sash. They are to make the sacred garments for your brother Aaron and for his sons to act as priests for me. [5]They themselves are to get the gold, the blue, purple, and scarlet thread, and the fine linen."

[Verses 6–43 give the details on these various items.]

29:1"This is what you are to do for them in consecrating them to act as priests for me. Get one steer of the herd and two whole rams, 2and flat bread and loaves mixed with oil, and flat wafers spread with oil; make them of choice wheat flour. 3Put them in one basket and bring them forward in the basket, with both the bull and the two rams. 4Aaron and his sons you are to bring forward to the doorway of the meeting tent and wash them with water. 5Get the garments and clothe Aaron with the tunic, the ephod robe, the ephod, and the breastplate, and fasten the ephod on him with the ephod's creative work. 6Place the head-dress on his head and put the sacred emblem on the headdress. 7Get the anointing oil and pour it on his head, and anoint him. 8And his sons: bring them forward, clothe them with tunics 9and wind sashes on them, Aaron and his sons, and tie caps on them. The priesthood will be theirs by a rule in perpetuity. You are then to ordain Aaron and his sons."

[Verses 10–37 give the details of the sacrificial rituals this involves.]

I shall shortly have completed forty years teaching in seminary, and a bit longer than this in being a priest and pastor. A few years after I started seminary teaching, I became embarrassed to realize that I no longer believed that within Christian faith there is such a thing as a theology of ordination, a theology of priesthood—or at least that there is a theology that you could call scriptural. It is common in different denominations for there to be just one particular designated person in a congregation who can celebrate Holy Communion and/or preach, or for there to be one "senior pastor" who has ultimate authority and responsibility under God for a congregation. This common practice stands in tension not only with the practice in the New Testament but also with the theological convictions of the New Testament.

Eventually I came to see why the church felt the need of priests and how God might look at this. The dynamics of Scripture with regard to ministry are similar to those with regard to sanctuaries. In Genesis there were no priests, and as Israel arrived at Sinai, Exodus 19:1–8 affirmed the whole people's priestly relationship with God. Then Exodus 19:9–25 referred to some people called priests, and now we find God issuing detailed instructions for the ordination of priests. The church likewise moved on from the New Testament's affirmation that the whole people was priestly and went about appointing priests and senior pastors within congregations. The dynamic of that move parallels the one with regard to sanctuaries. God is not identified with a place but with a people, but God becomes willing to meet us in a designated place because we find that helpful. That gives us a clue to what happened with regard to priests. God doesn't need there to be priests, but the people of God are inclined to shy away from too much responsibility or too much freedom in relation to God, and so with a shrug of the divine shoulders, God plays along with our need for mediators and leaders, appoints some, and seeks to get them to operate in ways God can live with. (God has to do a lot of shoulder shrugging with us.)

Theologically and chronologically, the people's priesthood comes first. A priest such as Aaron embodies what the people are. The description in this chapter relates in particular to the clothing of Aaron and thus of the person who will later be called the chief priest. He is the one who undertakes the special roles associated with occasions such as the Day of Atonement (Exodus refers only briefly to the simple garb that other priests would wear for more regular occasions). People are invited to look at the senior priest and to see themselves. They are involved in making the garments he will wear. His wearing special clothes as he is set apart for his service corresponds to Israel's being a special people set apart for God's service. The clothes are for splendor and beauty, because Israel itself is a people who are splendid and beautiful in God's eyes.

Like the instructions for building the sanctuary, the instructions about ordaining the first priests were eventually put into writing for the sake of the later community. How far did Israelites ever see these garments being worn? It is plausible to think of these chapters being written during the **exile**, when temple worship was suspended and no one had seen a priest actually performing. The chapters are then a prescription for what needs to be done if the temple is rebuilt one day, or a vision of how it might be, or a promise from God of what could or will be. They are a work of the imagination, and we learn by imagining what the priest would be like and reflecting on the significance of his dress and his actions. I have just watched the Israeli animated movie *Waltz with Bashir*, about someone seeking to regain his lost memories of the Israeli invasion of Lebanon. Animation enabled its themes to be expressed more powerfully, more symbolically, than would have been the case if the invasion had merely been reenacted in the manner of other war movies. So it is with this imaginative picture of the Israelite priest.

Among the garments, the ephod, the robe, the woven tunic, and the sash are special versions of ordinary clothes, a little like a shirt, a tee shirt or sweatshirt, a bathrobe, and a belt. The headdress would mark the priest as an important person. Usually a breastplate protects the wearer, but this one was different. There were twelve precious stones attached to it, representing the twelve Israelite clans. The breastplate symbolized how the priest undertook his service on behalf of the whole people. When he stood before God, he took the whole people with him. This was symbolized further in the engraving of the twelve clans' names on two onyx stones attached to the ephod's shoulder pieces. At the same time, the anointing symbolized the fact that the priest belonged to God. He brought together God and people. The breastplate also incorporated a pouch for the Urim and Thummim, means of God's responding to the people when they needed a question answered or needed guidance (maybe they were inscribed with signs that indicated "Yes" and "No").

Consecrating Aaron and his sons involves a rite of **purification**, to make sure of removing any taint that has come upon them through contact with something impure. That is also the significance of offering the steer, which is described as a purification offering. The offering of the goats is special to ordination, but the first is a version of a regular burnt offering, a pure gift to God that symbolizes the way the priests are being given to God. The blood of the second is applied to Aaron and his sons, again implying purification, consecration, and God's identification with the priests. It is also an offering shared by God and the priests, and it thus initiates the way priests share in some of the offerings; similarly, they eat the bread. The term "ordain" literally means "fill the hand," which might suggest both giving them a share in the offerings and giving them authority to act as priests.

EXODUS 29:38–30:37

How to Start and End the Day

[38]"This is what you are to offer on the altar: two sheep, a year old, regularly each day. [39]Offer one sheep in the morning and offer the second sheep at twilight, [40]with a tenth of fine flour mixed with beaten oil (a quarter of a measure) and a libation (a quarter of a measure of wine for one sheep). [41]When you offer the second sheep at twilight, offer it in the same way as the morning grain offering and its libation: a nice smell, a gift to Yahweh, [42]a regular burnt offering through your generations at the doorway of the meeting tent before Yahweh, where I will meet with you to speak to you. [43]I will meet with the Israelites there. It will become sacred through my splendor. [44]I will consecrate the meeting tent and the altar, and I will consecrate Aaron and his sons to act as priests for me. [45]I will dwell among the Israelites, I will be God for them, [46]and they will acknowledge that I am Yahweh their God who brought them out of Egypt to dwell among them. I am Yahweh their God."

[Exodus 30:1–37 gives instructions for building the incense altar and its use, for making the incense, the anointing oil, and the basin, and for everyone paying half a shekel each year to the sanctuary.]

When my wife died, we "celebrated" her life and marked her death at a memorial service where we burnt lots of incense, not something we regularly do in our church. One striking aspect of the burning of incense is the smell, which is a bit pungent if you are not used to it. Another is the sight of the little clouds of smoke hovering about. Burning incense was a prominent feature of Israelite worship, though the Old Testament never explains why this is so. The New Testament associates incense with prayer: Revelation 5:8 and 8:3–4 picture "living creatures," elders, and an angel offering incense along with the prayers of God's people, so that the smoke wafting upwards suggests their prayers rising up to God, mingled with their praises. I loved the idea that our praises for my wife and our prayers for ourselves—my prayer for myself and my family—in the context of our loss and sadness were rising up to God as certainly as the incense was wafting around the church. It fits with this that Luke 1:10–13 describes Zechariah as a priest making the incense offering when it was his turn, because he is then told that his prayer has been answered (his prayer for Israel's deliverance and his prayer that he and his wife might have the baby for whom they have longed for many years).

Incense comes from sources such as the wood, bark, fruit, and resin of various trees, which produce a fragrance when you burn them. God here specifies the herbs to be used in making the special incense for use in worship and instructs Moses about the making of the incense **altar** to be placed within the sanctuary. Only this specially prescribed incense is to be used, and it is not to be used for the everyday purposes of generating a nice fragrance. God similarly prescribes the constituents of the oil to be used for anointing the priests and the various parts of the structure to mark them as belonging to God, and again forbids the use of this special anointing oil for everyday purposes as if it were ordinary makeup.

The regular burning of incense is to take place in the context of the twice-daily regular sacrifices in the sanctuary, at dawn and dusk. As dawn breaks and a new day begins, Israel offers itself to God, offers the day to God, and seeks God's blessing for the day. It does so not merely in its thinking and its words but by its actions. The sacrifice and the offering of bread and wine give body to Israel's giving of itself to God. They are forms of worship that Israel gets nothing out of, because a burnt offering is simply given over to God. Then as the day ends and the night comes, once again Israel offers itself to God, offers to God the day that has passed, and seeks God's presence and protection for the night. The question this pattern raises for us is, How can we together mark the beginning and the end of the day with shared praise and prayer like that? It doesn't need to mean we are physically together; often Israelites would be miles away from the sanctuary, but they would know that this was the moment for prayer and praise and that they could join in from a distance. There is some parallel with the old Christian idea that the minister rang the church bell when Morning and Evening Prayer were about to begin, so that people who were still out in the fields could join in. The Israelite pattern also raises the question of how our prayer and praise can be not merely feelings and thoughts, words and music, but something that involves the whole person and something that involves a cost to us.

This worship indeed involves all the people. In prescribing what Moses is to do, God promises, "I will meet with you," and the "you" is plural. After promising, "I will speak with you," where the "you" is singular and refers to Moses, God again says, "I will meet with the Israelites there." The people can be assured that God speaks to Moses, so the people who subsequently read the **Torah** can be assured that what they read there issues from God's actual speaking to Moses and his successors. They are not left on their own, without guidance as to what God expects of them. They can also be assured that God is in *their* presence, God is with *them*. People like Moses and Aaron do not stand between them and God, so that God meets with them but not with ordinary people. God meets with the whole people. This sanctuary really is God's earthly home. As you visit other people and are welcomed into their yard for a barbecue (not into their private rooms, of course), so you visit God and are welcomed into God's yard for a barbecue.

So the structure Israel will erect becomes a sacred place. God's splendor is manifested there. What would that be like? How would it happen? The splendor or glory of God is the outward manifestation of God's holiness. The Old Testament often speaks of this splendor in terms of a cloud appearing that simultaneously reveals and conceals God's presence. At the heart of the cloud is a shining brightness such as would blind you if you looked at it, but the cloud mercifully masks this brightness while also confirming that it is there. Exodus 16 spoke in these terms in connection with the gift of manna and quail; Exodus 24 did so in connection with God's appearing on Sinai. Here Exodus 31 promises that God's presence with the people will not be confined to occasional events or unique events such as the appearing at Sinai. God will always be there in the sanctuary. God makes no reference here to the cloud. The people who read Exodus know there is not a visible manifestation of God every time they come to meet with God in the sanctuary, but this promise still applies. God is there, all right. The relation between them and God is secure: "I will be God for them." That is underscored by the further reference to their acknowledging God as the one who brought them out of **Egypt** to dwell among them. The exodus was a manifestation of God's splendor, and as they tell the story of that event, it is a continual reminder and reaffirmation of God's glory.

Exodus mentions two other adjuncts to the priests' work. In the sanctuary yard, between the sanctuary and the sacrificial altar there was to be a copper basin where the priests could ceremonially cleanse their hands and feet before entering the sanctuary or making an offering at the altar. God also prescribes that adult Israelites are to contribute a half-shekel each year towards the sanctuary's upkeep. The sum is not large and is the same for rich and poor: everyone has equal status and responsibility in this connection.

EXODUS 31:1–18

The First Spiritual Gifting

¹Yahweh spoke to Moses: ²"See, I have summoned by name Bezalal son of Uri son of Hur, of the clan of Judah. ³I have filled him with a divine spirit of insight, discernment, knowledge, and every craft, ⁴for making designs for working with gold, silver, and copper, ⁵and in cutting stone for setting and carving wood, for working in every craft. ⁶Further, I have myself given him Oholiab son of Ahisamach of the clan of Dan, and into the mind of everyone who is insightful in mind I have given insight. They will make everything I have commanded you: ⁷the meeting tent, the chest for the declaration, the expiation cover on it, all the accoutrements of the tent, ⁸the table, its accoutrements, the pure-gold candelabra, all its accoutrements, the incense altar, ⁹the altar for the burnt offering, all its accoutrements, the basin, its stand, ¹⁰the braided garments, the sacred garments for Aaron the priest and his sons' garments for acting as priests,

[11]the anointing oil, and the aromatic incense for the sanctuary. Just as I have commanded you they are to do."

[12]Yahweh said to Moses: [13]"You yourself, speak to the Israelites: 'Nevertheless, my Sabbaths you are to guard, because that is a sign between me and you through your generations, for acknowledging that I Yahweh have consecrated you. [14]You are to guard the Sabbath because it is sacred for you. The person who treats it as ordinary is absolutely to be put to death. When anyone does work on it, that person is to be cut off from among his kin. [15]Six days work is to be done. On the seventh day is a day of complete stopping, sacred for Yahweh. Anyone who does work on the Sabbath day is absolutely to be put to death. [16]The Israelites are to guard the Sabbath, making Sabbath through their generations, a covenant in perpetuity. [17]Between me and the Israelites it will be a sign in perpetuity. Because in six days Yahweh made the heavens and the earth and on the seventh day stopped and found refreshment.'"

[18]He gave Moses (when he had finished speaking with him on Mount Sinai) the two declaration tablets, stone tablets written by God's finger.

An amazing experience of parenthood is your children's ability to do things you cannot do. Whereas I can just about play three chords on the guitar but have to think through where to put my fingers at each chord change, our younger son astonished me before he was in his teens with his intuitive ability to play. Whereas for five minutes I can understand how the internal combustion engine works but then have lost it again, that same son could disassemble a car engine and reassemble it without having been told how to do this. At the same time as he was dazzling me with his guitar playing, his older brother was among the first generation that grew up with computers and was writing me a program to enable me to incorporate Hebrew in things I wrote. These are all gifts; they become spiritual gifts if you give them over to God. In other words, spiritual gifts are not divinely provided add-ons supplementing what we would be able to do "naturally." They are aspects of the way God in love and grace made us that can become gifts with which we serve God. (They may indeed be capacities that we never realized we had that get released and find expression in a way that would never have happened if the Holy Spirit not been at work in us in a new way.)

The cumbersome language Exodus uses helps make this point. God intends to take people who are already skillful, insightful, or talented in mind, heart, or spirit and put skill or insight or talent into their minds, hearts, or spirits. They would be unable to do the things they will need to do if God had not made them those kinds of people, but they would also be unable to do these things if God did not get involved with them now, inspiring them in their work. Bezalel will not have been someone who was hopeless at metalwork to whom God now gave this gift; he is someone with such gifts whom God now commissions to do the work that is needed.

God has come to the end of the instructions for making the sanctuary and now gives the two stone tablets, inscribed with the ten commands that form the declaration, for putting into the chest in the sanctuary. Before that, the instructions add a surprising footnote. How many days a week is it okay to serve God by building the sanctuary? Surely the answer is "seven." It's God's work. It's to make something beautiful for God. It's to construct the place where God will come and dwell among the people.

Actually, no. Even in doing this work for God, you work only six days each week. The Sabbath is still sacred, holy ground. God has claimed it. You have to keep your feet off it. To underscore the point, God gives it a new significance. The Sabbath is a sign, like the rainbow or the eating of flat bread at Passover, that reminds people of their special relationship with God. The peoples among whom the Israelites will live in **Canaan** or in **Babylon** did not observe the Sabbath and sometimes consciously or unconsciously tried to compromise the Israelites' observance. Keeping Sabbath was a weird thing to do; it was countercultural. Precisely because of that, it was hugely important, a symbol of the Israelites' special relationship with God. If they ignored this sign, they were compromising and imperiling their special position. Hence the seriousness of the sanctions Exodus speaks of. There are many references to Sabbath breaking in the Old Testament but only one story of a Sabbath breaker being put to death. As with other offenses, making Sabbath breaking a capital offense is a way of saying not what a court should do but what a terrible offense Sabbath breaking is, because it compromises Israel's distinctive position as God's people.

So the Sabbath needs guarding. It is always in danger. There are things you cannot avoid doing on the Sabbath, such as looking after the children, herding the sheep, or offering the daily sacrifices. God is not legalistic. But there are things you can avoid doing. The temptation to assume that working for God is okay on the Sabbath is a particularly subtle one. The point is underlined further by a new and bold comment about why God stopped working on the Sabbath. Exodus 23:12 bade Israelites to make sure that the servants and immigrants who work for them have a chance to find refreshment on the Sabbath. Now Exodus says that the first Sabbath was when God found refreshment. It is not implying that God was tired, but like Genesis it does imply that there was something valuable for God in standing back and contemplating the achievements of the week. It doesn't argue that we should guard the Sabbath because it will be good for us (we might then think we don't need it) but because of our concern for other people and our vocation to be Godlike.

EXODUS 32:1–29

How to Pray for Rebels

¹The people saw that Moses was shamefully long about coming down from the mountain. So the people assembled against Aaron and said to him, "Up, make us gods who will go ahead of us, because this Moses, the man who brought us up from Egypt—we don't know what has happened to him." ²So Aaron said to them, "Tear off the rings of gold on the ears of your wives, sons, and daughters, and bring them to me." ³So the entire people tore off the rings of gold in their ears and brought them to Aaron. ⁴He took [the gold] from their hand and shaped it with a tool and made it into the figurine of a calf. They said, "Israel, these are your gods who brought you up from Egypt." ⁵When Aaron saw this, he built an altar in front of it. Aaron proclaimed, "Tomorrow is a festival for Yahweh!" ⁶So early next day they offered up burnt offerings and brought fellowship sac-

rifices. The people settled down eating and drinking, and set about enjoying themselves.

⁷Yahweh spoke to Moses: "Get yourself down, because your people have ruined things. ⁸They have quickly turned aside from the way I commanded them. They have made themselves the figurine of a calf and bowed down to it and sacrificed to it and said, 'Israel, these are your gods who brought you up from Egypt.'"⁹ Yahweh said to Moses, "I have looked at this people. There: it is a stiff-necked people. ¹⁰So now, let me be, so that my anger may burn against them and I may consume them, and make you into a great nation." ¹¹Moses sought to calm Yahweh his God: ¹²"Why should the Egyptians say, 'It was to bring disaster that he brought them out, to slay them in the mountains and finish them off from upon the face of the ground'? Turn from your angry fury. Relent of bringing disaster on your people. ¹³Be mindful of Abraham, Isaac, and Israel, your servants, to whom you swore by your own self: 'I will make your offspring as numerous as the stars in the heavens, and this entire country of which I spoke I will give to your offspring, and they will possess it in perpetuity.'" ¹⁴So Yahweh relented of the disaster he said he would do to his people.

[In verses 15–29 Moses goes down the mountain with the tablets, sees the calf and the dancing, smashes the tablets, and destroys the calf. He challenges Aaron about what he has done and challenges people to take God's side. The clan of Levi respond, and he urges them to kill people who are involved in the calf celebration, which they do.]

You could say I came to the United States to avoid the responsibility of leadership. I was the head of a seminary and got paid more than my colleagues because it was my job to lie awake worrying about its future. Metaphorically speaking, on my desk sat that notice saying "The buck stops here." When I arrived in my new post to resume being just an ordinary professor, for the first term I would go to my office and look for the stacks of paper to deal with and find there were none; so I would go off to the library. Occasionally I would be aware that the dean or provost had to deal with some problem, and I would think, "That used to be me, and now it isn't," and then I would go off to the library again. In England I remember especially clearly one spring when the number of students applying to begin ordination training was low and our seminary was affected by this. The faculty got concerned about the seminary's future and their own future and their jobs, and one or two came to confront me in my office. Didn't I realize there was a terrible crisis? Why wasn't I doing something about it? I didn't sleep that night. (Everything sorted itself out okay in the end.)

So I sympathize with Aaron. Against the background of that idyllic scene on the top of the mountain, with Moses memorizing the instructions for the sanctuary that the people are to construct so that God can come to dwell among them, at the bottom of the mountain the people are engaged in something close to the opposite, point by point, to what God has in mind. Moses seems to have gotten lost in his wonderful spiritual experience with God; here they are stuck in the wilderness with nothing to do and no idea what is supposed to happen now. They need to take responsibility for themselves. Previously, they had a God who was concerned about them and a leader who mediated that God's guidance. Now they have neither. So they turn to the leader's apparent next-in-command and urge him to take action, and Aaron tries to find some action that will satisfy them without compromising their faithfulness too much.

The Hebrew word for "God" and "gods" is the same. Usually there is no ambiguity because the context makes clear which meaning applies, but the built-in ambiguity enables the people and Aaron to have different views of what is going on in this story. The people talk about "gods," but Aaron makes only one figurine and subsequently proclaims a festival "for **Yahweh**." Maybe the people do not see themselves as giving up on Yahweh, the God of Israel. Maybe they see these other "gods" as representatives or subordinates of the real God. Much later in Israel's history, when other gods are worshiped in the temple, that will likely be the way people see it (remember again that these are the people for whom the story is written and by whom it is read). Certainly Aaron doesn't see himself as abandoning Yahweh. Yet the people are conveniently putting out of mind the first commandment, about not having other gods over against Yahweh, and Aaron is conveniently putting out of mind the second commandment, about not making a statue or anything to help people in worship, whether it is a statue of Yahweh or of another "god."

Between them they have put out of mind the most basic requirements of their faith. God has to be incensed. Moses knows God is right. He destroys the tablets inscribed with those commands because the people have destroyed the relationship they embody. He encourages people who are on God's side to exact terrible punishment of the people involved in the apostasy. But first he confronts God. God's inclination is simply to abandon the people and start again with Moses, as God had once abandoned the world as a whole and started again with Noah. Moses says, "You can't do that. What will the **Egyptians** say? What about the promises you have bound yourself by?" And God relents.

This exchange is another exercise in doing theology by telling a story, like the account of the conflict between Moses and Pharaoh (which thinks its way around the relationship between God's sovereignty and human responsibility). The theological question here is, How is God to respond to the rebelliousness and failure of the people of God? It would be appropriate to abandon the people, but God cannot do that. God faces two conflicting obligations. God is torn between the obligation to cast off and the obligation to be merciful. (When such conflicts happen to us, we can at least comfort ourselves with the fact that it happens to God, too. Being God does not make everything straightforward.)

At the same time, this exchange suggests something significant about prayer. In prayer we are like children begging our parents to do what we want. Sometimes children fail in such attempts, but sometimes they succeed. Significantly, however, Moses is not praying for himself but for the people, and he is praying about God's own honor. Significantly, he is not praying that the God who is inclined to be merciful should be tough but that the God who is inclined to be tough should be merciful. Is prayer about conforming our will to God's will? Moses thinks prayer is about conforming God's will to our will; or rather, Moses knows that God's will is not always inexorably fixed, that God has to wrestle with conflicting obligations, and that God makes the decision about which obligation has priority only on a 51 to 49 basis. It might be easy to push the figures the other way. When God announces a determination to bless us, there is no way you can get God to have a change of mind about that, as Balaam points out to Balak in Numbers 23. But when God announces a determination to punish, it is always worth a try, as Abraham assumed about Sodom, and as prophets such as Amos and Jeremiah will assume.

EXODUS 32:30–33:11

How to Check Things Out with God

[30]Next day, Moses said to the people, "You have committed a great wrong, but now, I will go up to God. Perhaps I may be able to make expiation for your wrongdoing." [31]So Moses went back to Yahweh and said, "Oh, it was a great wrong this people committed when they made a gold god for themselves. [32]But now, if you could carry their wrongdoing. . . . But if not, you can erase me from the book that you wrote." [33]Yahweh said to Moses, "Whoever offended against me I will erase from my book. [34]So now, get going, lead the people where I told you. There: my aide—he will go in front of you, and on the day I attend to them, I will attend to them in respect of their wrongdoing."

[35]So Yahweh smote the people because they made the calf that Aaron made, [33:1]and Yahweh said to Moses, "Get going, go up from here, you and the people that you brought up from Egypt, to the country I swore to Abraham, Isaac, and Jacob, saying, 'To your offspring I will give it.' [2]I will send an aide in front of you and drive out the Canaanites, the Amorites, the Hittites, the Perizzites, the Hivvites, and the Jebusites, [3]a country flowing with milk and sweetness, because I will not go up in your midst, because you are a stiff-necked people, in case I consume you on the way." [4]When the people heard this tough message, they went into mourning and no one put on their finery.

[5]So Yahweh said to Moses, "Say to the Israelites, 'You are a stiff-necked people. Were I to go up in your midst for one moment, I could finish you. So now, take your jewelry off you so I may decide what I should do with you.'" [6]So the Israelites stripped off their jewelry from Mount Horeb on.

⁷Now Moses would take a tent and pitch it outside the camp, some distance from the camp. He called it the meeting tent. Anyone seeking something from Yahweh would go out to the meeting tent outside the camp. ⁸When Moses went out to the tent, the entire people would get up and stand at their tent doorway and watch Moses until he went into the tent. ⁹When Moses went into the tent, the cloud column would come down and stand at the tent doorway, and he would speak with Moses. ¹⁰The entire people would see the cloud column standing at the tent doorway, and the entire people would get up and bow down, each person at their tent doorway. ¹¹Yahweh would speak to Moses face to face, as someone speaks to a friend, and he would go back to the camp, though his attendant, Joshua, son of Nun, a young man, would not move from the tent.

Throughout most of my life, I have had a particular place where I pray each day. At the moment it is an ancient recliner chair sitting in front of my desk. Next to it is a little table where I keep a Bible and a prayer notebook and so on, and on the other side of the chair is a little shelf where I put my cup of coffee. Across from the chair is a sofa where I sometimes think of God sitting as I read and ruminate and talk to God and ask God things and seek to see if God has anything to say to me. I know God is also present at this desk as I write and is present in other parts of the house, and I talk to God there, too, but it helps me that there is a particular place where I am used to talking to God.

Maybe some equivalent dynamics apply to Israel and God. The meeting tent for which Moses has received very lengthy specifications in Exodus 25–31 has not yet been built, but a meeting tent evidently already exists. Exodus does not clarify the relationship between the meeting tent that **Yahweh** is commissioning and this meeting tent that is already available. It is another indication of the laid-back process whereby the **Torah** came into existence, without a continuity person to make sure everything fitted together neatly. God could teach Israel things through the instructions for building the elaborate meeting tent, especially as readers contemplate the similarity and the differences from the First and **Second Temple**. God could also teach Israel things through the account of this simpler meeting tent, a place where people could go to talk to God on their own, perhaps to get God's advice about a problem, to pray for healing when a child got sick, or to talk to God about a conflict with the people in the next tent. Literally, Exodus speaks of people "seeking Yahweh," but the way the Old Testament uses this expression makes clear that it means seeking guidance or help from Yahweh.

The reference to everybody being free to go there is background to the description of Moses going there. As the people's leader, he has special reason for seeking God's guidance. Most of the Torah's teaching is described as given by God's initiative on top of Sinai, but some is described as given on Moses' initiative when he has to deal with an issue. This story suggests how he might gain God's guidance in this connection. It suggests a model of Israel's ongoing life. Ordinary Israelites could always go and talk to God at the sanctuary, as a person like Hannah does (1 Samuel 1). Moses' successors, leaders such as judges, elders, priests, kings, and prophets, could always go and talk with God there, as Moses does, when they have to deal with issues that arise and they need to know what God will say to his people as new circumstances arise. Their responsibility is not merely to work out what to do but to consult God about it. We may guess that the material eventually collected in the Torah issued from a process like this.

The picture of God's accessibility stands in poignant juxtaposition to the further story of Moses' seeking God's forgiveness for the people's wrongdoing at Sinai. Once more the sequence of events is jumpy. Why is Moses doing this when he has already had the conversation with God on the top of the mountain? Is Exodus 32:35 referring to the same slaughter as the preceding verses, or is God threatening another one? The jumpiness again reflects the way Exodus is a collection of separate, overlapping stories. God and Israel did not want to lose any of them, so Exodus simply strings them together.

Not long ago, Pharaoh had to beseech Moses to "carry" his wrongdoing and plead with God on his behalf (Exodus 10:1–20). There is thus some humiliation about Moses' having to beseech God to carry Israel's wrongdoing, but God and Moses will have to get used to the idea. God had to put up with the world's wrongdoing and the ancestors' wrongdoing, and will henceforth have to put up with Israel's and with the church's. Yet Moses speaks like someone who is brash and audacious. He is totally committed to Israel. In the exchange on top of Sinai, God had proposed abandoning the people and starting again with Moses, but Moses had argued God out of it. Here he goes beyond resisting that idea and says, "If you won't have them, you can't have me at all." God's "book" might be simply God's list of the people who belong to Israel or, perhaps specifically, God's plans about whom to use in fulfilling the purpose to take Israel to its destiny and bring blessing to the world. Either way, Moses says, "Cross my name out if you're crossing their names out." He may mean "Cross my name out and leave theirs in"; but this involves some reading into his words. Either way, this time God resists Moses' argument in order to make another point that needs making. There is such a thing as individual human responsibility. Moses has to let his people accept theirs.

The commission to get going on the journey to **Canaan** makes clear that the story has not derailed, even though the people are "stiff-necked," like an ox that doesn't want to wear a yoke to make it go the way the farmer wants. That is true even if God resists Moses' pressure, and even if God punishes the people, and even if God needs to be careful about coming too close to Israel in case they behave so objectionably it will be impossible to resist coming down on them like a ton of bricks. It is also true even if the people have to live rather more soberly in light of what has happened. God is still committed to taking them to Canaan and throwing out the peoples who have forfeited the right to stay there because of their wrongdoing (there is again no reference to killing them). But God will lead them and act by means of an **aide** rather than in person.

EXODUS 33:12–23

Rock of Ages Cleft for Me

[12]Moses said to Yahweh, "Look, you are saying to me, 'Take this people up,' but you yourself have not made known to me whom you will send with me. And you yourself said, 'I have

acknowledged you by name; indeed, you have found favor in my eyes.' [13]So now, if I have actually found favor in your eyes, will you let me know your way, so I may acknowledge you, in order that I may find favor in your eyes? Look, because this nation is your people." [14][Yahweh] said, "My face will come, and I will give you rest." [15][Moses] said to him, "If your face does not come, do not take us up from here. [16]By what means would it be acknowledged, then, that I have found favor in your eyes, I and your people, unless by your coming with us, so that we may be distinct, I and your people, from any other people on the face of the ground?" [17]Yahweh said to Moses, "This thing, too, that you have spoken of, I will do, because you have found favor in my eyes and I have acknowledged you by name."

[18]He said, "Will you show me your splendor?" [19][Yahweh] said, "I myself will pass all my goodness before your face and proclaim in the name of Yahweh in front of you: I will show grace to whomever I will show grace, I will show compassion to whomever I will show compassion." [20]But he said, "You cannot see my face, because humanity cannot see me and stay alive." [21]Yahweh said, "There: a place with me. Stand on the rock. [22]When my splendor passes, I will put you in a crack in the rock and lay my hand over you until I have passed by. [23]Then I will take away my hand and you will see my back, but my face will not be seen."

In the County of Somerset in the West of England there is a canyon called Cheddar Gorge (yes, where the cheese comes from). One day in 1763 a young minister was caught in a tumultuous thunderstorm in the cliffs nearby. The minister, Augustus Toplady, took refuge in a cave and found himself reflecting on the way the "rock of faith" provides us with a shelter from the storms of life (he in fact died of TB when he was thirty-eight). The words of the hymn "Rock of Ages, Cleft for Me" formed themselves in his mind there. Its opening line is a riff on this story from Exodus. The story and the hymn have in common the insight that there are aspects of God's own being that would be a threat to us but that God in person saves us from these. The hymn, however, is preoccupied by God's righteousness and our sin while the story is preoccupied by God's supernatural splendor and our mortal ordinariness. It constitutes another example of Exodus thinking its way round a theological profundity by telling a story.

This particular theological mystery surfaces several times in Exodus, especially in Exodus 24. What do we mean by being in God's presence or seeing God? Is this possible when God is the almighty, supernatural, transcendent creator and we are just ordinary mortals? There is also that moral problem. God has pointed out how dangerous God's "literal" presence with wayward Israel would be. God would be continually battling to be tolerant toward them and might not always succeed. It would be better if God commissioned an **aide** to accompany them and if God kept a little distance. So here, Moses' opening question may be "Who is this aide?" or it may be "Okay, there is this aide ahead of us clearing the way, but who will be with me?" The question is not so different from the one he asked when God first appeared to him (Exodus 3). One can hardly blame Moses for asking. Leadership is a lonely business. How does sending him off on his own as Israel's leader fit with God's talk of acknowledging him and showing favor to him?

God's answer again involves referring to the name **Yahweh**. Exodus has often used the word "acknowledge," usually in connection with people acknowledging God, though God has "acknowledged" Israel's oppression. When the Old Testament elsewhere speaks of God's acknowledging Abraham, Israel, and Jeremiah, it means God fixes an eye on them, recognizes them, chooses them as servants. In Exodus the *idea* of God's acknowledging Moses (and Israel) has been present, though the actual *word* has not appeared in this connection. Nor has Exodus explicitly spoken about God's showing favor to Moses, though Genesis used that expression of Abraham and of Noah, and again in substance God was doing this in Exodus 3 (even if Moses was not inclined to see God's commission as a favor).

That being true, Moses says, I need you to show me your way. The dynamic of the conversation again recalls Exodus 3. God's way (as opposed to God's "ways"—plural) suggests the characteristic nature of who God is and of how God acts. If it seems odd for Moses to request such a revelation after all this time, we need to remember that Exodus's concern is not to give us biographical information about Moses' spiritual development but to help us understand who God is and how we may relate to God. Exodus (like the rest of the Bible) will often take more than one run at an issue to help us understand it.

God's response, "My face will come, and I will give you rest," has similar implications to "I will be what I will be." There is nothing concrete about it, just a general promise, with an implied invitation to trust and not to feel overburdened by the responsibility. (The seminary where I used to work in England was called St. John's Theological College, and when I was leaving, one of the college children apparently asked if it would now change its name. When I felt overburdened by the responsibility of being in charge, I had to try to remember it wasn't John's college; actually God bore responsibility for it.)

God also gives a paradoxical reassurance: "I myself will not go with you—but my face will go with you." It sounds like a distinction without a difference. But the promise means that people will be protected from the kind of reality of God's presence that would be a threat but will be granted a reality of God's presence that will be a blessing. (Hebrew does not have a special word for "presence"; the word for "face" covers the idea of presence. Linked to that is the idea that when God's face shines on us, God blesses us.)

The reality of God's presence, however, is not enough for Moses; he wants to see God's splendor. That is an unrealistic aspiration, because it would be like looking at the sun. It would be bound to blind him. As a gesture of love, then, God takes Moses as close as possible to that experience yet protects him from its mortal danger. God will proclaim the goodness, grace, and compassion associated with the name Yahweh in their wide-ranging reach ("whomever"). These are the characteristics associated with the face or presence of God, and they are another way of indicating God's "way."

Yet God then identifies the "face" with the "splendor" and says it is too dangerous for Moses to see it! If we feel confused, it is a sign that we are seeing the point. It is a mysterious business, trying to think about the presence of God. You can hardly avoid saying things that seem contradictory. What the story does is assure Moses, Israel, and us that God's presence really goes with us—and so do God's goodness, compassion, and grace—and that we need not be afraid. We are protected from what would overwhelm us as human beings and (Toplady's concern) as sinners.

EXODUS 34:1-26

Now I Will Seal a Covenant

[1]Yahweh said to Moses, "Carve yourself two stone tablets like the first ones, and I will write on the tablets the words that were on the first tablets, which you broke up. [2]Be ready by the morning, and come up Mount Sinai in the morning and present yourself to me there on the top of the mountain. [3]No one is to come up with you, nor is anyone to appear anywhere on the mountain, nor are flocks or herds to graze in front of the mountain." [4]So he carved two stone tablets like the first ones. Early in the morning Moses went up Mount Sinai as Yahweh commanded him, taking the two stone tablets in his hand. [5]Yahweh came down in a cloud, took his stand with him there, and proclaimed with the name Yahweh. [6]Yahweh passed before his face. Yahweh proclaimed, "Yahweh, God compassionate and gracious, long-tempered, big in commitment and truthfulness, [7]keeping commitment to thousands, carrying waywardness, rebellion, and shortcoming, he certainly does not acquit, visiting the waywardness of parents on children and grandchildren, thirds and fourths."

[8]Moses quickly bowed down to the ground [9]and said, "If I have indeed found favor in your eyes, my Lord, will my Lord go in our midst? Because this is a stiff-necked people, pardon our waywardness and our offense. Possess us." [10][Yahweh] said, "Now. I am going to seal a covenant. In front of all your people I will do wonders that have not been created in all the earth or among all the nations. All the people in whose midst you are will see how awesome is the deed of Yahweh that I am going to do with you."

[God repeats the promise to drive out the inhabitants of Canaan and the declaration that Israel must not make any covenant with them because that will lead to sharing their religious commitment. Rather Israel must destroy their forms of worship. God goes on to reaffirm a set of further basic commitments expected of Israel, mostly restating expectations in Exodus 20–23.]

Visiting Jerusalem brings many striking experiences for sober-minded Westerners. The celebration of a bar mitzvah or bat mitzvah at the Western Wall is an occasion of enthusiastic rejoicing, dancing, and singing as **Torah** scrolls are carried around in excited, boisterous procession. The fervor of this event also features in the Jewish people's great celebration each September/October called "Rejoicing in the Torah." There are processions around the synagogue with the Torah scrolls, singing, and dancing, and many people may share in carrying the scrolls around, reading from them, and declaring a prayer of blessing over them. The singing and dancing may spread out into the streets. These celebrations seem to have begun in the Middle Ages, but they are in keeping with the Old Testament attitude to the Torah. Whereas Christians often assume that the law must have been a burden and still is a burden to Jews, neither Old Testament Israel nor modern Jews see it that way.

Exodus 34 gives us one clue why that it so. The Israelites have imperiled their relationship with God, with potentially fatal results. That is symbolized by Moses' breaking the tablets inscribed with God's commands. Those tablets were to be deposited in the sanctuary as a symbol of the relationship between God and people, but the people have broken the commands, and Moses has broken the tablets. It is as if the relationship is over. But God is prepared to start again, and reinscribing the commands on two new blocks of stone is an expression of that. The renewed gift of the commands is a reason for enthusiastic rejoicing. The relationship is not irretrievably broken.

The implications are worked out in God's self-description, a succinct summary of systematic theology, of a doctrine of God, that is often referred to in the Psalms and the Prophets. What is God like?

1. God is compassionate. The word is related to the Hebrew word for the womb, so it suggests that God has the feelings of a mother for Israel. How can a mother cast off the children of her womb? So how could God cast off Israel?
2. God is gracious. Grace means showing favor to someone when there is nothing about the person to merit it. Israel's

righteousness was not the reason that God chose Israel; its failure therefore does not mean God unchooses Israel.

3. God is long-tempered. If it did not look like that in Exodus 32, the readers of Exodus can look back over Israel's story (and the church's story) and see how God's not casting off the people shows how long-tempered God is.

4. God is big in **commitment**. Like grace, commitment means God gets involved with Israel even though there is nothing special about them. It goes beyond grace in declaring that God maintains commitment even though people forfeit any right to expect that God would do so.

5. God is big in truthfulness. God stays faithful and steadfast. What God says, happens. When God makes promises, they come true.

6. God keeps commitment to thousands—to judge from what follows, this likely implies thousands of generations, which takes us up to our own day and way beyond.

7. God carries waywardness, rebellion, and shortcoming. When the child rebels or disobeys, the mother rolls with it, leans into the wind. When the child hurts itself by doing something stupid and disobedient, the mother comforts the child and bandages the wound, accepting responsibility for the waywardness rather than saying, "Serves you right, deal with it."

8. God does not acquit. After numbers one to seven, this is a surprise. Mother's temper does not hold forever. She may say, "That's it," and let the child suffer for a while.

9. Indeed, God can pay us a visit as a result of our waywardness. It is a wondrously, frighteningly mafia-like image. Like a visit from the mafia, it may implicate not merely the offender but the family, because the fate of families is bound up together.

The good news is that you can take God for granted. The bad news is that you cannot take God for granted. A relationship with God is like any other personal relationship. When the other person is loving and gracious, you must be wary of thinking that your response to this counts for nothing. When you have done wrong, you may get into trouble, but you can remind yourself that love and commitment are more basic to the other person than anger or jealousy.

Above the Western Wall when Jews are celebrating bar mitzvah and bat mitzvah is the Haram al-Sharif with the Dome of the Rock, where Muslim worshipers in the mosque might make one think of the way Moses prostrates himself in response to God's appearing. They show how kneeling is a serious, whole-body business, not a graceful leaning on the pew in front. Once again Moses begs God to go with him and his people. God's response is to talk about sealing a **covenant**. It is the first time God has done so in Exodus. Exodus 24 did involve a kind of re-sealing of the covenant relationship in light of the exodus, but only here does God make this explicit. It is a significant gesture. Israel has imperiled the covenant by its action. Moses has broken the covenant tablets. Does the covenant still hold? Has it been annulled? In uttering these gracious words, "I am going to seal a covenant," God reaffirms the covenant commitment notwithstanding Israel's imperiling of it. Grace can trump justice.

EXODUS 34:27–40:38

The Magnificent Presence

[27]Yahweh said to Moses, "Write yourself these words, because on the basis of these words I have sealed a covenant with you and with Israel." [28]He was there with Yahweh forty days and nights; he did not eat food or drink water. He wrote on the tablets the covenant words, the Ten Words. [29]When Moses came down from Mount Sinai with the two tablets of the declaration in Moses' hand as he came down from the mountain, Moses did not know that the skin of his face emanated through his speaking with him. [30]Aaron and all the Israelites saw Moses: there, the skin of his face emanated. They were afraid to come near him. [31]Moses called to them, and Aaron and all the leaders of the community came back and Moses spoke to them. [32]Afterwards, all the Israelites came near and he gave them as commands all that Yahweh spoke with him on Mount Sinai. [33]When Moses had finished speaking with them he put a veil on his face. [34]So when Moses went in before Yahweh to speak with him he took the veil off until he came out. When he came out,

126

he spoke to all the Israelites what he had been commanded. [35]The Israelites would see Moses' face, how the skin of his face emanated, and Moses would put back the veil on his face until he went in to speak with him.

[Exodus 35:1–40:33a relates how Moses led the Israelites in implementing the instructions for building the sanctuary.]

[40:33b]So Moses finished the work, [34]the cloud covered the meeting tent, and Yahweh's splendor filled the dwelling. [35]Moses could not go into the meeting tent because the cloud dwelt over it and Yahweh's splendor filled the dwelling. [36]When the cloud lifted from over the dwelling the Israelites would set out, during all their journeying. [37]If the cloud did not lift, they would not set out until the day it lifted, [38]because Yahweh's cloud would be over the dwelling by day and the fire would be in it by night, in the sight of all the household of Israel during all their journeying.

When I sit in my ancient recliner aware that God is there with me, in the way I described in connection with Exodus 32:30–33:11, I do not have experiences that leave my face radiating in such a way that later in the day students are afraid to draw near to me (there must be other reasons for their fear). When I go to church and rejoice in arriving to celebrate what God has done for us, I do not sense an overwhelming manifestation of God's splendor that makes me wary about going into church. Ought God to give us experiences like that, or ought we to be able somehow to generate them or earn them? Some things that happen in the Bible should also happen today, and some things that people did in the Bible are the kind of things we should do today, but many stories about Moses and the Israelites (or Jesus) are there to inspire us not because we expect the same things to happen but because we are not to expect them.

While Moses' face shining as it did was very important for the Israelites, the expression is a puzzling one. The Hebrew word that I have translated "emanate" is related to the word for a horn and thus looks as if it denotes Moses' putting out horns. Maybe he radiated something hornlike, something like the rays of the sun, that dazzled people and threatened to blind them.

This would fit with the idea that God's splendor is something people needed protection from. When Moses goes into the meeting tent to consult God about an issue, something of God's splendor attaches to him. For the Israelites that would be scary but also encouraging. It means he really has been in God's presence and really can mediate God's answer concerning whatever the issue was. It symbolizes the supernatural and trustworthy nature of the results of Moses' (and his successors') consulting God, which Israel has in the **Torah**. That's why what matters for Israel and for us is not having an experience like Moses', but having the Torah (and the rest of the Scriptures) that reflect how certain people were in special touch with God like that. (Paul riffs on this story in 2 Corinthians 3 to make a different point. He has Moses putting on the veil "so that the Israelites would not see the end of what was passing away." He may be taking up the way the story was understood by the Jewish people in his day. Moses then comes to stand for the Jewish people as a whole. Their not recognizing Jesus as Messiah suggests that a veil stops them from seeing God's splendor in Jesus' face. The light goes on for them only when they turn to the Lord.)

Nearly all of Exodus 35–40 then simply repeats Exodus 25–31 in the past tense (except that the priests' ordination will not come until Leviticus 8–9). One might have thought the Holy Spirit could economize on space or use the space to give us (say) a solution to the problem of evil or the relationship of divine sovereignty to human free will. Yet the repetition is an encouragement. We could be disheartened by the people's rebellion and waywardness, but here they do exactly as God says. Once more it is helpful to read the story from the perspective of its Israelite readers. We could think of people in Haggai's day feeling that their circumstances made it too tough to set about restoring the temple after the exile. To them, it is a challenge to follow their forebears' example in their detailed obedience to God's instructions.

The people's detailed obedience also raises suspense: what will God think of it? Is God interested in the sanctuary any more, after what happened in Exodus 32–34? They may build, but will God come? Exodus's closing paragraph constitutes a "Yes" to that question. God has not said, "Forget those instructions about building a sanctuary; I'm outta here." As God had reaffirmed a commitment to Israel by sealing a **covenant**, now the cloud comes when Moses has finished the work. Once again it both reveals and conceals God's presence, indicating that God was truly there but was preventing people from being blinded by looking at that presence. The cloud had accompanied Israel from **Egypt** via the Reed Sea to Sinai and then settled over Sinai when God was to speak there. Now it covers the tent and God's splendor fills the sanctuary. Henceforth God is there. Only when it is time for the people to move does God signal this by the cloud's moving.

The cloud descended like that again when the Jerusalem temple was first built, though there is no such description when people responded to Haggai's exhortation and restored it after the exile. It is again not something the readers experienced, but the story reassures them that God did so come and give this manifestation of the divine presence when the wilderness sanctuary was built and when the temple was built. Even if they did not see the cloud, God was there all right. On that basis they can live their lives, sure of God's presence in their midst.

LEVITICUS 1:1–2:16

Giving to God

[1]Yahweh called to Moses and spoke to him from the meeting tent: [2]"Speak to the Israelites and say to them, 'When one of you presents an offering of livestock to Yahweh, you may present your offering from the herd or from the flock.

[3]"'If his offering is a burnt offering from the herd, he is to present a whole male. He is to present it at the doorway of the meeting tent so he may find acceptance before Yahweh. [4]He is to put his hand on the head of the burnt offering so that it may be acceptable for him, in making expiation for him. [5]He is to slaughter the animal before Yahweh, and Aaron's sons, the priests, are to present the blood and cast the blood over the altar at the doorway of the meeting tent, all round. [6]He is to skin the burnt offering and cut it into its parts. [7]The sons of Aaron the priest are to put fire on the altar and arrange wood on the fire, [8]and Aaron's sons, the priests, are to arrange the

parts, with the head and the suet, on the wood that is on the fire on the altar. [9]He is to wash its innards and its legs in water and the priest is to turn the whole into smoke at the altar as a burnt offering, a gift, a nice smell, for Yahweh.

[10]"If his offering is from the flock, from the sheep or the goats, as a burnt offering, he is to present a whole male. [11]He is to slaughter it on the side of the altar to the north before Yahweh, and the sons of Aaron, the priests, are to cast its blood over the altar, all round. [12]He is to cut it into its parts, and with the head and the suet the priest is to arrange them on the wood that is on the fire on the altar. [13]He is to wash the innards and legs with water and the priest is to present the whole and turn it into smoke at the altar. It is a burnt offering, a gift, a nice smell, for Yahweh.'"

[Leviticus 1:14–2:16 gives equivalent instructions for offering a dove or pigeon, and for the grain offering.]

In our seminary in England, faculty and students worked as teams in planning and leading worship. While this was a great privilege and I enjoyed it when it was my team's turn, my heart would also sink somewhat when our period of duty arrived because it would take hours to discuss and sort out and practice what we were going to do. Our seminary in California has a different system, but when I am taking part in leading worship in some way, I get a sequence of e-mails about the arrangements, then a request to show up half an hour early for sound check. In both settings the music group will have spent hours rehearsing so as to get things absolutely right. Getting the details of worship right is really important to us.

When people set about reading through the whole Bible, the opening of Leviticus is often where they get stuck, partly because it discusses different details from the kinds that preoccupy us. It first assumes that worship and prayer are naturally expressed in concrete external ways. The Old Testament assumes that feelings, words, and music are important, but they are not enough. In human relationships, if I had told my wife I loved her but never gave her a birthday gift, she would have a basis for wondering how real my love was.

God's instructions concerning the sanctuary have described the offerings made each morning and evening. While the priests offered those on behalf of the whole community, the people themselves would not usually be there. Here it describes gifts an individual might want to make for personal reasons. Stories about people making these offerings suggest they might simply be an expression of commitment and love, or might accompany prayer for blessings, favor, healing, or forgiveness. Leviticus itself mentions expiation, which might imply this particular focus or simply the recognition that whatever the reason people bring offerings, they need to make sure that they have found cleansing if their offerings are to be acceptable.

Sometimes the gifts we give one another are extravagant, and sometimes they are small, and the latter may be just as meaningful. The same is true with offerings to God. It would be really extravagant to sacrifice a steer and somewhat extravagant to offer a sheep or a goat. Leviticus 3 allows just as happily for a person to offer some grain, raw or baked as bread or griddled or fried. This would be much less costly, an everyday kind of offering. For Israelites, eating meat would be an occasional and not an everyday experience; bread would be their everyday staple. Offerings work in a similar fashion. Ordinary people might never be in a position to offer a steer, a sheep, or a goat, but they could know that God was happy for them to make an everyday offering. Either way, they are bringing God gifts relating to their ordinary lives—the animals that are in a sense part of their family, the grain they grow, and the bread they eat. Indeed, it is quite okay to offer a dove or pigeon, which presumably costs nothing (this is the offering Mary brings in Luke 2). It is a little like picking a bunch of wildflowers as a gift.

You do have to remember that only a good example of a particular offering will do as a sacrifice. If you are offering an animal, a male will do, even though males are less valuable to you than females, but it needs to be one that is whole. A deformed animal would suggest you're trying to look impressive (you're giving an animal, not just some grain), but you're doing it on the cheap. Further, the wholeness of an offering corresponds to the wholeness of God, of the sanctuary, and of creation.

Leviticus makes clear the respective roles of priest and offerer. The offerer brings the animal into the courtyard to the doorway of the sanctuary, God's dwelling, to "show" it to God as an offering God can properly accept. He puts his hand on it as a sign of identifying it as his, kills it, skins it, cuts it up, and washes it (to urbanized Westerners this does not seem a very attractive aspect of worship, but it would be natural to a farmer). The instructions about the offerer's role link with Leviticus's opening description of its teaching as meant for the people as a whole. In Israel's worship, the people do not just sit there while worship leaders do the worship for them.

Yet there is good reason why this book is called Leviticus. Much of it concerns the responsibility of the priests, the members of the clan of Levi. They do anything involving the **altar**. They throw the blood over it as a way of giving the animal's life back to God, fuel the altar fire, arrange the wood, put the parts of the animal on the altar, and make it burn so the barbecue smell ascends to God. These tasks need fulfilling in the right way, so the priest undertakes them.

Although Leviticus is a separate book from Exodus, in content things carry straight on. The last part of Exodus has described how the sanctuary was built. Leviticus opens with instructions about how to offer the sacrifices there.

LEVITICUS 3:1–4:35

Enjoying Fellowship and Gaining Cleansing

[1]"If his offering is a fellowship sacrifice: If he is presenting something from the herd, whether a male or a female, whole, he is to present it before Yahweh, [2]put his hand on the offering's head, and slaughter it at the doorway of the meeting tent, and Aaron's sons, the priests, are to cast the blood over the altar, all round. [3]He is then to present from the fellowship sacrifice as a gift to Yahweh the fat covering the innards, all the fat above the innards, [4]the two kidneys and the fat on them, at the loins, and the lobe on the liver (he is to remove it with the kidneys). [5]Aaron's sons are to turn it into smoke at the altar, with the burnt offering on the wood that is on the fire, a gift, a nice smell, for Yahweh.'"

[Verses 6–17 gives equivalent rules for when the fellowship sacrifice is a sheep or goat.]

⁴:¹Yahweh spoke to Moses: ²"Speak to the Israelites as follows: 'When a person offends by mistake with regard to any of Yahweh's commands about what should not be done, and does one of them: ³If it is the anointed priest who offends and brings liability on the people, he is to present to Yahweh for the offense he committed a bull from the herd, whole, as a purification offering. ⁴He is to bring the bull to the doorway of the meeting tent before Yahweh, put his hand on the bull's head, and slaughter the bull before Yahweh. ⁵The anointed priest is to take some of the bull's blood and bring it to the meeting tent. ⁶The priest is to dip his finger in the blood and sprinkle some of the blood seven times before Yahweh, in front of the sanctuary curtain. ⁷The priest is to put some of the blood on the horns of the altar of aromatic incense before Yahweh, in the meeting tent, and all the rest of the bull's blood he is to pour out at the base of the altar of burnt offering at the doorway of the meeting tent.'"

[Verses 8–35 gives more detail on what the priest is to do with the different parts of the bull, then prescribes equivalent rules for when the offense attaches to the whole people, or to a leader, or to an ordinary person.]

I just had an invitation to a Thanksgiving dinner and was in a quandary about how to respond. Our first one or two Thanksgivings were very meaningful because we were thankful for God's goodness in connection with our move here. We could identify with the Pilgrim fathers and mothers in some small way. Then that feeling got overlaid with another awareness. To a foreigner, someone outside the culture, the dinner was a strange ritual. Through the rest of the year, I would never eat roast turkey or pumpkin pie, and the ritualized sharing of reflections on the past year seemed, well, ritualized—which for an outsider means artificial. It's my problem, of course. There is nothing wrong with the ritual if you are an insider.

Worship is ritualized, as comes home to us when we take part in another Christian tradition's worship. Israel's sacrifices are also ritualized. As at Thanksgiving, it is important to do the right thing (which in large part means the traditional thing) in the right way at the right time, and it is important to eat the right thing. This does not make it meaningless. For an insider it makes it meaningful and valuable (as happens with thankful reflections over the past year at Thanksgiving). In addition, the ritual can be a means of bringing home some truths. In the **Torah**, that is more explicit with regard to Passover, but it is implicit in the regulations about sacrifice.

The trouble is that leaving things implicit may mean people don't get the point or they misunderstand the meaning behind the ritual. Such uncertainty is a special problem if you are outside the culture where the ritual takes place. As a result there are aspects of the sacrifices that we do not understand and aspects about which there are differing opinions. In my comments on the sacrifices, I am giving one set of understandings. They are mainstream understandings, not weird ones that I have invented, and the overall picture is not controversial. The details, however, are subject to debate.

Thus "fellowship sacrifice" is only one possible title for the offering in Leviticus 3, but it is clear that this offering was not one the offerers simply gave over to God but one they shared with God. With whole burnt offerings (as the name implies), you gave the entire animal to God. It was a gift. If we give someone a gift we will share, we know we have cheated. Grain offerings were only slightly different, in that part went to the priests on God's behalf as an element in their "salary" for being priests, because their work meant they had no opportunity to grow their own food. With fellowship sacrifices, only part went to God; most of it the offerers themselves ate. It truly was a fellowship sacrifice, involving fellowship between the offerers and God and fellowship among the offerers themselves.

As with aspects of a U.S. Thanksgiving or a British Christmas, the reasons for some aspects of the ritual (such as giving the fat to God, which is also a custom among some other peoples) have long been forgotten. When Israelites gave God the liver and kidneys, it might bring two facts home. The liver and the kidneys stood for the inner person, the emotions and attitudes. Putting one's hand on the animal's head, so as to identify it as one's own, and then giving these to God could mark this act of worship as involving not just the outward person but (as Western people would put it) the heart. The other fact is that other peoples examined an animal's liver as a means of divining the future (like reading palms or tea leaves). Giving it to God could imply surrendering that way of trying to discover or control the future.

Again, "**purification**" offering is only one possible title for the offering in Leviticus 4. Translations traditionally refer to it as the "sin offering," but it does not cover what we would think of as sin. It is concerned with accidental offenses. If you have deliberately done wrong, you cannot deal with it by a mere sacrifice. All you can do is acknowledge the wrongdoing, throw yourself on God's mercy, and hope that God will then treat your offense as if it were something accidental (because now you do not mean it). The next chapter will tell us more about the kind of offense that the sacrifice is designed to deal with.

This chapter makes two things clear. One is that just because you didn't mean to do something, it doesn't alter the fact that what you did has consequences that need to be dealt with. You can't just shrug your shoulders. The other is that the bigger you are, the more disastrous are the consequences of your wrongdoing. When religious leaders or political leaders are involved in a scandal, it is much bigger news than if ordinary people are. It can have big ramifications in national and religious life. Yet here, the differences between the offerings are striking. For the priest or the whole community, the offering is a bull; for a leader or an ordinary person, it is a goat. A leader is no more important than an ordinary person! On the other hand, the priest's offense imperils the whole people. He "brings liability on the people."

Whoever the offenders are, the sanctuary is affected when they come there. It is vital that the sanctuary be cleansed by this ceremony. Otherwise God could hardly deign to be present. The effect of the offenses would be cataclysmic. So the blood of the sacrifice is not applied to the person who committed the offense but sprinkled before God, applied to the incense **altar**, and poured out below the sacrificial altar. It is they that need cleansing.

LEVITICUS 5:1-6:7

Making Reparation

[1]"'When a person offends if he has heard the proclaiming of an oath and he is a witness who saw or knew something—if he does not speak up, he carries his waywardness. [2]Or when a person touches something taboo (the carcass of a taboo wild animal or a taboo domestic animal or a taboo creature that moves along the ground) and it escapes him, though he is taboo: he is liable. [3]Or when he touches something human that is taboo (of any of the things that would be taboo for him, which would make him taboo) and it escapes him, though he knew it: he is liable. [4]Or when a person swears, blurting with his lips, to do bad or good, in connection with anything a human being may blurt out in an oath, and it escapes him, though he knew it: he is liable, with regard to one of these matters. [5]When he is liable with regard to one of these matters, he must make confession of how he has offended with regard to it, [6]and bring his reparation to Yahweh for the offense he committed, a female from the flock, sheep or goat, as a purification offering. So the priest is to make expiation for him because of his offense.'"

[Verses 7–13 make rules for people who could not afford a sheep or goat.]

[14]Yahweh spoke to Moses: [15]"When a person commits a trespass and offends by mistake in any of Yahweh's sacred things, he is to bring his reparation to Yahweh, a ram, whole, from the flock, convertible into silver shekels by the sanctuary shekel, as reparation. [16]For the matter in which he offended in connection with the sacred thing he is to make restitution and add to it a fifth and give it to the priest, and the priest will make expiation for him with the reparation ram, and there will be pardon for him."

[Leviticus 5:17–6:7 extends this regulation to areas where a person is not sure about the trespass and then to trespass that involved deceiving another human being but swearing one has done no wrong.]

When my wife and I knew we were in love and wanted to get married, my wife's parents opposed the match for various reasons. I was a mere would-be pastor with no career prospects to compare with Ann's as a physician. I was too informal and not polite enough; I didn't shake hands, I didn't wear a suit, and I had long hair. In Ann's parents' culture, I was behaving in an offensive and disrespectful fashion. Although I wore casual fashion, it "escaped me" that I was causing offense by not wearing a suit. Being a young man, my response would in any case have been "Tough, we are going to marry anyway, deal with it," which would have rather proved their point. Since then, I have learned in some ways, but I still get into trouble because of not understanding people's expectations. I have discovered that many U.S. students are sensitive about professors using certain four-letter words. It is easy to offend people accidentally, behaving in an offensive way through not realizing the way other people think. It can "escape you" that you are acting offensively. Westerners do this routinely in other cultures.

What kind of thing offends God? Leviticus gives four examples. They look random, illustrating a common feature of the **Torah**'s rules. It does not seek to legislate comprehensively for every eventuality in life. Instead, it gives you sample cases, because it is not really a code of laws, which as such would be expected to cover a broad range of eventualities. It more resembles a teaching device that works by saying, "You see these examples? Now, learn to think in light of them, so you can see how to approach the different circumstances that will occur in life."

First, imagine there is a dispute that the community elders are trying to sort out (for instance, an argument about which member of the community is responsible for some wrongdoing), and you were a witness but did not show up to speak (maybe you didn't realize what the dispute was about or you got preoccupied by something else), and the case is wrongly decided. You then "carry your waywardness"—that is, God holds you responsible. Or imagine you touched the carcass of an "unclean" or **taboo** animal (Leviticus will explain later what that means), and you didn't realize it was taboo. Or imagine you had been in contact with some human taboo (Leviticus will also explain later what that involves—but contact with a corpse would be an example), and you didn't realize, or you forgot. Or imagine you made a promise and forgot it. All these are offenses that would mean you defile the sanctuary by your presence there.

Western people would see two of these offenses as purely ceremonial and might not think of them as raising a problem in relation to God; the other two are more like ones we could recognize as raising a moral or relationship problem. Other parts of Leviticus make clear its recognition that deliberate failure to testify or to fulfill promises raise moral and relationship questions. In connection with the **purification offering**, the Torah's concern is different. Even moral issues raise religious questions. The four offenses it mentions here, and all the other offenses of which they are just examples, raise problems because these actions are for varying reasons incompatible with who God is. They make it impossible for people affected by them to come into God's presence at the sanctuary; or if people do, they bring their offenses with them and leave a trace of them there. So the people and the sanctuary need to be cleansed from their effect. The purification offering is God's provision for ensuring that.

Leviticus 5 goes on to talk more systematically about reparation as well as purification, as it moves to discussing the "reparation offering." Traditionally it is the "guilt offering"; it is concerned with how you make restitution when you are guilty of some wrongdoing or "trespass." The idea of trespass is that a person has rights of various kinds (to their honor or their land or their personal space or the contents of their refrigerator) and we have infringed these. We have treated their rights as something we could play fast and loose with. In relation to God, Israel could commit trespass by praying to other gods (and thus failing to recognize **Yahweh**), but the Torah's concern here is with the way people treated sacred things such as offerings. As usual, the regulations offer no way of putting that right by sacrifice. There is no way you can get out of the consequences of deliberate wrongdoing by a sacrifice. All you can do is cast yourself on God's mercy. But Leviticus does offer you sacrifices for when you commit a trespass accidentally. You might, for instance, fail to bring the regular tithes or offerings. When you realize you have done that, you must then bring them, but you also give something extra to make up for the failure. The requirement of a reparation offering would be an incentive to filling in your tax form correctly the first time.

Reparation offerings also apply to wrongs against another human being. Here, when you come to own the wrong you did and repent of it, again you must put things right with the other person. If you stole something, or defrauded someone of something, or kept something on the basis of finders keepers, you must restore it. In addition, you must add an extra fifth to its value. The regulation provides a vivid example of the Torah's way of viewing what we would call crime. The offense is not against the state, so the individual does not pay a fine or go to prison. The offense is against another member of the community, so the person must restore what was defrauded and add something to it.

The reason for dealing with this matter in these chapters is that in addition to making restitution to the other person, you have to make a reparation offering. Deceiving the other person involved "a trespass against Yahweh." There is a general sense in which that is true. When you steal something, you are ignoring what God said. But here (and often) there is a particular sense in which it is true. The verses refer to the person's having sworn falsely in connection with the deceit or theft. He or she has taken an oath in God's name in denying the wrongdoing and has thereby trespassed against God's honor as well as deceived the other person. The wrongerdoer must have to put things right with God as well as with the victim. It is not exactly that sacrifice puts the matter right between the wrongdoer and God; the wrongdoer must come to God in repentance and contrition. But the offering constitutes the objective reparation.

LEVITICUS 6:8–7:38

Being Grateful, Keeping a Promise, Being Generous

[8]Yahweh spoke to Moses: [9]"Command Aaron and his sons as follows: 'This is the instruction about the burnt offering. The burnt offering is on the hearth, on the altar, all night until the morning; the altar fire is to be kept burning on it. [10]The priest is to put on his linen garment and the linen undergarments next

to his body and take up the ash that the fire consumes (the burnt offering on the altar) and put it by the altar. [11]He is to take off his clothes, put on other clothes, and take the ash outside the camp to a clean place. [12]The fire upon the altar is to be kept burning on it [the hearth]; it is not to go out. The priest is to feed wood to it morning by morning, arrange the burnt offering on it, and turn the fat parts of the fellowship sacrifices into smoke upon it. [13]A continual fire is to be kept burning on the altar; it is not to go out.'"

[Leviticus 6:14–7:10 gives similar instructions about how the priests handle the grain offering, purification offering, and reparation offering.]

[7:11]"'This is the instruction about the fellowship sacrifice that one presents to Yahweh. [12]If he presents it as a thanksgiving, he is to present in addition to the thanksgiving sacrifice flat loaves mixed with oil, flat wafers spread with oil, and fine flour blended [so as to make] loaves mixed with oil, [13]in addition to the loaves of leavened bread. He is to present his offering, in addition to his thanksgiving fellowship sacrifice. [14]From it he is to present one from each kind of offering as a contribution to Yahweh, to the priest who casts the blood of the fellowship sacrifice: it will be his. [15]The meat of the thanksgiving fellowship sacrifice is to be eaten on the day of its offering. He is not to leave any of it till morning. [16]If the sacrifice he offers is a vow or voluntary offering, it is to be eaten on the day he presents his sacrifice, though what is left of it may be eaten on the next day, [17]but what is left of the meat of the sacrifice is to be burnt in the fire on the third day. [18]If any of the meat of the sacrifice is eaten at all on the third day, the one who presents it will not find acceptance. It will not be counted for him. It will be offensive. The person who eats of it will carry his waywardness.'"

[Verses 11–38 give further instructions about technical aspects of dealing with sacrifices: about not eating fat or blood; about the particular role of the offerer of a fellowship sacrifice; and about the parts of sacrifices that go to the priests.]

When my wife died, I was touched by the way people wanted to give something in thanksgiving for her life. One obvious object for that was the MS Society, because MS was the illness by means of which she had served God and glorified God over many years. Someone else wanted to give something to our church in Pasadena because he knew how much it had cared for Ann over the twelve years we have belonged to it; and I have mentioned that we had plans (among other things) to improve handicapped access in the church, which I had hoped would help Ann (and me!). One message that gave me particular delight was a card saying that as their thanksgiving some friends had donated five ducks to a two-thirds-world family by sending money to an organization that arranges that kind of thing.

Leviticus 7 explains that thanksgiving is at the heart of what a fellowship sacrifice is about. There are three motivations for bringing a fellowship sacrifice. One is straightforward thanksgiving because God has done something for you. A woman might bring such a sacrifice when she has safely given birth to a child. (Here as usual I leave the translation of Leviticus in its gendered form, and one can imagine that the male head of the family might commonly take the lead in bringing a family's sacrifice, but stories such as those of Hannah, in 1 Samuel 1, and Mary make clear that "he" does not exclude "she.")

The second reason for bringing such a sacrifice would also relate to thanksgiving but would involve a difference. When Hannah longs for a baby and prays for this gift, she promises she will actually give him back to God to minister in the sanctuary. We might think that sounds suspiciously like an attempt to bribe God, but apparently it is okay with God, because God answers her prayer. Eventually she comes back with the baby and with a sacrifice. More commonly, people would simply promise that if God answered their prayers, they would indeed bring a sacrifice. Their fellowship sacrifice would then be a fulfillment of that promise.

The third reason for bringing a fellowship sacrifice is—well, you just feel like it. It is what translations traditionally refer to as a freewill offering. In many churches, you pledge your offerings for the year, and each week you fulfill your pledge, but sometimes you also make a freewill or voluntary offering over and above your pledge. We thus follow Israel's way of doing things. There is a regular round of offerings that the community is thus committed to, but there are other offerings you make simply as a gesture of worship and love.

The remaining parts of Leviticus 6–7 concern what happens to sacrifices when the sacrifice is over. The remains of the burnt offering must be disposed of reverently. There are rules for how the priests may partake of other offerings, because these belong to God and some reverence is appropriate, and rules for who else apart from the priests (such as their family or laypeople) may partake of the different sacrifices. There is a reminder that people must not consume the fat of animals or their blood. There is a reminder that the **altar** fire is never to be allowed to go out. There might be the practical reason for this—it might be difficult to get it going again (for instance, if it is raining), but Leviticus 9 will tell us how the altar fire is set going by God, so this rule may be designed to ensure that the altar fire stands in continuity with that. All this contributes to taking God very seriously and also to taking worship in its various facets very seriously.

We have come to the end of the rules about sacrifice in Leviticus 1–7. One striking feature is that they have little to do with sin. In Christian thinking the main point about sacrifice is to deal with sin. Actually, even when the rules are concerned with sin, they focus on accidental offenses and on the way these bring **taboo** on the sanctuary. In Leviticus, sacrifice is a multifaceted way of making worship not just something that involves words and feelings but something that is concretely expressed. Christian worship usually costs us nothing. David determined he would not offer God burnt offerings that cost him nothing (2 Samuel 24:24). Leviticus's assumptions about worship, praise, prayer, and fellowship fit with that attitude.

LEVITICUS 8:1–10:20

Ordination and Disaster

[Leviticus 8:1–9:21 relates how Moses ordained Aaron and his sons in keeping with the instructions in Exodus 29 and how Aaron and his sons began their priestly ministry by offering their first purification offerings, burnt offerings, grain offering, and fellowship sacrifice.]

⁹:²²Then Aaron lifted up his hands towards the people and blessed them, and came down after offering the purification offering, the burnt offering, and the fellowship sacrifice. ²³Moses and Aaron went into the meeting tent, and came out and blessed the people. Yahweh's splendor appeared to all the people, ²⁴and fire came out from Yahweh's presence and consumed the burnt offering and the fat parts on the altar. The people saw, and resounded and fell on their faces.

¹⁰:¹But Aaron's sons, Nadab and Abihu, each took his censer, put fire in it, placed incense on it, and presented before Yahweh alien fire, which he had not commanded them, ²and fire came out from Yahweh's presence and consumed them. They died before Yahweh. ³Moses said to Aaron, "This is what Yahweh spoke of: 'In the people who come near to me I will manifest holiness, and before the face of all the people I will manifest splendor.'" Aaron was silent, ⁴but Moses summoned Mishael and Elzaphan, sons of Aaron's uncle, Uzziel, and said to them, "Come near, carry your relatives from before the sanctuary outside the camp." ⁵They came forward and carried them in their tunics outside the camp, as Moses said. ⁶Moses said to Aaron and his sons Eleazar and Ithamar, "Do not bare your heads, do not tear your clothes, so you do not die and wrath come on the whole community. Your relatives, the whole household of Israel, can weep for the burning Yahweh has brought about. ⁷Do not go out of the doorway of the meeting tent in case you die, because Yahweh's anointing oil is on you." They did as Moses said.

⁸Yahweh spoke to Aaron, ⁹"Do not drink wine or liquor, you or your sons, when you go into the meeting tent, so you will not die. It is a rule in perpetuity, through your generations, ¹⁰so that you can distinguish between the sacred and the ordinary and between the taboo and the clean, ¹¹and teach the Israelites all the rules Yahweh has spoken to them by means of Moses."

[Verses 12–20 give further instructions on what the priests are to do with different parts of the sacrifices afterwards.]

There's a joke that describes the pastor as six days invisible and one day incomprehensible. My first sermon after I was ordained had five points all beginning with the letter *p*. They were long or tricky words too—the only one I can remember is *paradox*. The

143

five points got three or four minutes each (twenty minutes may be short for a Baptist, but it's quite long in the Church of England), and they left the congregation exhausted if not bemused. From Monday to Saturday I was expected generally to spend the mornings studying and preparing (those were the days!), so I was invisible then. In the afternoons I would generally visit people in their homes or in places such as a hospital, so I was visible to one or two people. In the evenings I would be at youth meetings or Bible studies or committee meetings, so I would be visible to larger groups of people. (I did have Tuesday off.)

It is easy to assume that an Israelite priest's main responsibility was the parallel public one of offering sacrifices. That was indeed when he was visible to the whole congregation, but there were lots of priests, and they took turns offering sacrifices, so any individual priest did not do so very often. (Luke 1 describes how Zechariah had this responsibility on one occasion because it was his section's month on duty and because the responsibility then fell to him by lot.) The closing verses translated above give us some insight about the priests' broader responsibilities.

Their work involves being able to distinguish between the sacred and the ordinary, and between the **taboo** and the clean or pure, and also being able to teach people about that. Their teaching contributes to ensuring that things happen in the sanctuary with proper reverence for who Yahweh is. Christians may have a similar concern, though we probably fulfill it on a different basis. We may think that people should be quiet in church or wear certain kinds of clothes there, and that we should be reverent about what we do with the bread and wine that are left after a Communion service. Israel had equivalent ways of marking the special significance of the sanctuary and the sacrifices; the sanctuary was not just an ordinary place, and the sacrifices were not everyday food. Likewise it was important to distinguish the taboo and the clean or pure. Priests needed to be able to evaluate the animals people brought as sacrifices and to decide whether a disease that someone had meant that he or she should not come into the sanctuary. Leviticus 10 concerned dealing with dead bodies, an important issue in connection with purity and taboo.

Leviticus will go on to show how holiness and cleanness extend to many aspects of everyday life; moral and other behavioral matters are part of Israel's distinctiveness over against other people and part of its purity. All this gives the priests an important teaching role. So (Moses says), watch your drinking habits. The fellowship sacrifices and the libations would give priests the chance for overindulgence, and that would make them incapable of properly fulfilling their vocation.

All this supplies background to the horrific story that opens Leviticus 10. It begins by suggesting a contrast with the previous chapters, which emphasized that the priests were ordained "as Yahweh had commanded Moses"; at point after point, it reexpresses Exodus 29, underscoring that point.

We don't know what then made the fire "alien," but it was somehow different from what God had commanded, and that is the point in relation to the exhortation about distinguishing between the sacred and the ordinary and between the taboo and the clean. The offensive fire was unholy or impure. Terrible consequences followed from offering it. Priests of later centuries needed to learn the lesson of the story.

It also has a broader implication. Every time God does something new (creation, calling Abraham, the exodus, meeting Israel at Sinai, sending the Holy Spirit on the disciples), that is soon followed by people making it go wrong. There is wonder at what God has done but also an awareness that we still look to the future for the fulfillment of God's purpose.

When the Israelites looked back on events such as the garden-of-Eden story, or the gold calf and its aftermath, or Nadab and Abihu, I don't know whether they asked themselves whether it really happened; one could ask the same question about our reading in Acts of Ananias and Sapphira, who were struck dead for falsifying their pledges. If the Israelites did assume it actually happened, perhaps they also knew that things like that didn't happen much in their own day. Maybe God acted in different ways at those crucial early points in the story of Israel and the church. Because things like that don't happen much in the experience of modern Western people, we may be inclined to think that the story is more like parable than history. Maybe we are right; maybe we are wrong. Whichever it is, the story functions to underline the importance of the ministers fulfilling their ministry in a way that follows the directions God has given.

LEVITICUS 11:1–12:8

You Are What You Eat

[1]Yahweh spoke to Moses and Aaron, saying to them, [2]"Speak to the Israelites as follows: 'These are the creatures you may eat among the animals on the land: [3]among the animals, any that has a divided hoof (that has a cleft in its hoofs) and that brings up its cud—you may eat them. [4]These, however, you may not eat, of those that bring up their cud and of those that have divided hoofs: the camel, because it brings up its cud but does not have a divided hoof—it is taboo for you. [5]The rock badger, because it brings up its cud but does not have a divided hoof— it is taboo for you. [6]The hare, because it brings up its cud but does not have a divided hoof—it is taboo for you. [7]The pig, because it has a divided hoof (it has a cleft in its hoof) but does not chew its cud—it is taboo for you. [8]You are not to eat of their meat or touch their carcass—they are taboo for you.'"

[Verses 9–47 gives similar rules about other kinds of creatures. People can eat water creatures only if they have both fins and scales. They cannot eat birds such as the eagle, ostrich, seagull, pelican, and stork. They cannot eat creatures that have both wings and legs unless their legs are jointed; thus they can (for instance) eat locusts. They cannot eat other land animals such as mice, lizards, and crocodiles. It also includes rules about dealing with a situation in which such creatures come into contact with human beings or with things that human beings use.]

[12:1]Yahweh spoke to Moses: [2]"Speak to the Israelites as follows: 'When a woman brings forth offspring and gives birth to a male, she is to be taboo for seven days; she is to be taboo as in the days of her menstrual infirmity. [3]On the eighth day the flesh of his foreskin is to be circumcised. [4]For thirty-three days she is to stay in blood cleansing. She is not to touch anything sacred or go into the sanctuary until the completion of her days of cleansing. [5]If she gives birth to a female, she is to be taboo for two weeks as in her infirmity and to stay for sixty-six days in blood cleansing. [6]At the completion of her days of cleansing, for a son or a daughter she is to bring to the priest a year-old lamb as a burnt offering, and a pigeon or dove as a purification offering. [7]He is to present it before Yahweh and make expiation for her, and she will be clean from her flow of blood. This is the instruction about someone giving birth to a male or a female. [8](But if her means are not sufficient for a sheep, she is to take two doves or two pigeons, one for the burnt offering and one for the purification offering, and the priest will make expiation for her, and she will be clean.)'"

We had squirrels in our garden in England and on our patio in California, and in both places I have threatened to make squirrel casserole. Ann protested because she likes the squirrels; other people protest because they are repelled by the idea. In Britain rabbit features regularly in the supermarket butchery, but not in California. In France they eat frogs and snails, which makes Brits feel funny. The Scots eat haggis, which starts with sheep intestines, and that makes English people feel funny. My father took lard sandwiches to work; I wasn't too thrilled when one day at high school I found I had picked up his sandwiches by mistake. In the north of England a traditional breakfast delicacy is black pudding, made basically of pig's blood and suet (the Irish version adds pig's liver). I'm not enthusiastic about that either.

Food is an expression of identity. God takes that fact and makes it contribute to the forming and articulating of Israel's identity. Jews don't eat pork; it's one of the things that makes them stand out and keeps them separate. Thus "you are to consecrate yourselves and be holy, because I am holy" (Leviticus 11:44). The rules about what Israelites can eat are not merely its version of the kind of rules that every culture has. These are brought into a relationship with Israel's distinctive vocation to be God's people. God is holy, which means being different, being set apart. Israel is holy, which means being different, being set apart, as the Jewish people have always been. They were called to point toward God, and their distinctiveness was one way they would do that. They did not have to live separately from other peoples, but their distinctive customs meant they were always distinguishable from other peoples.

These rules about food brought this home to them. People would rarely think of eating rock badgers, mice, bats, or many of the other creatures mentioned (both ones they could eat and ones they could not). The lists are as much a teaching tool as instructions that revolutionized people's diet. They remind them that they need to stay distinctive. God's missional purpose worked via their being distinct in this way. (In Acts, God changed this and started drawing other peoples to faith by the opposite means, abolishing rules such as these in Leviticus 11 so that Jews who believed in Jesus could mix more easily with Gentiles.)

To make Israel stand out in this way, the rules could have been quite arbitrary, but Leviticus points to several forms of rationale for them. They have little if anything to do with hygiene; not all the outlawed creatures are threats to human health and not all creatures that might be threats to human health are outlawed. Further, if hygiene were an important basis of the rules, they would hardly be abolished in the New Testament. They may have something to do with economics; in Israel's mountain country, keeping pigs is not very practical. What Leviticus makes explicit is that creatures are allowed or disallowed according to whether they belong to proper categories, such as having divided hooves and digesting by ruminating (chewing the cud), or having both fins and scales. Creatures with one characteristic but not the other are anomalies. This observance brings home that humanity lives in a structured and ordered world, not one that is random and chaotic. It is a created world, a cosmos.

In connection with these rules and then the rules about childbirth, translations traditionally use the word "unclean," which gives a false impression about childbirth, menstruation, and womanhood. The word is a positive one denoting the possession of a quality, not a negative one indicating the absence of something (that is, the absence of cleanness). It suggests that there is something mysterious, extraordinary, perplexing, and a bit worrying here. I use the word *taboo*, which has some of those resonances. In Jewish thinking, handling the Scriptures makes you taboo. There is certainly something mysterious, extraordinary, perplexing, and worrying abut childbirth. In a traditional

148

society it is a very dangerous process. Many women die in childbirth; there are no painkillers to help take you through it; and many babies die at birth. The Church of England's service traditionally called "the churching of women" thus makes no reference to the popular idea that women were "unclean" after childbirth and instead gives as the service's main title and theme "The Thanksgiving of Women after Child-birth."

One of the perplexing aspects of giving birth is that it intertwines opposites, death and life. God is the God of life and not of death, yet birth brings the two into close connection. A woman may lose considerable blood in childbirth, and losing blood suggests death, yet this happens in the context of giving life. So after giving birth the mother stays home for a week and holds back from going to the sanctuary for another month. As happens when a man has had to bury someone, her association with death makes it inappropriate to go too close to the place where the living God dwells. The taboo period is twice as long for a baby girl because this baby herself will eventually be involved in the same experience in which life and death are intertwined.

LEVITICUS 13:1–14:57

Distinguishing Life from Death

[1]Yahweh spoke to Moses and Aaron: [2]"When there is a swelling or rash or spot on the skin of a person's body and it becomes an outbreak of scaliness on the skin of his body, he is to be brought to Aaron the priest or to one of his sons, the priests. [3]The priest is to look at the outbreak on the skin of the body. If the hair in the outbreak has turned white and the outbreak's appearance is deeper than the skin of his body, the outbreak is scaliness. When the priest sees it, he is to declare him taboo. [4]If it is a white spot on the skin of his body and its appearance is not deeper than the skin and the hair has not turned white, the priest is to confine the person who has the attack for seven days. [5]On the seventh day the priest is to look: there, if the outbreak has stood still as far as he can see, and the outbreak has not spread on the skin, the priest is to confine him for seven more days. [6]The priest is to look at him again on the seventh

day: there, if the outbreak has faded and the outbreak has not spread on the skin, the priest is to declare him clean. It is a rash. He is to wash his clothes and he will be clean. [7]If the rash actually spreads on the skin after his appearing to the priest to be declared clean, he is to appear to the priest again. [8]If the priest looks and there, the rash has spread on the skin, the priest is to declare him taboo. It is scaliness."

[Verses 9–59 deal in a similar way with other skin abnormalities such as discolorations, boils, burns, lesions, spots, and hair loss, and with analogous moldlike abnormalities in fabrics.]

[14:1]Yahweh spoke to Moses: "This is to be the instruction for the person with scaliness, on the day of his cleansing. He is to be brought to the priest; [2]the priest will go outside the camp. The priest will look, and there, if the outbreak of scaliness has healed from the person with the scaliness, [4]the priest is to command that they get for the person being cleansed two live clean birds, cedar wood, scarlet yarn, and hyssop. [5]The priest is to command that they slaughter one bird in a clay pot over fresh water. [6]The live bird he is to take, with the cedar wood, the scarlet yarn, and hyssop, and dip them with the live bird in the blood of the bird that was slaughtered over the fresh water. [7]He is to sprinkle it over the person being cleansed from the scaliness, seven times, and cleanse him. He is to send off the live bird over the open country."

[Verses 8–57 further describe the process whereby the person with the scaliness returns to ordinary life and freedom to come to the sanctuary, and makes rules for the treatment of houses with analogous moldlike abnormalities.]

The first funeral I did in the United States was for a friend in his thirties whose wedding I had conducted. We buried him within about a year, after he died of a brain tumor. I admire the way U.S. funerals commonly have the dead person present in the coffin with its lid open, which is rarer in Britain. At the end of this service everyone in the congregation filed past the coffin saying their last goodbyes. I stood watching the variety of expressions on people's faces and talked to some of them about this afterward. Death is a scary business. We are not sure we want to get too close to it. I buy my clothes from the thrift store, which means I am often wearing dead men's clothes, but I don't think about that too much.

A useful starting point for understanding Leviticus 13–14 is a story about Moses and Aaron's sister Miriam, in Numbers 12. Miriam gets afflicted by scaliness like the one these chapters are concerned with, and Aaron appeals to Moses, "She mustn't become like a dead person who comes out from his mother's womb and half his flesh is eaten away!" Moses cries out to God accordingly, and in due course she is restored. The **Torah** is concerned about this scaliness because it makes the flesh look as if it is being eaten up as happens after one dies or when a child is stillborn. The affliction is traditionally referred to as leprosy, which originally denoted a scaly skin affliction but then came to denote a disease that eats up a person's limbs. This translation gives a misleading impression in the Bible, where the word refers to a skin disease that gets special treatment because it resembles death and thus raises similar questions to those raised by childbirth. There, the process of giving birth is uncomfortably associated with the possibility of dying and with the signs of dying (loss of blood). Here a living person looks like a dead person. No two things could be more different than death and life. Yet in our experience, it can be hard to distinguish them. The debate about abortion involves questions about when a fetus becomes a living person; the debate about end-of-life issues involves questions about the boundary between life and death.

God therefore encourages Israel to have ways whereby people make clear to themselves that death and life really are different. Quarantining someone with a scaly affliction that makes him or her look like someone dead is an example. The parallel regulations about deathlike phenomena in fabrics and houses further underline the point and reflect how Leviticus is not thinking of scaliness as an illness.

Affirming the distinction between death and life is important for the reason noted in connection with Leviticus 11–12. Yahweh is the God of life, the living God. "He is not the God of the dead but of the living" (Mark 12:27). Jesus works with this rule: after healing some men quarantined because they are afflicted by scaliness, he sends them to the priests to be certified as clean, in accordance with Leviticus (Luke 17:11–19).

Yahweh is in control of the realm of the dead. The **Canaanites** believed there was a god of the dead, among many other
gods, and also that it was possible for gods to die. The Israelites
knew there is only one God, who is in control of death as of anything else. Yet they also knew that death is alien to God. To bring
home that point, Israelites could have nothing to do with the
realm of death. Other peoples had ways of making contact with
the spirits of dead family members by the means with which
we are familiar in "spiritualism"; Israelites were forbidden to do
so, though they often ignored this rule. Leviticus's rules quaran-
tine people whose experience was redolent of death so that their
taboo status did not come to affect other people. This brought
home the importance of having nothing to do with the realm
of death. In particular people needed to avoid incurring taboo
status if they wanted to be able to go to the sanctuary.

Leviticus envisages an affliction that would come on a person
only temporarily (Miriam was quarantined for a week), and thus
adds provision for restoring the person to the community when
the affliction goes away. The ceremony deals with the affliction
in two ways, offering a double reassurance to the person, the
person's family, and the community. A bird is slaughtered as in
a **purification offering**, to purify the person and give assurance
that he or she is okay. Another bird is sent off as a way of expel-
ling the affliction from the community and assuring everyone
that it is gone.

Two other aspects of attitudes to scaliness are significant.
In other cultures, it was often attributed to demons; Leviticus
implicitly assures people that this is not so. Further, it is sometimes seen as divine punishment for sin; Leviticus also implicitly assures people that this is not so. It is "just one of those
things." You have to deal with it but not be overwhelmed by it.

LEVITICUS 15:1-33

Sex and Taboos

¹Yahweh spoke to Moses and Aaron: ²"Speak to the Israelites
and say to them, 'When any man is discharging from his flesh,
in connection with his discharge he is taboo. ³This will be his

taboo because of his discharge (whether his flesh runs with his discharge or his flesh seizes up through the discharge, it is his taboo): [4]any bed that the man who is discharging lies on is to be taboo. Any object that he sits on is to be taboo; [5]a person who touches his bed is to wash his clothes, bathe in water, and be taboo until evening.'"

[Verses 6–15 prescribe in more detail the process for purifying the man and anything or anyone who has physical contact with him.]

[16]"'When a man has an emission of semen from himself, he is to bathe his whole body in water and be taboo until evening. [17]All cloth or leather that has the emission of semen on it is to be washed in water and be taboo until evening. [18]As for the woman that the man sleeps with involving emission of semen, they are to bathe in water and be taboo until evening. [19]When a woman is discharging, if her discharge in her flesh is blood, she is to be in her infirmity seven days. Anyone who touches her will be taboo until evening.'"

[Verses 20–27 prescribe the process for purifying the woman and anything or anyone who has physical contact with her. They also cover discharge of blood not associated with menstruation.]

[28]"'When she is clean from her discharge, she is to count for herself seven days, and afterwards she is to be clean. [29]On the eighth day she is to get herself two doves or two pigeons and bring them to the priest at the doorway of the meeting tent. [30]The priest is to make one a purification offering and one a burnt offering, and the priest is to make expiation for her before Yahweh, from her taboo discharge. [31]You are to keep the Israelites away from their taboo so they do not die through their taboo, through bringing taboo on my dwelling in their midst.'"

[Verses 32–33 summarize the contents of the chapter.]

"Sexual intercourse began / in nineteen sixty-three / (which was rather late for me)," the poet Philip Larkin wrote in his poem "Annus mirabilis." It was the decade when the pill made it possible to separate sex from procreation. My prospective in-laws were horrified when they discovered that their prospective son-in-law had been discussing contraceptives with their daughter. Then we learned a few months after we married that the separation was more complicated than we thought. When the *British Medical Journal* reported that the particular contraceptive pill Ann had been taking was less effective than some others, we had already proved this.

Like Genesis, Leviticus keeps sex and procreation in association. Judaism has never manifested the ambivalence about sex that the church has sometimes shown. The open way the **Torah** discusses it shows this lack of ambivalence, as does the Song of Songs. Yet the Torah is bothered about sex because it knows that sex and procreation are linked, but that the link is inefficient. Most times a man has sex with his wife, it does not result in procreation. His semen is wasted. Leviticus may also refer to nocturnal emissions; even more obviously his life-giving semen is then simply wasted. The same would be true of masturbation and coitus interruptus. So a man is **taboo** after any of these happenings, not because there is something wrong about the sexual act itself but because there is something unnatural about the wasting of life-giving semen. It's not a big deal; you just have to wash the bedclothes, bathe, and stay out of the sanctuary that day.

Parallel but more complicated questions are raised by menstruation (here and throughout Leviticus 15, "flesh" is a euphemism for the genitals). The questions are more complicated because menstruation involves blood, which adds to its worrying and mysterious nature. It is a paradoxical event because it is simultaneously a sign of life (menstruation signals that a woman could be the bearer of new life) and a sign of death (losing blood is a sign of death). Like the emission of semen, then, menstruation makes someone taboo, but the greater level of mystery and taboo about menstruation means the process of cleansing is more complex than that for emission of semen. The Torah does not imply a link between menstruation and sin, or any need to avoid being in the presence of menstruating women and thus to isolate them, or any link between menstruation and demons. All these attitudes have been taken in different cultures, reflecting male fear of menstruation, and there are hints in the Old Testament that Israelite men could share these instincts, but the Torah sets boundaries to them. Menstruating women are not isolated from their families, homes, or work. You just have to avoid direct physical contact if you want to go to the sanctuary that day.

Emission of semen and menstruation are what one might call regular, natural events, even though they convey taboo. The chapter also covers irregular discharges such as male gonorrhea. Again, it does not suggest that these imply sin or treat them as illnesses requiring treatment. As with those "regular" events, the concern is with the taboo they bring, the way they make it inappropriate to come into the sanctuary and the implications they could have for other people who come into contact with the taboo person.

In another sense all this is a big deal. Not only do you have to go through frequent times when you hold back from going to the sanctuary and/or avoid physical contact with people and/or go to make an offering (at a sanctuary miles away, when Israel is in **Canaan**; and you could spend the whole week washing bed-clothes and so on, and where do you get the water?). We have noted that many of the regulations in the Torah do not look as if they were designed for literal implementation. They were more like teaching tools. Of course many Jews give themselves to proper literal observance of these rules—though again, after the destruction of the temple and the cessation of sacrifice, the rules could not be observed as they stand. However far they were designed for literal implementation, they were *also* teaching tools.

In Western Christian culture, the key question about sex may seem the moral one about whether you are having sex with the right person, and menstruation is just something a woman has to manage. Actually sex and menstruation deserve some awe on the part of both men and women. For some women, their monthly period is a reminder that once again they have failed to conceive. They are very aware of the link between menstruation and procreation and their menstruation is a sign of life and a sign of death; it is life wasted. So is their husbands' emission of semen.

LEVITICUS 16:1–34

The Expiation Day

¹Yahweh spoke to Moses and Aaron after the death of Aaron's two sons when they drew near to Yahweh and died. ²Yahweh said to Moses, "Tell your brother Aaron that he is not to come at any time into the sanctuary, within the curtain, in front of the expiation cover on the chest, lest he die, because I appear in the cloud, over the cover. ³In this way Aaron is to come into the sanctuary, with a bull from the herd as a purification offering and a ram as a burnt offering. ⁴He is to put on a sacred linen tunic, with linen undergarments next to his body, wind on a linen sash, and wrap on a linen headdress. These being sacred garments, he is to wash his body in water and then put them on. ⁵From the Israelite community he is to get two goats from the flock as a purification offering and a ram as a burnt offering. ⁶Aaron is to present the bull that is his purification offering and make expiation for himself and for his household, ⁷and to get the two goats and set them before Yahweh at the doorway of the meeting tent. ⁸Aaron is to put lots on the two goats, one lot for Yahweh, one lot for Azazel. ⁹Aaron is to present the goat that the lot came on 'for Yahweh' and make it a purification offering."

[Verses 10–19 give more detail on the procedure.]

²⁰"When he has finished making expiation for the sanctuary, the meeting tent, and the altar, he is to present the live goat. ²¹Aaron is to put both his hands on the head of the live goat and confess over it all the wayward acts of the Israelites and all their rebellions in connection with all their offenses, put them on the head of the goat, and send it off in the charge of an appointed person into the wilderness."

[Verses 22–28 give further detail on the procedure.]

²⁹"This is to be a rule for you in perpetuity: in the seventh month on the tenth day of the month you are to discipline yourselves and not do any work, the citizen and the alien who resides in your midst. ³⁰Because on this day expiation is made for you to cleanse you from all your offenses; you will be clean before Yahweh. ³¹It will be a total stop for you. You are to discipline yourselves; it is a rule in perpetuity."

[Verses 32–34 are a summary conclusion.]

I climbed Mount Sinai in September 1973, near the beginning of the seventh month in the Jewish year as Leviticus computes it (counting from Passover), and thus just after the New Year on the modern Jewish calendar. It was five days before Yom Kippur, the Day of Atonement, the most solemn occasion in the year. Israel virtually closes down: there is no public transport; the movie theaters, stores, and businesses are closed; and television and radio are suspended. On the Day of Atonement that year, five days after I had been in Sinai, Egypt and Syria launched an attack to reclaim land occupied by Israel and won an initial advantage by their surprise move. Jews were scandalized at the attack on Israel's holiest day, but I guess all is fair in love and war, especially when you want to get your land back; and if religion becomes a "get-out-of-jail-free" card, it becomes prostituted.

The Day of Atonement or **Expiation** Day is indeed the holiest day of the year. Coming just after the celebration of the New Year and just before the Feast of Sukkot (Shelters), which again commemorates the exodus, it looks both backward and forward. It clears the slate, so it is possible to go into the New Year with confidence because things have been sorted out with God. In Leviticus, the focus of the occasion is cleansing the sanctuary. God's presence or absence there means life or death to the community. If God is there, they can go and meet with God, offer their worship, bring their prayers and their thanksgivings, and live in relationship. If God were to leave the sanctuary, the center of their lives would have gone.

They know, and God knows, that it is quite possible for junk between them and God to accumulate in such a way that God has to say, "I can't stay here any longer." The action of Aaron's sons reported in Leviticus 10 was one obvious major threat to God's willingness to stay; hence this chapter's starting point. Maybe this rite initially relates to that event, but if so, it becomes an annual observance. On this one occasion in the year the high priest goes into the inner sanctuary to make sure the presence of junk in the sanctuary does not affect it. The object of many of the rules either side of Leviticus 10 is to prevent this from happening in more gradual ways. The junk is material that stands in conflict with who **Yahweh** is—things

157

redolent of death and disorder. There is no way of ensuring that all these things are dealt with through the year. Who knows how many people have ignored rules or accidentally contravened them without anyone knowing? So God sets up this annual observance that constitutes a thorough cleaning out of the sanctuary to ensure it is possible to stay.

The distinctiveness of the observance lies in what happens to the two goats, though it is an enhanced version of the actions with the two birds in chapter 14. At one level the actions with the two goats provide two ways of dealing with the same problem; one of their functions would be to reassure people that God really has dealt with it (twice!). Offering one goat to God would be the regular and familiar way of providing cleansing for the sanctuary, but when God needs to deal with something as big as this, the action with the second goat makes doubly sure. In case it seems that offering the goat to deal with the offenses that would bring **taboo** on the sanctuary was not enough or did not seem enough, the second goat carries them off into the wilderness, into a place where they can do no harm. Or perhaps the two actions deal with two aspects of the problem. Sacrificing the one goat deals with the need to cleanse the sanctuary; the action with the second goat deals with Israel's rebelliousness and its effects on its broader relationship with God.

Only in this chapter does Leviticus talk about Israel's "rebellions"; it is a strong term to describe its wrongdoing. It suggests much more than accidental trespass into the sanctuary area when you should keep out because of a taboo. So the observance involving the second goat signifies Israel's repentance, its forsaking of its waywardness and its desire to be rid of it, and it signifies God's providing for its removal so it does not get in the way between God and Israel. If you put an object such as a bag of wheat on an animal, it carries the burden off. When the high priest puts his hands on the goat's head, he is identifying the goat as belonging to the people whom he represents and as in some sense representing them. (Putting both hands on something is unusual, but it also happens when— for instance—Moses commissions Joshua as his successor, so maybe it signifies that this is a very important act.) God lets that be the way the people's rebellions are invisibly transferred

158

to the goat for it to carry. The normal principle is that if you do wrong you "carry your waywardness." You bear responsibility for it, and you are liable to have to pay for it. But now the goat will "carry all their acts of waywardness" and take them off into the wilderness (verse 22).

In later Jewish literature Azazel is a demon, but we have noted that if anything, Leviticus wants to avoid Israel's being demon preoccupied like other peoples, as if there were powers of evil that rivaled Yahweh in their power. If Azazel is a demon, he has been demythologized, as happens when we ourselves speak of "gremlins" or "evil forces," whether or not we believe in demons. In later Jewish writings Azazel refers to the place where the goat was sent, or it can be a term to designate the animal as the "scapegoat." Whatever it means in itself, it signifies an assurance that Israel's wayward acts are taken off to a place where they can do no harm. It parallels the picture in Micah 7:19 of offenses being thrown into the deepest sea. This is effective not only for Israelites but also for any aliens who choose to identify with Israel.

LEVITICUS 17:1–18:30

The Life Is in the Blood

[1]Yahweh spoke to Moses: [2]"Speak to Aaron and his sons and to all the Israelites. Say to them, 'This is the word Yahweh commanded. [3]"Any man of the household of Israel who slaughters an ox or sheep or goat in the camp or slaughters it outside the camp [4]and does not bring it to the doorway of the meeting tent to present as an offering to Yahweh before Yahweh's dwelling, blood will be counted to that man. He has shed blood. That man is to be cut off from among his people. [5]It is so that the Israelites may bring their sacrifices that they are making in the open country and bring them to Yahweh at the doorway of the meeting tent, to the priest, and offer them to Yahweh as fellowship sacrifices, [6]and the priest may cast the blood over Yahweh's altar at the meeting tent doorway and turn the fat into smoke as a nice smell for Yahweh, [7]and they may no more offer their sacrifices to goat-demons after whom they are straying. This is to be a rule in perpetuity, through their generations.'"

⁸You are to say to them, 'Any man of the household of Israel or of the aliens who reside in your midst who offers up a burnt offering or sacrifice ⁹and does not bring it to the doorway of the meeting tent to offer it to Yahweh, that man is to be cut off from his kin. ¹⁰Any man of the household of Israel or of the aliens who reside in your midst who eats any blood: I will set my face against the life of the person who eats the blood and cut him off from among his people, ¹¹because the life of the flesh is in the blood, and I myself have given it to you on the altar to make expiation for your lives, because it is the blood that makes expiation by means of the life.'"

[Verses 12–16 give further detail and equivalent rules for game and animals that die naturally or through another animal's attack.]

¹⁸ˑ¹Yahweh spoke to Moses: ²"Speak to the Israelites; say to them, 'I am Yahweh your God. ³You are not to act in accordance with the practices of Egypt where you lived, and you are not to act in accordance with the practices of Canaan where I am bringing you. You are not to live by their rules. ⁴You are to implement my decisions and guard my rules by living by them. I am Yahweh your God. ⁵You are to guard my rules and my decisions, by which the person who implements them may live. I am Yahweh. ⁶No man may approach any of his own flesh to reveal nakedness. I am Yahweh.'"

[Verses 7–30 are more specific about the people this applies to, add further rules, and then again emphasize that Israelites are not to live like Canaanites.]

A month ago a woman came to see me to talk about the general difficulties of her life. Her mother had died some time previously. She was barely on speaking terms with her father. She certainly was not on speaking terms with her married adoptive brother. She longed to be married but seemed to set her sights on people with whom it was never going to happen, such as the celibate priest of her Roman Catholic church. Eventually the basis for her anger with her brother emerged, and along with it (I suspected) something that underlay her other difficulties in relationships and her ambivalent attitudes to them. Her adoptive brother had had sex with her several times when he was eighteen and she was sixteen. She adored him, and he had not forced her, but her father had discovered and had thrown the boy out. It was neither a biologically incestuous relationship nor an illegal one (she was above the age of consent in their state), but it was a toxic one.

Overlapping dynamics underlie the concern about sexual relationships in Leviticus 18. "Revealing someone's nakedness" is a term for having sex with them, and the chapter bans a wide range of sexual relationships with one's own flesh—that is, within the household, such as the relationship I have just described. Its concern is not that the relationships are biologically incestuous, and as well as extramarital sex its ban would cover marriage (for instance, after a woman's original husband had died). Such relationships threaten disruption within the household and raise questions about power such as are illustrated in the story of Absalom and his father's secondary wives, with whom he has sex as a sign of claiming to take over David's position. Both this chapter and that story illustrate how we have to think of the family in the Old Testament in a different way from the one that is customary in the West. The household, people who live close together (not in the same house, but in adjacent houses) is more like what we would call the extended family.

God associates the forbidden practices with **Egypt** and **Canaan**. As far as we know, these two peoples were not distinctively perverted. They are mentioned because they are the countries on either side of Israel, the one Israel left and the one they are on their way toward. The people of God need to stay aware that sexual relationships in the culture in which they live are likely to be perverted and that they need to shape their own lives on the basis of concern for the family and in awareness of those questions about power. Otherwise Israel will end up in the same predicament as these other peoples. The inclusion of a ban on homosexual acts (18:22) likely marks this as another way Israel was expected to be different. The cultures around them accepted same-sex relationships, which dissociate sex from marriage and procreation. The **Torah** sets sex in the context of marriage and procreation.

Leviticus 17 focuses on a concern with blood, which is closely linked with life. If you bleed and don't stop, you die. The life of the flesh is in the blood, so there is something sacred about blood, because life comes from God. Therefore Israel has to be careful what it does with blood. Shedding blood and thus killing an animal is a questionable procedure; it involves behaving as if life were under our control. As The Smiths' album title put it, *Meat Is Murder*, or almost. At the beginning, God gave humanity no authority to kill animals (and thus eat them), but humanity took that authority. God rolled with it as God often does with human acts but sought to safeguard their consequences. So God here requires the killing to happen at the sanctuary, so it actually becomes a fellowship sacrifice, an occasion of sharing between the family and God. Recognizing that blood is key to life and death and is thus a sign of the life that comes from God and belongs to God, the offerers give God the blood as well as the fat. Leviticus adds the further consideration that on a broader front blood is key to **expiation** by means of sacrifices, because shedding blood denotes causing the animal to give up life and die. There is a broader reason to be reverent about blood.

Once again the rules apply to non-Israelites who become part of the community; Israel is always open to other peoples coming to join if they commit themselves to living by the same obligations as Israel. Conversely, if they then ignore these rules, they risk being "cut off from the community." Either God may cast such people off or the community may throw them out. You don't have to be an Israelite to belong to God's people, and being an Israelite doesn't guarantee your position within God's people.

Another consideration surfaces in the reference to sacrificing to goat-demons. If people must bring their sacrifices to the sanctuary, the priests can keep an eye on what is going on. Yet there is no way that Israelites spread all over the country will be able to come to the sanctuary every time they want to slaughter an animal, and other strands of the Torah make provision for what might be called secular slaughter, killing an animal at home. Notwithstanding the comment about this being a rule in perpetuity, that is one example of the way God often gives different instructions about the same issue within the Torah, because different social contexts require different compromises.

LEVITICUS 19:1–18

Be Holy as I Am Holy

[1]Yahweh spoke to Moses: [2]"Speak to the entire Israelite community and say to them, 'You are to be holy because I, Yahweh your God, am holy. [3]Everyone is to revere their mother and father and guard my Sabbaths. I am Yahweh your God. [4]Do not turn to idols and do not make figurines of gods for yourselves. I am Yahweh your God. [5]When you offer a fellowship sacrifice to Yahweh, sacrifice it so you may find acceptance. [6]It is to be eaten on the day you sacrifice it, or the next day, but what is left until the third day is to be burnt up in fire. [7]If it is actually eaten on the third day, it will be offensive. It will not find acceptance. [8]The one who eats it will carry his waywardness, because he has treated as ordinary something sacred that belongs to Yahweh. That person will be cut off from his kin.

[9]"When you reap the harvest of your land, you will not finish off harvesting the edge of your field or gather the gleanings of your harvest [10]or scour your vineyard or glean the windfall of your vineyard. You are to leave them for the weak and the alien. I am Yahweh your God. [11]You will not steal. You will not deceive or cheat one another. [12]You will not swear deceitfully by my name and treat the name of your God as ordinary. I am Yahweh. [13]You will not defraud your neighbor or commit robbery. The wages of an employee will not stay with you until morning. [14]You will not belittle the deaf or put an obstacle in front of the blind but revere your God. I am Yahweh. [15]You will not do wrong in giving judgment: you will not be partial to the poor or deferential to the great; you will give judgment for your kin with faithfulness; [16]you will not live as a slanderer among your kin; you will not take the stand against your neighbor's life. I am Yahweh. [17]You will not repudiate your relative in your thinking; you will firmly rebuke your kin; you will not carry liability because of him. [18]You will not take redress or hold onto things in relation to members of your people, but care for your neighbor as for yourself. I am Yahweh.'"

163

Today's newspaper reports on the release from a detention center in Iraq of a twenty-seven-year-old man, after eighteen months there. He was given a letter to say that his case had been concluded and the occupation authorities had decided he needed to be released. He is among 90,000 detainees who have been freed. One of them comments on the way he, an apparently innocent guy, was thrown into prison and lost his job, how his family went hungry, and how they (people in general, I think) have refused him a job when he got out. His friends are afraid to associate with him in case he really is guilty, or the powers-that-be think he is, or he has become a Western agent, or he has now signed on to work for a militia, and lest in connection with any of these possibilities they are then assumed to be his associates. In seeking to bring order in Iraq, we had to take steps to confine people who might be contributing to disorder, but what sort of priorities should we have in seeking to care for people who are innocent until proved guilty?

Leviticus 19–22 comprises a wide variety of imperatives, though the "you will not" form makes them look as much like a description or definition of what it means to be an Israelite as is the case with the Ten "Commandments." Yet they are indeed strong imperatives, as when a parent says to a child, "You will not do that!!" They often seem to be in a quite random sequence, though there may be some logic about how they came to be in this sequence, and a vision for the community emerges from them. One aspect is a concern for justice. Most Israelites through Old Testament times lived in villages that might typically comprise about a hundred people belonging to about three kin groups or (very) extended families. The "weak," the "alien," and the "employee" are then people who have somehow ended up in the village although they came from elsewhere, so they are not members of one of the families. Most people in the village were not employees of anyone; they worked on the family farm. Outsiders may be employed by a family; if not, they are dependent on its generosity if they are to survive. One way or the other, the extended family is the safety net for the society.

Justice is in the hands of the community's senior members, who meet in the village square to sort out conflicts and problems. The **Torah** is aware of the temptation for the community court to ignore the rights and needs of the powerless and the alien and to work in favor of people with resources and power, people like the members of the court themselves. Here it warns against taking that kind of exhortation too far and ruling in favor of the poor when right is not on their side. There is to be favoritism neither to poor people nor to important people.

Responsibility for sorting out conflicts rests with the whole community, not just with the senior members. It starts with the individual: with avoiding acts that will cause conflict, like stealing a sheep belonging to another family; cheating when you are bartering produce with another family, or swearing you have not done so when you have; taking advantage of the handicapped; or lying to the meeting of the elders in some case they are trying to resolve in order to profit from the result yourself (in a way that may imperil the life of someone else). If all that is to happen, it requires your inner attitude to be right. You must not repudiate someone in your thinking; then you will not repudiate that person in your actions.

If you are the victim and not the perpetrator when something wrong happens, or if you discover that someone has committed a wrong, your job is to talk straight and confront the person rather than come to share in the guilt because you have been complicit. If you are the victim, your obligation is not to hold onto your grievance and look for a chance to take matters into your own hands; that is what the gathering of the elders is for. You are to care for your neighbor even when your neighbor does wrong.

Translations traditionally refer to "hating" and "loving" in verses 17 and 18, but the Torah is referring to something that involves action as well as feeling; hence I translate "repudiate" and "care for." The Torah gives no scope for "hating your enemy"; it is your enemy you are bidden to love or care for. Jesus' exhortation to love your enemy brings out the Torah's own implication. The Torah also makes clear (as Jesus does) that loving or caring may require confrontation.

Leviticus offers two considerations to motivate you in your relationships, especially when there is conflict. One lies in the way it describes other people in the community. They are your neighbors, fellow members of the community; the community

165

will collapse if people are not on speaking terms with one another. They are also your kin, members of the same clan and the same people, your brothers and sisters. Usually instinct tells us to be committed to members of the family and more tolerant of them, and the Torah invites us to make that our model for relationships in the local community.

The other consideration lies in God. The section begins with the expectation that you will be holy because God is holy. In itself, God's holiness lies in God's deity, God's distinctiveness, God's extraordinariness, and Israel is to be distinctive over against other people in some ways that may seem random. **Yahweh**'s distinctiveness also lies in qualities such as integrity and love, and Israel is expected to mirror those. Reminders such as "I am Yahweh" also recur in this section of Leviticus. The logic is the same as that in the Ten Commandments: "I am God, and I am your God, and I claim the right to tell you what to do, so just do it even if you don't like it." That will be the way you go about "revering" your God. Again, translations often refer to "fearing" God, but that gives the wrong impression. Revering God expresses itself in being considerate to weak people.

LEVITICUS 19:19–20:27

Improving on Creation

[19]"'You are to keep my rules. You will not mate two kinds of cattle; you will not sew your field with two kinds [of seed]; you will not put on cloth woven of two kinds [of yarn]. [20]When a man sleeps and has sex with a woman and she is a servant designated to someone and she has not actually been redeemed or given her freedom, there is to be an inquiry. They will not be put to death because she had not been freed, [21]but he is to bring his reparation offering to Yahweh to the doorway of the meeting tent, a ram as a reparation offering, [22]and the priest is to make expiation for him with the reparation offering ram before Yahweh for the offense he committed, so there will be pardon for him for the offense he committed. [23]When you come into the country and you plant any kind of edible tree, you are to treat its fruit as uncircumcised. For three years it is to be uncir-

cumcised for you, not to be eaten, [24]in the fourth year all its fruit will be holy as an expression of great praise to Yahweh, [25]and in the fifth year you may eat its fruit—so as to increase its harvest for you. I am Yahweh your God. [26]You will not eat anything with the blood. You will not practice divination or augury. [27]You will not trim the side of your head or clip the side of your beard. [28]You will not make a gash on your flesh for someone or the mark of a cut on yourselves. I am Yahweh. [29]Do not degrade your daughter by making her act immorally, so that the country may not become immoral and full of wickedness. [30]You will keep my Sabbaths and revere my sanctuary. I am Yahweh."

[Leviticus 20 expounds further rules on the same issues as arise in chapter 19.]

When a man and his wife are about to go out and the wife asks whether she looks okay, the appropriate answer is "You look lovely" (not "Maybe that dress and those shoes don't go together"). If she then says, "Is that what you really think?" the answer is "My dear, you really look lovely." It is unlikely that suggestions for improvement will be welcome. Something equivalent in relation to God may be implied by the opening ban in these verses. For ten dollars, the Shaatnez Inspection Service of Seattle will inspect your suit to make sure it does not have both linen and wool in it, and for another ten dollars it will remove the *shaatnez*; this is the word translated "woven" in verse 19. No one really knows what the word means, but its implications are clear. The Shaatnez Service notes that the **Torah** does not explain the reason for this ban and comments that Jews will obey it anyway (if God says so, that is reason enough), but it speculates that the problem with the banned mixtures is that they imply we think we can improve on creation. This seems an insult to God, who at the end of creation looked over it and thought it was quite beautiful.

Further, God made everything work according to its "kind"; by its species, we might almost say. That word recurs in Genesis 1 and in Leviticus 11. When you plant an apple tree, you don't have to wonder whether next year it might grow carrots. There is a consistency and order about the world God created. Work with that fact, Leviticus says. It at least makes us ask questions about times when we improve on creation. Remember that I made you to be different from other peoples, Leviticus also says. Be wary about the way you get mixed up with other peoples. Don't lose your identity.

The rule about fruit trees is related. The fruit of a tree's first three years of life is to be treated as if it were an uncircumcised foreskin; you wouldn't regard it as proper, and you would in fact cut it off. In year four the tree starts becoming mature, so you could eat it, but it is now like the first fruits of a harvest, and you therefore give it to God as a praise offering. You start eating it yourself in year five. Then you will have a fruitful tree. The rule combines sensible husbandry and tangible recognition of God as key to success in growing things.

Other themes run through these miscellaneous collections of rules. They relate to themes that came earlier in Leviticus. In other words, Leviticus 1–16 was sometimes dealing systematically with issues that are dealt with more occasionally in Leviticus 19–20 as it collects material illustrating what holiness look like.

The rule about a particular sexual offense is related to our laws about sex with a minor. The kinds of circumstances that the rule is designed to apply to are those also presupposed by Exodus 21. Suppose a family gets into economic difficulties and can no longer support itself, and a father seeks to safeguard his children by letting them become servants to another family. With a girl, the assumption will be that she will eventually marry the head of her new family or one of his sons, unless the family gets back on its feet and her father is able to redeem her and free her from her bond service. Suppose meanwhile another man has sex with her. That could start quite a fight between her father, her master, and the seducer, perhaps even a lynching. Further, is she to be treated as complicit? The rule forestalls the fighting and protects the girl by regarding her as a minor. It presupposes that the man's action is not merely a wrong against the girl, her father, her master, and the village community as a whole, but a wrong against God, so he has to make reparation to God. Chapter 20 then makes clear that adultery is much more serious than this kind of extramarital sex, as are various other illicit unions. Saying they warrant execution is a way of indicating how wrong they are.

The other rule about a girl presupposes that the family's situation deteriorates rather than improves. Now in general, women engage in the sex trade because they are economically desperate. Suppose a father is desperate but could feed his family if he let his daughter engage in the sex trade. No, says the Torah, letting her enter service with a commitment to marry her master or his son is one thing, but this other crosses a line. Again, it is not merely a matter of her rights but of the whole people's relationship with God. Impurity on the people's part brings **taboo** on the sanctuary. Sexual immorality on the people's part makes the very country reek of immorality. Elsewhere Leviticus points out that this was the kind of thing that got the **Canaanites** thrown out of the country.

Presumably the situations these rules cover did not occur frequently, though other sorts of questions about sex did arise and cause scandal. Their presence in the Torah presupposes a case-law approach to sorting out issues in the village. They give the whole community, and the elders in particular, examples of how God requires particular situations to be dealt with, to guide people's thinking and help them deal with different but related situations.

Several of the other rules presuppose further ways in which Israelites must not follow the natural instincts that peoples such as the Canaanites follow. Divination and augury are equivalents to astrology in the Western world, techniques to discover what the future holds, what troubles may threaten, and what may be done to avert them. Israel is to go straight to God about such questions and not think they can handle them by such techniques. Other passages make explicit that trimming hair and gashing oneself are "for the dead." They are pagan practices connected with staying in relationship with dead family members in order to get their advice and help, and/or with seeking the help of deities who are in control of the world of the dead. They probably do not imply a ban on purely decorative tattoos, though they would imply we had to ask about the implications of various practices in our culture and whether it was appropriate to follow them. The rule about sacrifice to Molech in chapter 20 has related significance, since Molech was the god the Canaanites believed to be in charge of the realm of death; hence also the ban on mediums and spiritists in the chapter.

LEVITICUS 21:1–22:33

Some Responsibilities of Priests

[Leviticus 21:1–22:16 covers priestly obligations. Priests have to be more restrained than laypeople in caring for dead family members, in the trimming of hair and self-gashing that could suggest pagan observances, in whom they marry, and in taking care how their offspring behave. The senior priest has to be even more restrained. Members of the priestly clan with physical defects may partake of the sacrifices that are the priests' food but may not take part in the key priestly duties. All members must be careful to be in a pure state when they eat of the sacrifices. Laypeople may not eat them unless they belong to a priest's family.]

[17]Yahweh spoke to Moses: [18]"Speak to Aaron and his sons and all the Israelites. Say to them: 'Any man of the household of Israel or of the aliens in Israel who presents his offering in connection with any of their vows or voluntary offerings that they offer to Yahweh as a burnt offering, [19]so you may find acceptance: [it is to be] a male from cattle or sheep or goats that is whole. [20]Any that has a defect you will not present because there will not be acceptance for you. [21]When someone presents a fellowship sacrifice to Yahweh to fulfill a vow or as a voluntary offering, from the herd or the flock, it will be whole, in order to find acceptance, with no defect in it. [22]Blind or injured or maimed or with sore or scab or boil: you will not present these to Yahweh or put any one of them on the altar as a gift for Yahweh. [23]You may make as a voluntary offering an ox or sheep with a limb that is extended or shortened, but for a vow it will not be acceptable. [24]You will not present to Yahweh something with testicles bruised, crushed, torn, or cut. You will not do this in your country [25]or present as your God's food any of these [obtained] from the hand of a foreigner. There is a deformity in them, a defect in them. They will not be acceptable for you.'"

[26]Yahweh spoke to Moses: [27]"When an ox or sheep or goat is born, it is to be with its mother for seven days. From the eighth day on, it will be acceptable as an offering, a gift to Yahweh. [28]You will not slaughter a cow or sheep with its offspring on the same day. [29]When you make a thanksgiving sacrifice to Yahweh, offer it so that you may find acceptance. [30]It is to be eaten on that day. You will not leave any of it until morning. I am Yahweh.

[31]"You are to guard my commands and do them. I am Yahweh. [32]You will not treat my holy name as ordinary, so that I may remain holy in the midst of the Israelites. I am Yahweh, who made you holy, [33]the one who brought you out from Egypt to be your God. I am Yahweh."

When you give people presents, you can get into a lot of trouble, some of which you deserve. You can spend time and money finding what you hope will be just right for someone and find it was just the wrong thing: "You think I'm that size? You think I like that kind of thing?" (I've done that). You can buy someone the record you want to listen to or the book you want to read or the food processor you want them to use or that you yourself want to experiment with (I've done that). You can give on the cheap by using a discount coupon you carefully saved (I've done that) or by buying from the thrift store (I've done that). You can pick a bunch of flowers from someone's garden and give those to your beloved; that would get you into trouble if you got found out (let alone what the garden's owner thought). But you could pick a bunch of wild-flowers that also cost you nothing and get away with it (I've done that). Giving needs to be a bit selfless, and it should be the best you can do.

When it comes to offerings to God, parallel considerations apply. You can't fulfill a promise to God by attempting to pass off a sick or lame animal that is less use to you than a healthy and whole animal. As Malachi puts it, try offering them to the government when you are paying your taxes—you think that would work? If not, doing it to God is an insult. The comparison also helps us see the background to the extra expectations of the priests, detailed in chapter 21. The special position of people who have a responsibility to the king or the governor places special obligations on them. Their position of privilege involves forfeiting some of the freedoms of ordinary people. And like the servants of a king or governor, the sacrificers need to be healthy and whole like the sacrifices.

The sacrifices, after all, are "your God's food." Every Israelite knew that God did not really eat, though no doubt they sometimes forgot and assimilated their God to the gods of other peoples who behaved in more humanlike ways, so the **Torah**'s phrase is a brave one. But when you offer a sacrifice, especially a fellowship sacrifice when people join in a meal together in God's presence and give part of the animal to God, it is *as if* God were eating with them. That highlights the insult. If you invite the boss for a meal, you give him or her the best.

Typically, the rules then turn out to have some inbuilt flexibility. Suppose you're under no obligation to make an offering (it's not a tithe or the fulfillment of a promise), but you're just making a voluntary offering; it's then okay to give an animal with something slightly odd about it. When the people join in eating the sacrifice, this kind of imperfection isn't going to spoil it; nor is God obsessional about perfection. Analogously, priests who cannot take part in offering sacrifices still share in the sacrifices.

As usual the same rules apply to aliens—not foreigners staying in Israel temporarily, maybe as traders, but people who may be just as foreign but are permanent residents in the community. They count as members of it, with the same privileges and obligations. They can make offerings to God but must do so the same way as natural-born Israelites. (The "foreigner" from whose hand an offering might come will be someone from whom an Israelite or an alien bought a defective animal cheap.)

The rules about animals and their offspring tweak God's expectations in a different direction. The Torah repeats three times a rule that you mustn't cook a kid goat in its mother's milk, so it was evidently important, but frustratingly the Torah doesn't give a rationale for it. Considered in light of Leviticus 22, one of its functions is to encourage us not to be inhumane in the way we treat animals even as food, like killing a baby and its mother on the same day.

LEVITICUS 23:1–24:9

How to Celebrate

[In this translation the ellipses indicate where the chapter goes into detail about the observance of the various events.]

¹Yahweh spoke to Moses: ²"Speak to the Israelites and say to them, 'These are Yahweh's set times, which you are to proclaim as sacred occasions, my set times. ³For six days work is to be done. On the seventh day there is a total stop, a sacred occasion. You will not do any work. It is a Sabbath for Yahweh in all your dwellings.

⁴"'These are Yahweh's set times, the sacred occasions, which you are to proclaim at their set time. ⁵In the first month on the fourteenth day of the month at twilight is Yahweh's Passover, ⁶and on the fifteenth day of this month the flat bread festival for Yahweh. For seven days you are to eat flat bread. ⁷On the first day there is to be a sacred occasion for you. You will not do any servile work. ⁸You are to present gifts to Yahweh for seven days. On the seventh day, a sacred occasion, you will not do any servile work.'"

⁹Yahweh spoke to Moses: ¹⁰"Speak to the Israelites and say to them: 'When you come into the country I am giving you and reap its harvest, you are to bring the first sheaf of your harvest to the priest. ¹¹He is to elevate the sheaf before Yahweh. . . . ¹⁵You are to count off seven Sabbaths from the day after the Sabbath, from the day you bring the elevation sheaf. They are to be complete; ¹⁶you are to count them until the day after the seventh Sabbath, fifty days, and present an offering of new grain to Yahweh. ¹⁷From your dwellings you are to bring two loaves of elevation bread. . . . ²⁴ᵇIn the seventh month on the first day of the month there is to be a rest for you, a commemoration with horn blasts, a sacred occasion. ²⁵You are to do no servile work. You are to present a gift to Yahweh.'" ²⁶Yahweh spoke to Moses: ²⁷"Now. On the tenth day of this seventh month is the day of complete expiation. . . . ³⁴ᵇOn the fifteenth day of this seventh month is the shelters festival for Yahweh for seven days. . . . ⁴²You are to live in shelters for seven days. Every citizen in Israel, they are to live in shelters, ⁴³so that your generations may acknowledge that I made the Israelites live in shelters

173

when I brought them out from Egypt. I am Yahweh your God." [44]Moses proclaimed Yahweh's set times to all the Israelites.

[Leviticus 24:1–9 adds further instructions about providing oil for the sanctuary lamps and presence bread for the sanctuary table, prescribed in Exodus 25.]

When my parents could afford it, two or three times as a teenager I was able to go to "camps," as they would be called in the United States (I am glad to say there were no tents in sight; we slept in school dormitories). It was at one of these camps that I sensed God was calling me to be a pastor. About four years later, as a university student I went to another camp for Christian students from all over Britain, and it was there I met my wife. Four years later, when I was a young assistant pastor, a highlight of our teenagers' program was a week's camp during the Easter break that was often a transforming experience for people. Another four years later I started taking my own sons to an annual Christian weekend celebration of music, drama, worship, and teaching (which unfortunately did involve tents). Nowadays my son takes his own family to an annual week of teaching and celebration (which also involves tents; in fact he has just come back from it and says he has never seen such rain). Such events can be great celebrations that take people forward in their understanding of the faith and occasions God uses to break into their lives in new ways (perhaps even introduce them to the love of their life).

Leviticus 23 develops the outline of the annual cycle of such events in Israel's life that was presented in Exodus 23. As well as having occasional residential events like the ones I have just described, the Christian church developed an annual cycle of observances and celebrations, a calendar equivalent to Israel's, comprising Advent, Christmas, Epiphany, Ash Wednesday, Lent, Holy Week, Easter, and Pentecost. Both calendars make it possible to instill deep in people's consciousness the fundamental elements of their faith.

Israel's calendar starts with the Sabbath, which in some ways is equivalent to the Christian Sunday, though its stress lies on stopping work rather than on worshiping. In Israel, most of the annual occasions are called "festivals," a word that implies going on pilgrimage to the sanctuary; when the word first appeared in the **Torah**, it referred to the Israelites' leaving Egypt to meet God at Sinai. These are Israel's annual "holy-days." As is the case with our holidays, setting them up would involve considerable stress. People would have to make arrangements for the journey, get other people to look after things at home, think about care for the children, sort out where they were going to stay, and make sure of having something to eat. . . . But once they had covered all that, they could relax and unwind in God's presence and have their faith deepened and their understanding built up. So the festivals combined the functions of the church's calendar and of those more occasional residential events. One would not do any "servile work," which perhaps denotes hard work of the kind that could be avoided. The prohibition might not exclude preparing dinner, whereas on the Sabbath it was possible to expect a complete stop for one day.

The year begins with Passover in the spring, the celebration of the people's ceasing to be Pharaoh's servants and starting to be God's servants. It was associated with the flat bread festival, which reminded them of one aspect of the exodus story. That is also set in association with the people's arrival in **Canaan**. The barley harvest begins about then, and at this time they are also to lift up the first sheaf of barley to God as an "elevation offering." It is a statement of faith whereby people give to God the first sheaf and give thanks for the harvest before they know how good it will be, even if it looks as if there will not be one. Thus this celebration brings together the great historical acts of God that brought about the people's deliverance and entry into the country with the ongoing acts of God whereby the people were able to grow the food they needed each year.

Seven weeks later, in early summer, comes Pentecost, the time when the grain harvest should be complete and when there is thus basis for another celebration. Leviticus adds the reminder that people are not to be too careful about reaping their harvest but to let the edges of their fields remain unharvested and resist the temptation to go back to pick up grain they dropped. They must instead leave something for people who have no land to harvest. The calendar brings together worship and concern for the needy as well as God's great once-for-all acts and God's regular annual provision.

In early fall come what Jews call the "High Holidays," which nowadays begin with the New Year. The New Year is not mentioned in the Torah, though the beginning of the seventh month is specially marked, perhaps because such important observances take place in this month. On the tenth day is Yom Kippur, the day of complete expiation (see Leviticus 16), not a pilgrimage occasion but one that people follow at home while the observance happens at the sanctuary. On the fifteenth day is Sukkot, the festival that involves living in homemade "shelters." It marks the completion of the fruit harvest. The shelters are a practical resource, making it possible to stay out in the fields during the harvest, but they also commemorate the way the Israelites had to live in such shelters after the exodus. This festival most explicitly combines a celebration of that great act of God in the past that remains important for them in the present, and God's continuing provision year by year.

LEVITICUS 24:10–23

An Eye for an Eye

[10]Someone with an Israelite mother and an Egyptian father went out among the Israelites, and the man with the Israelite mother got into a fight in the camp with an Israelite. [11]The man with the Israelite mother cursed the name and belittled it. So they brought him to Moses (his mother's name was Shelomit, daughter of Dibri, of the clan of Dan) [12]and they kept him in custody for things to be made clear by the mouth of Yahweh. [13]Yahweh spoke to Moses: [14]"Take the belittler outside the camp. All the people who heard are to put their hands on his head, and the whole community is to stone him. [15]You are to speak to the Israelites as follows: 'Anyone who belittles his God will carry his offense. [16]The person who curses the name of Yahweh is definitely to be put to death. The whole community is to stone him. Alien and citizen alike, on cursing the name he is to be put to death. [17]Anyone who strikes and kills a human being is definitely to be put to death. [18]Someone who strikes and kills an animal is to make restitution, life for life. [19]Some-

one who causes an injury to his fellow: as he did, so it is to be done to him, [20]fracture for fracture, eye for eye, tooth for tooth. As he causes an injury to the person, so it is to be done to him. [21]Someone who strikes down an animal is to make restitution for it, but someone who strikes down a human being is to be put to death. [22]There is to be one decision for you; it is to be for alien and citizen alike, because I am Yahweh your God." [23]Moses spoke to the Israelites and they took the belittler outside the camp and pelted him with stones. The Israelites did as Yahweh commanded Moses.

Two or three years ago, the Archbishop of Los Angeles was attacked one night near the cathedral as he went out to mail a letter. His assailant simply went up to him, punched him, pushed him to the ground, and kicked him. He was bruised but not seriously hurt. He did not report the incident to the police but referred to it in speaking to some of his clergy a few weeks later, and this is how it eventually got into the newspapers. Obviously if he had reported it to the police and they had been able to find the man, he would have been tried, convicted, and punished for the assault.

It is appropriate both that a person who has been assaulted should resist any temptation to get his or her own back and that the community should be concerned that a person who has done wrong should "pay for it." As Jesus points out, the principle of an eye for an eye is not one that we are entitled to claim when we are assaulted by someone (Matthew 5:39). The point about that principle is to provide the community with guidance when it is seeking to deal with the consequences of wrongdoing. For us as individuals, Jesus also points out, the judgment we apply to others will be the one applied to us (Matthew 7:2). The first great avenger, Lamech, boasted that he killed someone who had injured him (Genesis 4). The principle of an eye for an eye, of proportionate redress administered by the community and not private vengeance without restraint, has been important in holding societies together over the millennia.

One challenge it presents to the modern West is that we treat wrongdoing as an offense against the state and accordingly punish wrongdoing by fines paid to the state and by incarceration.

The **Torah**'s principle is that a wrongdoer has to "pay for it" to the person wronged. So if I kill your animal, I must give you an animal to replace it. If I take a life, I must in some way compensate for that. "Fracture for fracture, eye for eye, tooth for tooth" is a traditional and poetic formula; the Torah hardly means that the community should literally break a person's leg to make up for that person's breaking someone else's leg. People could presumably see that this gets no one anywhere except by giving the hurt person a Lamech-like satisfaction that does no real good. When it talks about doing something to the offender equivalent to what the offender did, it implies getting the person to make restitution in a way equivalent to the damage done. If the individual broke someone's leg, then until it mends the wrongdoer is going to have to "be that person's leg," helping him or her to get around, plow the ground, harvest the crops. If you killed someone, it would cost you your whole life. You could be executed or (other elements in the Torah imply) your family could arrange things so that either you or they would give the equivalent of a life in serving the family that you robbed of one of its members. The rule could also ensure that rich people cannot kill with impunity because they can always make monetary compensation for the wrongdoing. One result of making restitution will be that the offender gets rehabilitated as a human being even while the person who was hurt is enabled to cope with the consequences of the wrongdoing. Another is that the families affected also have opportunity to find reconciliation within the community.

It's not clear why this declaration about proper restitution and restoration is set in the midst of the story about the man who curses God. Perhaps it's because that started off with a fight and someone's being injured. The story makes clear that killing another person is not the only wrongdoing that might cost you your life. When the Torah first discusses murder, in Genesis 9, what it finds appalling is that attacking another human being means attacking the God in whose image the human being was made. To us, physically attacking a human being may seem much worse than verbally attacking God. To the Torah, cursing God is a horrifying offense and a dangerous one. Suppose God were to take the hint and leave? Cursing

God might imperil the community more than killing one of its members. The story likely assumes that the death penalty for cursing God could be presupposed; the waiting on God concerns whether it applies to someone who is not a full Israelite and/or concerns the method of execution. The form of execution involves the whole community, which thereby disassociates itself from the curse.

Presumably it is significant that the man who curses God is half Israelite and half **Egyptian**. The Old Testament is not against mixed marriages (David's father had an Israelite father and a Moabite mother). Their danger is that the couple may not be sure to which community and God they belong. They have to make up their minds.

The introduction to this story perhaps points to a tragic aspect to the man's story. From where does the man who is half Egyptian and half Israelite come out into the midst of the Israelites? Just from his own tent? From the area where the mixed crowd who came out from Egypt have their quarters? Or even from Egypt itself? Whichever of these applies, there is some ambiguity about where he belongs, about which side of his ancestry he wants to identify with. He reminds us of Moses when he went to find out how things were among the Israelites after growing up in the Egyptian palace. Is this man Moses' alter ego? (Moses also got into a fight and got into trouble as a result.) Has he actually just made up his mind who he is, like Moses, and does his "coming out" indicate this? If so, the fight leads him to somersault in the opposite direction. Or perhaps there is another piece of background. Later Judaism thinks that people count as Jews if they have a Jewish mother, but we have no evidence that this was so in Old Testament times. Its implication is rather that you can only have a share in the land if your father is Israelite. Does he know that there is no way he can ever be a full member of the community with a family to which **Yahweh** gives its own share of the land as its own?

Losing his life for cursing God is not the ultimate tragedy. The ultimate tragedy in a murderer's life is the committing of the murder, not the execution that may follow. The ultimate tragedy for the curser is not his execution but his actual uttering of the curse.

LEVITICUS 25:1–26:2

The Jubilee

¹Yahweh spoke to Moses on Mount Sinai: ²"Speak to the Israelites as follows: 'When you come into the country I am giving you, the country is to observe a Sabbath for Yahweh. ³Six years you may sew your fields and six years you may prune your vineyard and gather the produce, ⁴but in the seventh year it is to be a total Sabbath for the country, a Sabbath for Yahweh. You will not sew your field, prune your vineyard, ⁵reap your harvest's aftergrowth, or pick the grapes of your unpruned vines. It is to be a year of cessation for the country. ⁶The country's Sabbath will be food for you, your male and female servant, your employee and your resident living with you, ⁷and for your cattle and the wild animals that are in your country, all its produce will be for eating.

⁸"You are to count off seven Sabbaths of years, seven times seven years, so that your seven Sabbaths of years are forty-nine years. ⁹You are to sound a blaring horn in the seventh month, on the tenth of the month; on the day of complete expiation you are to sound the horn throughout your country. ¹⁰You are to sanctify the fiftieth year and proclaim release in the country for all its inhabitants. It is to be a jubilee for you. You are to return, each person, to his holding, and to return, each person, to his family. ¹¹The year, that fiftieth year, is to be a jubilee for you. You will not sew or reap its aftergrowth or pick its unpruned vines, ¹²because it is a jubilee. It is to be sacred to you. You are to eat from the produce of the field. ¹³In this year of jubilee you are to return, each person, to his holding. ¹⁴So when you sell property to your fellow, or buy from what he possesses, one person is not to wrong his relative. ¹⁵It is by counting the years since the jubilee that you are to buy from your fellow; it is by the number of the years of produce that he is to sell to you.'"

[The rest of the passage gives more detail on how the jubilee is to work, then reminds people of basic requirements concerning images, the Sabbath, and the sanctuary.]

The other day, I heard a story about a couple who have just had their home repossessed. Part of the story's sadness was that it is not only the house where the wife had been born but the house where her father had been born. The couple had inherited it from her parents and lived there happily until they got into economic difficulties two or three years ago and took out a second mortgage. Then everything went wrong with the economy, and they hadn't understood the implications of the refinancing they had arranged. It meant they lost their house. The financial adviser who had worked with them commented that it was his job to sell mortgages, not to warn people about the moves they were making. One reason Israel has provisions like these concerning the jubilee is that people always need protecting from such experiences.

Like the detailed schedule for the annual festivals in Leviticus 23, these instructions for the Sabbath year and the treatment of the poor (including the ban on lending money at interest) expand on the outline in Exodus 22–23. One of their underlying assumptions is that the land belongs to God. People recognize that the week belongs to God by holding themselves back from one day in seven, and that offspring belong to God by dedicating the first fruits of the womb, and that the harvest belongs to God by giving tithes, and they recognize that the land belongs to God by keeping off it for one year in seven. The idea would be scary. How can one expect to survive on that basis? As happens with those other observances, God promises they will be provided for. They can't treat the Sabbath year's growth as a regular harvest or store some of it away for the future, but it will provide them enough to eat. God does not promise that they will do as well as their neighbors but does promise that they will have enough. Whereas Exodus 23 provided a humanitarian rationale for the Sabbath year and the Sabbath itself, Leviticus makes it simply something people do as part of their acknowledgment of God's ownership of the land.

The same principle underlies the jubilee idea. Our word "jubilee" comes from the Hebrew word used here. In origin, it refers to blowing a ram's horn, the signal that the year has arrived. The jubilee idea again presupposes that the land belongs to God. You cannot sell it as you can sell a house in the city (you cannot sell a house in a village, because that is an adjunct to the land that people are there to farm). It also presupposes that God

181

allocated the land to the people by their clans and extended families; that excludes any people becoming big landowners. Some will be better or more hardworking farmers than others or will have better luck than others and will be able to make those others an offer for their land that they cannot refuse, especially when lazier or poorer or unluckier farmers cannot make ends meet. The prophets'. admonishments show that exactly this happened in Israel. Leviticus sets in place procedures designed to prevent it. On the assumption that the **Torah** developed over the centuries as God guided the community in facing the needs that arose in different social contexts, one can imagine that its regulations were worked out in light of the experience of such dynamics.

Like its Sabbath-year teaching, the Torah is not directly concerned here with the impoverished farmers themselves. Restoring the land to the families that owned it happens only once every fifty years, so people who lost their land are not likely to live long enough to have a practical interest in farming again by the time the jubilee comes round. Perhaps Leviticus presupposes that their predicament was likely to be their own fault. Its own concern is with God's purpose, not with poor farmers. God had a plan for the country, and God does not want it derailed by the incompetence of some and the greed of others. At the same time, for the people themselves there is hardly a question more basic to their lives than the question of land. It is hard for an urbanized society to grasp this idea. There is no supermarket down the street, and you have no money. Being able to live depends on being able to grow your food, and being able to grow your food depends on possessing land.

The Torah sets forward no ideal whereby everyone has the same assets and income, the same degree of wealth. Rather it assumes that wealth places obligations before people. Farmers who do well are not to make that the basis for enlarging their farms but the basis for helping people who do not do well, without asking questions about why they failed. What the well-off do is take over the land of failed farmers on a temporary basis. They are to do so in a fair way in light of where the people are in relation to the previous jubilee and the next one. In the meantime, they will be able to see the land is properly farmed.

Its nominal owners will now work more like employees than owners of land. Their new boss is to treat them well, not as if they were servants or aliens but as family members (servants and aliens were treated as members of the family, but evidently not in quite the same sense). Yet they have lost their independence, and their land has lost its proper steward.

When this happens, one possibility is that someone else from their own extended family may be in a position to act as their "restorer" or "redeemer" by giving back to the new "owner" whatever he has provided for the impoverished man and his family; or maybe they will get to a position where they can "restore" themselves. If that does not happen, in due course the jubilee brings a "release" to both people and land.

Leviticus points to another principle underlying the way successful farmers are to treat the unsuccessful. As the land belongs to God, so do the people. They are all God's servants. Therefore the successful cannot treat the unsuccessful as if they were servants. You can treat foreigners that way, Leviticus says, which might seem narrow-minded. It anticipates the way the New Testament expects people in the church to treat one another with more love than they treat outsiders; that is how family works. In the Torah, at least, the point may be a theoretical one. Its focus is on how people treat fellow Israelites who become impoverished. There would not be many foreigners in a village (apart from resident aliens, who come in a different category), and the point about foreigners is there only as a makeweight.

LEVITICUS 26:3–46

Promises and Warnings and Promises

[3]"'If you walk by my rules and guard my commands and do them, [4]I will give your rains in their season, so that the country will give its produce and the trees of the field their fruit. [5]For you threshing will overtake reaping and reaping will overtake sewing. You will eat your food to the full and live securely in your country. [6]I will put peace in the country and you will lie down with no one disturbing. I will eliminate harmful beasts from the country and the sword will not pass through your

country. [7]You will pursue your enemies and they will fall to the sword before you. [8]Five of you will pursue a hundred and a hundred of you will pursue ten thousand. Your enemies will fall to the sword before you. [9]I will look on you and make you fruitful and numerous. I will establish my covenant with you. [10]You will eat old grain then take out the old to make room for the new. [11]I will put my dwelling in your midst and my heart will not spurn you. [12]I will walk about in your midst. I will be God for you and you will be a people for me. [13]I am Yahweh your God who brought you out of Egypt to stop being servants to them and broke the bars of your yoke and let you walk erect.

[14]"'But if you do not listen to me and put into effect all these commands, [15]if you reject my rules and your heart spurns my decisions so as not to put into effect any of my commands and break my covenant, [16]I will also do this to you: I will appoint terror over you, wasting away and fever wearing out the eyes and consuming the heart. You will sew your seed in vain; your enemies will eat it. [17]I will set my face against you and you will stumble before your enemies. Your foes will dominate you and you will flee when there is no one pursuing you.'"

[Verses 18–41 warn of a continuing process whereby Israel's failure to respond to Yahweh's chastisements will lead to further chastisements designed to drag them back, culminating in their being thrown out of the country. Then at last they will turn back to Yahweh.]

[42]"'And I will be mindful of my covenant with Jacob, and my covenant with Isaac, and be mindful of my covenant with Abraham, and be mindful of the country. [43]The country will be left by them so that it may make up for its Sabbaths by being desolate without them, and they themselves will make up for their waywardness because—yes, because they rejected my decisions and their hearts spurned my rules. [44]But for all this, when they are in the country of their enemies I will not reject them or spurn them so as to finish them off, breaking my covenant with them, because I am Yahweh their God. [45]I will be mindful for them of the covenant with the original people I brought out of Egypt in the sight of the nations, to be God for them. I am Yahweh.'" [46]These are the rules, the decisions, and the teaching Yahweh established between him and the Israelites at Mount Sinai by means of Moses.

Yesterday a student from a two-thirds-world country came to see me to talk about wealth and poverty, about the idea that God exercised a preferential option for the poor, about whether it was okay for us to enjoy the wealth we have, and about what he should say to a friend who asked if it was okay to buy a BMW rather than a Honda (he didn't know I'd just bought a Honda). Discussing such issues with someone from the two-thirds world is different from discussing them with someone from the West, though this discussion was complicated by the fact that the student is in the United States because his family is well-to-do in his home country and can afford to send him to graduate school here. I talked about the fact that the Bible has no ideal whereby everyone has the same amount of wealth, but that having wealth is designed to make it possible to share it with others, and that people who want to spend a lot of their wealth on themselves would need to ask themselves what they expected to get out of doing that. The previous evening I had watched the movie *Confessions of a Shopaholic*, which at one level is simply a romantic comedy, but at the same time it raises questions about the rush that buying things gives us, like the rush you get from any addiction. By its nature, the rush is only momentary. Then we have to buy something else.

The **Torah** does not encourage a prosperity gospel promising that some people do really well through their obedience to God, so that they have a BMW while others drive a Honda. It does encourage the assumption that when the people of God live God's way, together they will do well. Jesus confirms that assumption (Matthew 6:33). Given the generous nature of God's work in creation, where it looked so good and God gave Adam and Eve so many great things to eat (even if veggie!), it is not surprising that God wants people to enjoy food, not to mention peace, security, and an awareness of God's walking about among them. Leviticus uses the same word as comes in Genesis 3 to describe that walking. In fact, it is almost promising a return to the garden of Eden. But then the same challenge applies to Israel as applied to Adam and Eve. God's plan will work out only if they live the way God directs. The chapter spends most of its time describing the horrible consequences that will follow if they do not.

It looks on through the story that will take Israel into exile, and it needs reading from the perspective of people reading it there. They can look back over Israel's story and see it has indeed been troubled by sickness and famine and by attackers such as the Moabites, Philistines, and **Assyrians**. The Assyrians terminated the life of **Ephraim**, and the **Babylonians** did that to **Judah**, destroying the temple in Jerusalem. The government, businesspeople, intellectuals, prophets, and priests were taken off to Babylon where they can no longer cause trouble. In **exile** it will not be surprising if they are discouraged, desolate, and dying of a broken heart. Is this the end? Moab and Philistia no longer exist. Is Israel going out of existence too? Other peoples get transported from their country. Will these Judeans ever see theirs again? Leviticus offers them various forms of good news, beginning, paradoxically, with the list of warnings about what will follow from disobedience.

When we ask, "Why did this happen to me?" we are looking for meaning. We can cope a little better with disaster if it makes sense than if it is simply random. It often does look random. Leviticus enables the exiles to see that in their case it was not. The grim things that had happened meant something. Being thrown out of the country made sense because they had ignored the rule about Sabbath years for centuries. God was now letting the country take its accumulated Sabbaths. It was an assertion of God's ownership of the country. This in itself meant that the exile need not be permanent. Israel needed just to make up for those Sabbaths.

Further, in general God's actions had been more like a parent's chastisements than a judge's punishments. They were reactions to the people's wrongdoing and were designed to win them back because of the **covenant** relationship between God and Israel. That's the difference between Israel and Moab, and why Moab can disappear and Israel cannot. (If this seems unfair, we can recall that God's keeping in covenant with Israel is the means of bringing about the salvation of the world, a process of which Christians today are all beneficiaries.) The fact that Israel breaks the covenant does not mean God will do so. God will remember not merely the covenant with Israel (which stressed the importance of its obedience) but the covenant with their ancestors (which issued purely from God's grace and was based purely on God's promissory commitment).

Maybe now at last God's chastisement can have its designed effect. Maybe now the government can own how its political policies left God out, the businesspeople can own how they left ethics out, and the intellectuals can own how they thought the same way as Edomite intellectuals. Maybe now the priests can own how they gave people the religion they wanted, and the prophets can own how they gave people false comfort. When the people turn back, Leviticus says, there is God waiting to welcome them.

LEVITICUS 27:1–34

Human Promises

[1]Yahweh spoke to Moses: [2]"Speak to the Israelites as follows: 'When someone makes an extraordinary promise to Yahweh equivalent to the assessment of a human being, [3]your assessment is to be [as follows]: A male from twenty to sixty years, your assessment is to be fifty silver shekels, by the sanctuary shekel. [4]If it is a female, your assessment is to be thirty shekels. [5]If it is someone from five to twenty years, your assessment is to be: a male twenty shekels, for a female ten shekels. [6]If it is someone from one month to five years, your assessment is to be: a male five silver shekels, for the female your assessment is to be three silver shekels. [7]If it is someone sixty years or over: if it is a male, your assessment is to be fifteen shekels, and for a female ten shekels. [8]If someone is too lowly for your assessment, they are to bring him in before the priest and the priest will assess him. In accordance with what the capacity of the person making the promise can manage, the priest is to assess him.

[9]If it is an animal, one of the ones that people may present to Yahweh as an offering, any of these that someone gives to Yahweh is to be holy. [10]A person may not exchange it or substitute for it, good for bad or bad for good. If he does substitute one animal for another, it and its substitute are to be holy. [11]If it is any taboo animal, one of the ones that people may not present to Yahweh as an offering, he is to bring the animal before the priest [12]and the priest will assess it. Good or bad, it is to be in

accordance with the priest's assessment. [13]If he does redeem it, he is to add a fifth to the assessment.

[Verses 14–34 lay down rules concerning fulfilling promises of houses and land, redemption of firstlings and tithes, and the impossibility of redeeming something that has been "devoted" or "proscribed."]

A distinctive feature of my seminary in the United States compared with my seminary in Britain is the high number of students who are "pastor's kids" or "missionary kids." I have wondered what lay behind this difference. It raises a question raised by other aspects of U.S. students' relationships with their parents: that is, whether they are tied to their parents for longer than is the case in Britain. If so, it could be read negatively (i.e., they take a long time to find their independence, partly because their parents are likely to be much more involved in funding their education) or positively (i.e., their family relationships are closer and they are under their parents' authority in a way that is also the case in a traditional society like Israel). There may, however, be a more specific reason for the higher number of U.S. students with parents who are pastors. Perhaps pastors here dedicate their sons and daughters to God in a way that we don't in Britain and pray for them to follow their parents in ministry or mission. I don't remember us praying that for our sons, and they didn't follow me into the ministry nor Ann into medicine.

In Israel, your children are among the people you might dedicate to God. The promise to do that is seen as an "extraordinary" one, and a good context to see such a promise is the story of Hannah (1 Samuel 1). This closing chapter of Leviticus is a kind of appendix dealing with a question that might arise in connection with the instructions for offerings that came near the beginning. One of these is the thanksgiving offering in connection with a promise you made to God; God has done what you ask, and you now fulfill that promise. In that connection we noted Hannah's promise to dedicate her baby to God, which did not mean going to a dedication service in the sanctuary and then taking him home but going to a dedication service at the sanctuary and then leaving him there. One can imagine Hannah agonizing over whether she could really bear to fulfill that promise. Other Old Testament stories show how such promises can get you into a lot of trouble. Jephthah infamously ended up apparently sacrificing his daughter to God (Judges 11). It was a sign of the degeneracy of his times that he didn't think of seeing if he could renegotiate the vow. Saul almost made the same mistake with Jonathan (1 Samuel 14), but fortunately his army was not as stupid as he was. Ecclesiastes 5 therefore warns you to think three times before you make a promise to God.

Leviticus 27 gives you a basis for renegotiating your vow. Instead of letting the person you have promised actually become someone who works in the sanctuary like Samuel or gets sacrificed like Jephthah's daughter, you make a gift to the sanctuary that may turn out to be even more useful to it. The **Torah** thus gives you an exchange rate, perhaps based on the person's capacity for physical work. We don't know the value of a shekel's weight in silver, but the amount of silver Leviticus is talking about would likely be equivalent to several years' wages, which again underlines that promises are not to be made lightly. The Torah then as usual avoids being legalistic by making the exchange rate flexible according to the capacity of the person making the promise. As Jesus will later put it, a widow's dollar may be more costly to her than a thousand dollars from a professor.

The parallel instructions for animals presuppose that not being able to sacrifice (say) a donkey doesn't mean there is anything wrong with donkeys or that the sanctuary has no need or use for them. They are, after all, the Israelite equivalent to a pickup truck. The instructions make explicit that the exchange rate is designed to facilitate the "redemption" of the promised gift (i.e., the substitution of cash for the animal), which makes it easier if you live a long way away and gives the sanctuary more flexibility in matching its resources to its needs (as when family members and friends give people gift cards rather than specific gifts at a couple's marriage). Something similar applies to the promise of a house or a piece of land.

On the other hand, there is apparently a kind of promise that explicitly involves forgoing any right to change your mind, as is the case with some airline deals (not to say Ticketmaster). If you have in this sense "devoted" or "proscribed" something, you are bound to fulfill your promise. "Devoting" in Exodus 22:20 denotes proscribing someone who sacrifices to another god, which would be another reason not to allow such a person to buy his or her way out of execution. Of course in connection with things or people that were to be "devoted" you could no doubt still throw yourself on God's mercy, and in some circumstances this may work, as I have found to be the case with airlines and concert tickets.

You cannot *promise* something that you *owe*, such as the firstborn of animals or the tithes of crops, though you may be able to redeem them. When you tithe your flock, you line up the animals and count them off, and numbers ten, twenty, and so on go to God. With a smile Leviticus then imagines a shepherd realizing that number twenty is his fattest sheep and number twenty-one is a sheep with a lame leg. Can he make a quick adjustment to the line? No; no substitutions are allowed. With that (apart from another note closing off the commands given through Moses), Leviticus ends.

GLOSSARY

aide

A supernatural agent through whom God appears and works in the world. Standard English translations refer to them as "angels," but this rather suggests ethereal figures with wings, wearing diaphanous white dresses. Aides are humanlike figures; hence it is possible to give them hospitality without realizing who they are (Hebrews 13). They have no wings; hence their need of a stairway or ramp between heaven and earth (Genesis 28). They appear in order to act or speak on God's behalf and represent God so fully that they can speak as if they are God (Exodus 3). They thus bring the reality of God's presence, action, and voice without bringing such a real presence that it would electrocute mere mortals or shatter their hearing. That can be a reassurance when Israel is rebellious and God's presence might indeed be a threat (Exodus 32–33), but they can themselves be means of implementing God's punishment as well as God's blessing (Exodus 12).

altar

A structure for offering a sacrifice (the word comes from the word for sacrifice), made of earth or stone. An altar might be relatively small, like a table, and the person making the offering would stand in front of it. Or it might be higher and larger, like a platform, and the person making the offering would climb onto it. The sacrificial altar is to be distinguished from the much smaller altar within the sanctuary, on which incense was burnt so that its smoke ascended to God.

Amorites

One of the original ethnic groups in **Canaan** (e.g., Exodus 3:8), though the term is also used to refer to the people of that country as a whole. Indeed, outside the Old Testament "Amorites" refers to a people living over a much wider area of Mesopotamia. "Amorites" is thus a little like the word "America," which commonly refers to the United States but can denote a much broader area of the continent of which the United States is part.

Apocrypha

The contents of the main Christian Old Testament are the same as those of the Jewish Scriptures, though there they come in a different order, as the **Torah**, the Prophets, and the Writings. Their precise bounds as Scripture came to be accepted some time in the years before or after Christ. For centuries, most Christian churches used a broader collection of Jewish writings, including books such as Maccabees and Ecclesiasticus, which for Jews were not part of the Bible. These other books came to be called the "Apocrypha," the books that were "hidden away"—which came to imply "spurious." They are now often known as the "deuterocanonical writings," which is more cumbersome but less pejorative; it simply indicates that these books have less authority than the Torah, the Prophets, and the Writings. The precise list of them varies between different churches.

Assyria, Assyrians

The first great Middle Eastern superpower, the Assyrians spread their empire westward into Syria-Palestine in the eighth century, the time of Amos and Isaiah, and first made **Ephraim** part of their empire. When Ephraim kept trying to assert independence, they invaded; in 722 they destroyed Ephraim's capital at Samaria, transported many of its people, and settled people from other parts of their empire in their place. They also invaded **Judah** and devastated much of the country, but they did not take Jerusalem. Prophets such as Amos and Isaiah describe how **Yahweh** was thus using Assyria as a means of disciplining Israel.

Babylon, Babylonians

A minor power in the context of Israel's early history, in the time of Jeremiah they took over the position of superpower from **Assyria** and kept it for nearly a century until conquered by **Persia**. Prophets such as Jeremiah describe how **Yahweh** was using them as a means of disciplining **Judah**. They took Jerusalem and transported many of its people in 587. Their creation stories, law codes, and more philosophical writings help us understand aspects of the Old Testament's equivalent writings, while their astrological religion forms background to aspects of polemic in the Prophets.

Canaan, Canaanites

As the biblical terms for the country of Israel as a whole and for its indigenous peoples, "Canaanites" is not so much the name for a particular ethnic group as a shorthand term for all the peoples native to the country. See also **Amorites**.

commitment

Commitment is the word *hesed*, which can be translated in many different ways—steadfast love, constant love, kindness, mercy, loving-kindness, grace, favor, loyalty, or just love. It denotes what happens when someone makes a commitment to someone else in one of two circumstances. One is when there is no prior relationship between the parties, so that someone makes a commitment that he or she was under no obligation to make. The other is when there is a relationship but one of the parties shows a commitment going beyond anything one might have expected. God behaves that way toward people and rejoices when they behave that way in response.

covenant

Contracts and treaties assume a quasilegal system for resolving disputes and administering justice that can be appealed to if someone does not keep a commitment. In contrast, in a relationship that does not work within a legal framework someone who fails to keep a commitment cannot be taken to court for this failure, so a covenant involves some formal procedure that confirms the seriousness of the solemn commitment one party makes to another. In covenants between God and humanity, in Genesis the emphasis lies on God's commitment to human beings, and to Abraham in particular. On the basis of God's having begun to fulfill that covenant commitment, Exodus and Leviticus also put some stress on Israel's responsive commitment at Sinai.

Egypt, Egyptians

The major regional power to the south of Canaan and the country where Jacob's family had found refuge, where they ended up as serfs, and from which the Israelites then needed to escape. In Moses' time Egypt controlled Canaan; in subsequent centuries it was sometimes a threat to Israel, sometimes a potential ally.

Ephraim

After the reign of David and Solomon, the nation of Israel split into two. Most of the twelve Israelite clans set up an independent state in the north, separate from **Judah** and Jerusalem and from the line of David. Because this was the bigger of the two states, politically it kept the name Israel, which is confusing because Israel is still the name of the people as a whole as the people of God. So the name "Israel" can be used in both these connections. The northern state can, however, also be referred to by the name of **Ephraim**, one of its dominant clans, so I use this term to refer to that northern state to reduce the confusion.

exile

At the end of the seventh century **Babylon** became the major power in **Judah**'s world but Judah was inclined to rebel against its authority. As part of a successful campaign to get Judah to submit properly to its authority, in 597 and in 587 BC the Babylonians transported many people from Jerusalem to Babylon. They made a special point of transporting people in leadership positions, such as members of the royal family and the court, priests, and prophets. These people were thus compelled to live in Babylonia for the next fifty years or so. Through the same period, people back in Judah were also under Babylonian authority, so they were not physically in exile but were also living in the exile as a period of time.

expiation

A key concern in Exodus and Leviticus is keeping the sanctuary pure. While God may be able to tolerate a small amount of impurity there (as we can tolerate a small amount of dirt), if the place people have made as a home for God becomes too much affected by things that are alien, then God can hardly carry on living there. So it is important to deal with impurity that comes on the sanctuary through the infringement of **taboos**. One way of conceiving this is to speak in terms of atonement (at-one-ment), which suggests the healing of a relationship. Another is to speak of propitiation, which suggests the mollifying of someone who was angry. In contrast, expiation relates to the thing that has caused the problem rather than to the person. It suggests the removal or wiping away of a stain. Of course the removal of the stain means that the threat to the relationship is gone and it is now possible for God to be in easy relationship with the people; in this sense expiation and atonement are closely related. On the other hand, "propitiation" is a more question-able idea in connection with Leviticus; while it does imply that God is offended by people and unwilling to associate with them, it does not speak of God's being angry with them because of their offenses.

faithfulness

In English Bibles the **Hebrew** word *sedaqah* is usually translated "righteousness," but it denotes a particular slant on what we might mean by righteousness. It means doing the right thing by the people with whom one is in a relationship, the members of one's community. Thus it is really closer to "faithfulness" than "righteousness."

Greece, Greeks

In 336 BC Greek forces under Alexander the Great took control of the **Persian** Empire, but after Alexander's death in 333 his empire split up. The largest part, to the north and east of Palestine, was ruled by one of his generals, Seleucus, and his successors. **Judah** was under its control for much of the next two centuries, though it was at the extreme south-western border of this empire and sometimes came under the control of the Ptolemaic Empire in **Egypt** (ruled by successors of another of Alexander's officers).

Hebrew, Hebrews

Whereas "Hebrew" became the term for the language of the Jewish people, it seems not to be an ethnic term in the Old Testament. Significantly, it is a word that the Pharaoh and his daughter use to describe the Israelites (Exodus 1:16; 2:6). While the Israelites might thus be termed Hebrews, they were not the only Hebrews. Other languages have related words, and all seem to be more sociological than ethnic, a little like the word "gypsy." They suggest people who do not belong to a regular, recognized political community.

Israel, Israelites

Originally, Israel was the new name God gave Abraham's grandson, Jacob. His twelve sons were then forefathers of the twelve clans that comprise the people Israel. In the time of Saul, David, and Solomon these twelve clans became more of a political entity; Israel was both the people of God and a nation or state like other nations or states.

After Solomon's day, this one state split into two, **Ephraim** and **Judah**. Ephraim was far bigger and often continued to be referred to as Israel. So if one is thinking of the people of God, Judah is part of Israel. If one is thinking politically, Judah is not part of Israel, but once Ephraim has gone out of existence, for practical purposes Judah *is* Israel, as the people of God.

Judah

One of the twelve sons of Jacob, then the clan that traces its ancestry to him, then the dominant clan in the southern of the two states after the time of Solomon. Later, as a **Persian** province or colony, it was known as Yehud.

Masoretes

The Jewish scholars who studied and preserved the tradition (*masora*) about the Old Testament text during the Middle Ages. Whereas the written Hebrew alphabet comprises only consonants, the Masoretes perfected and standardized a system of dots and dashes to indicate how the tradition understood the vowel sounds. They also standardized and preserved a division of the text into chapters and paragraphs (a different system from the one in English Bibles), a division into verses (English Bibles nearly always have the same system), and a system of signs that indicated the relationships between the words in sentences. The climax of this work was the production of a standard version of the Old Testament, the Masoretic Text, which is still the text that appears in Hebrew Bibles.

Mesopotamia

Etymologically, the country "between the rivers," the Tigris and Euphrates, though in practice it refers to the area they run through. The area is largely equivalent to modern Iraq. **Babylon** and Babylonia lie in its south; Ur, in its far south; **Assyria** and Nineveh, in its north; Elam and **Persia**, to its east.

Perizzites

One of the groups in **Canaan** whom the Israelites displaced or came to control and assimilate, they show up in several places in the Old Testament, and the word may be not so much an ethnic term as a sociological one (like **Hebrews**). The name resembles the word for an unfortified "settlement," so it might denote people who lived in such settlements rather than in cities, a bit like the English word "villagers."

Persia, Persians

The third Middle Eastern superpower. Under the leadership of Cyrus the Great, they took control of the Babylonian empire in 539 BC. Isaiah 40–55 sees **Yahweh**'s hand in raising up Cyrus as the means of restoring **Judah** after the **exile**. Judah and surrounding peoples such as Samaria, Ammon, and Ashdod were Persian provinces or colonies. The Persians stayed in power for two centuries until defeated by **Greece**.

purification, purification offering, *see* the comments on Leviticus 3:1–4:35.

restore

A restorer is a person who is in a position to take action on behalf of someone within his extended family who is in need in order to restore the situation to what it should be. The word overlaps with expressions such as next-of-kin, guardian, and redeemer. "Next-of-kin" indicates the family context that "restorer" presupposes. "Guardian" indicates that the restorer is in a position to be concerned for the person's protection and defense. "Redeemer" indicates having resources that the restorer is prepared to expend on the person's behalf. The Old Testament uses the term to refer to God's relationship with Israel as well as to the action of a human person in relation to another, so it implies that Israel belongs to God's family and that God acts on its behalf in the way a restorer does.

Second Temple

The first temple was Solomon's, devastated by the Babylonians in 587 BC; the second temple was the one rebuilt seventy years later (see Ezra 5–6). It was vastly remodeled and expanded by Herod in Jesus' time but destroyed by the Romans in 70 AD. The Second Temple period is thus the period from the late sixth century to New Testament times, the period when Judah was ruled by **Persia**, then **Greece**, then Rome.

taboo, *see* the comments on Leviticus 11:1–12:8.

Torah

The Hebrew word for the first five books of the Bible. They are often referred to as the "Law," but this label is misleading. Genesis itself is nothing like "law," and even Exodus to Deuteronomy are not "legalistic" books. The word *torah* itself means "teaching," which gives a clearer impression of the nature of the Torah. Often the Torah gives us more than one account of an event (such as God's commission of Moses), so that when the early church told the story of Jesus in different ways in different contexts and according to the insights of the different Gospel writers, it was following the precedent whereby Israel told its stories more than once in different contexts. Whereas Kings and Chronicles keep the versions separate, as would happen with the Gospels, in the Torah the versions were combined.

Yahweh

In most English Bibles, the word "LORD" often comes in all capitals, as does sometimes the word "GOD" in similar format. These actually represent the name of God, Yahweh. In later Old Testament times, Israelites stopped using the name Yahweh and started to refer to Yahweh as "the Lord." There may be two reasons. They wanted other people to recognize that Yahweh was the one true God, but this strange, foreign-sounding name could give the impression that Yahweh was just Israel's tribal god. "The Lord" was a term anyone could recognize. In addition, they did not want to fall foul of the warning in the Ten Commandments about misusing Yahweh's name. Translations into other languages then followed suit in substituting an expression such as "the Lord" for the name Yahweh. The downsides are that this obscures the fact that God wanted to be known by name, that often the text refers to Yahweh and not some other (so-called) god or lord, and that the practice gives the impression that God is much more "lordly" and patriarchal than actually God is. (The form "Jehovah" is not a real word but a mixture of the consonants of Yahweh and the vowels of that word for "Lord," to remind people in reading Scripture that they should say "the Lord," not the actual name.)